D1028263

OUR BETTER SELVES

A Memoir—From Secrets and Lies to Healing and
Forgiveness

KASEY ROGERS

Onward and upward!
Kasey Rogers
4/21/21

INDIES UNITED PUBLISHING HOUSE, LLC
P.O. BOX 3071
QUINCY, IL 62305-3071

Our Better Selves

A Memoir—From Secrets and Lies

to Healing and Forgiveness

By Kasey Rogers

Indies United Publishing House

Designed and printed in USA

Library of Congress Control Number: 2021934100

ISBN # 978-1-64456-282-6

ISBN (ePub): 978-1-64456-283-3

About the Cover

The Agave Pelona is a critically endangered succulent. The plant is native to Sonora, Mexico, and grows in harsh, mountainous conditions with little water but an abundance of sunlight. While it is a slow-growing plant, the brilliant display of red, orange, and brown spikes with toothless white thorns is a wonder to behold. For me, this plant symbolizes the courage it takes for individuals to flourish despite their adversities.

Dedication

*Resilience is knowing that you are the only one
that has the power and the responsibility
to pick yourself up.*

~ Mary Holloway

For The Beans

Acknowledgments

Writing this book was not a solitary adventure. After penning the first draft, several friends read the work and offered advice and encouragement to keep moving forward. Others read one or more drafts and helped me to revise and edit this memoir. I am very grateful to them all. This is a list of all the dear friends who helped, in alphabetical order.

Danna Bonner, Lynda D'Amico,
Jackie Flynn, Shelly Icardi,
Astrid Julienne, Vicki Lowery,
Loretta Meredith, Amy Myer,
Lesley Orr, Mary Anne Slack,
and Betina Spathis.

Author's Note

This book is a memoir. I have recreated these events from memories, journals, emails, and other private correspondence. To protect the privacy of those involved, I changed the names of many people and locations. While some of the events I've written about are unpleasant to reveal, my intention is only to shed light on the issues I detail. I hope this work will be read with that in mind.

Map of locations

6 hours from Alexandria to Blairstown, NJ
5 hours from Alexandria to Cobleskill, NY
6.5 hours from Alexandria to Marblehead, MA
1 hour from Marblehead, MA to Boston, MA

Part One

SEEDS OF DOUBT

March on. Do not tarry.
To go forward is to move toward perfection.
March on, and fear not the thorns,
or the sharp stones on life's path.

~ Khalil Gibran

Chapter One

A RELUCTANT FAREWELL

August 30, 2010 Alexandria, Ontario, Canada

T he red light flashed on the answering machine. I saw it blinking from the bathroom where I stood drying off from my shower. I wrapped a towel around my body and crossed through the door to the desk in the room. My hand hovered above the play button. Mentally, I listed the reasons I didn't want to listen to the message. Most likely, it was my husband, Phillip, calling to ask when I was leaving Alexandria. However, after twenty-four years of marriage, I knew that the question he asked and what he really wanted to know were two different things. While the question might be, "When are you leaving," what he wanted to know was if I'd finished packing. I wondered why he always seemed to think haranguing me would make me work faster. What it did, in reality, was piss me off. I stood there, debating whether to listen to the message at all.

I'd been alone for a few days after taking our twins, Jack and Lucy, to Vermont. My brother Jake and his wife Meredith were taking care of them for the week while I packed to move back to the States. While I was reasonably sure Phillip had left the message, I thought Jake could be trying to reach me, so I pushed the play button. I heard Phillip's familiar voice, heavy with recrimination.

"Well, I guess you've already left to go over to Jenny's. Funny how you always have time to spend with your friends. Don't bother calling me back tonight. I'm sure you'll be staying out late. Well, I have to get up early tomorrow because I work for a living. Call me tomorrow when you finish packing, so we...."

I erased the rest of the message without listening to the end. It would only be another reminder of the countless times during our marriage when Phillip insisted my desire to attend any social function was selfish, claiming that doing so made me a terrible wife and mother. What I finally had realized was that he was manipulating me with guilt. Those hurtful words had prevented me from going to baby showers, birthday parties, and countless other events I had wanted to attend. This latest ploy didn't work now because I'd learned it was another way he tried to control me.

"Screw him," I thought, flipping the answering machine the bird as I walked into the room to get dressed.

Sighing, I sat down and slumped across the mattress that was serving as my temporary bed, berating myself for telling Phillip in an email earlier in the day that I was going out in the first place. I should have known how he'd react. I was thankful I didn't tell him everything. Jenny was hosting a farewell dinner on my behalf and had invited several mutual friends. She'd also suggested I bring my laundry and spend the night. I wondered if Phillip knew that I did that frequently when Jenny's husband was away.

I looked down at Chubby Checkers, our small white Bichon-Lhasa mix, lying on the edge of the mattress. He looked up, wagging his tail.

"I'll bet you're looking forward to this evening as much as I am, Chub." I reached over to scratch his head, grateful for his company.

I wasn't used to being alone anymore. I felt untethered without a business to run and my kids to look after. Both kept me grounded and focused on the present. Now, I had too much time to think while I dismantled our life in Alexandria. Questions about the past and the future rattled around in my head.

I wanted to get to Jenny's before everyone else showed up, to talk with her about the ongoing saga of my troubled marriage. Things I had been blind to for decades were coming into sharp focus. Recollections of seemingly benign events were called into question and took on new meaning. I wasn't sure who Phillip was anymore. I was starting to think I never knew.

Reaching over, I picked up a small notebook lying on top of a cardboard box I was using as a nightstand. I was so busy over the last few days, I hadn't even told Jenny what I'd found under the desk. Earlier in the week, I'd received an email from Phillip asking me to help him recall all the dates of family birthdays and anniversaries. He couldn't locate the notebook where he kept all this information. Then I remembered seeing something on the floor beneath a desk in the office. He must have dropped it there on his last visit, which had been weeks ago.

I was delighted to find that not only did the notebook contain the dates of birthdays and anniversaries, but it also held all his usernames and passcodes. He had a horrible memory for such details. It wasn't long before I logged into his email account and was reading them without an iota of guilt.

What Phillip had written to various friends and members of his family left me numb. There was a tone of sheer hostility in his correspondence whenever he mentioned me. He made claims about my actions, or inactions, that revealed a resentment that was built on complete fabrications. Of particular note was an email he sent to his sister, Rachel. Phillip claimed I had squandered all the money from the sale of our house in the States on a "failed" business and that I had refused to follow through in contacting an attorney about our residency status in Canada. I wanted to scream when I read that. How dare he!

None of his claims were true. I had countless communications, in writing, from the Ottawa attorney filing documents on our behalf. I wondered why he didn't realize I had all our bank statements that included canceled checks to the attorney, and other financial records, that could show he was lying.

Reading this email allowed me to understand that his lies were another form of manipulation. I was starting to recognize that, by convincing his sister not to betray his confidences, he was assured she would never discuss this with me. His lies were actually a way for him to exert power and control over both of us.

His emails left me speculating, wondering why he was trying to frame the narrative beforehand. I began to wonder if he planned to file for divorce once the kids and I moved back to the U.S. It appeared he was trying to create the illusion I was the one at fault for all the problems between us in recent years. The whole matter made me eager to discuss what he'd written in them with Jenny. I was hoping we could talk in private so I could get her input.

I finished dressing and considered what I should do next. Jenny suggested we all gather around seven. Since it was only a bit after five, it was still too early to head her way. Confronting the piles of packed boxes cluttering the former tearoom downstairs was too daunting. There was little for me to do other than wait.

Earlier in the day I emptied shelves and disassembled various elements of my business, located on the main floor of the building. It was a bitter reminder of what I'd be leaving behind tomorrow when I traveled south. Even though the room was hot and stuffy, I avoided the unpleasantness of it all and stayed camped out in a room upstairs that once served as the office for my restaurant, The 2Beans Café and Tearoom.

Most people assumed 2Beans referred to coffee beans. But our twins were the real inspiration for naming the restaurant. We began calling them "the Beans" after Phillip and I saw their first ultrasound. They looked like two little kidney beans facing one another. It was a happy coincidence when it came time to name the restaurant nine years after they were born.

The opening of the restaurant was prompted by some decisions made after Phillip lost his job as a copywriter in February of 2005. The company he worked for in New Jersey merged with another ad agency and almost every employee was laid off. A year of unemployment forced us to make some hard decisions.

In October of 2006, we sold the old Victorian home we had lovingly restored in Blairstown, New Jersey. We moved into a rented apartment close to where the kids went to school and began looking for a way to start fresh.

We'd owned a vacation property in Quebec years ago, and Phillip's lifelong dream was to move to Canada permanently to reconnect with his French-Canadian heritage. He convinced me to purchase the property in Alexandria, Ontario, and we planned to open a family business. I thought reinventing our lives there would bring us closer together. Instead, the move fractured us in ways I never could have imagined.

We moved north at the end of June in 2007. Four months after we relocated, Phillip took a job back in the States, leaving the kids and me behind. He claimed it was because we needed the money. I vehemently disagreed because we still had plenty in the bank from the selling of our home in New Jersey. His absence left me raising the twins alone in a foreign country where I was also expected to operate the new business we were supposed to run together.

Phillip could only travel to Alexandria every few weeks. His visits and our conversations grew shorter and shorter as time and distance came between us.

"Hey. How was lunch today?" Phillip asked when he called each night.

"We were pretty busy," I would reply. I'd give him a brief rundown of the day and then ask, "How about you? Marco keeping you busy?"

"Yeah, I took work home. I have to work for a few more hours tonight. I was hoping I'd be able to come north this weekend, but it doesn't look like I'll have time. It makes little sense to travel six hours each way if I can't spend time with you and the Beans. Next weekend, though."

The excuses for why he couldn't come north were always the

same, and I believed him when he said he had to work, but it stung anyway. In the beginning, I tried to hide my frustration.

"That sucks. We all miss you," I would tell him.

"I know. I miss you, too. Are the kids there? I want to say hi," he'd reply.

I would put the phone on speaker so Phillip could talk to them both at the same time. I listened to him ask the same questions every night.

"How was school? Do you have lots of homework? What did you guys do today? How's Chubby?" When the list of banal questions were all answered, and silence filled the air, he'd say "goodnight," and "I love you. Can you put Mommy back on the phone?"

I believed then that the tenderness that came through the phone lines spoke of his loneliness. Back then, it left my heart melting. I both longed for him and hated him for leaving us behind. When I woke in the morning without him, my cycle of anger would begin again as I went through the day without him by my side.

ONE YEAR HAD TURNED into two, and there was always a reason Phillip said it made little sense for him to move north or for us to return south.

"How is Marco's business doing? Are things picking up at all?" I asked him often. It was my way of reminding him of his promise.

He responded, "Once the business is stable, you can all move back. Now is not the right time. We need to be sure my job is secure, and the business has been slow."

It never occurred to me to ask him, if Marco's business was so slow, why did he always have to work on the weekends?

After years of this, I grew immune to the loneliness in his voice and the hope that he'd visit. It hurt too profoundly to confront the reality that I had a husband I rarely saw and who our now eleven-year-old twins barely knew. He loomed over us like a distant rain cloud providing a break from the heat, but we knew the drenched earth would soon dry up and leave us all surveying the horizon, wondering when he would appear again.

I complained endlessly about the situation and expressed my anger with him to others. In reality, however, I missed him, and his choices hurt me. He was both the person who knew me best and a stranger. After decades of marriage, we had so much history together. Yet our lives had gone in such different directions.

I can't recall the exact moment it happened, but I suddenly realized I no longer had time to think about Phillip throughout my busy day. I was exhausted from hours of being on my feet. By the time I got into bed each night, the pains that ran down my back erased thoughts of Phillip.

Visits from him became further and further apart as he got busy, too. We were no longer a couple, with our lives immeasurably intertwined. We were two people who were married to one another, leading separate lives.

At first, he didn't need to be there physically to occupy a large part of my day. The rugs that lined the tearoom floor were the rugs that we had spent hours discussing before we purchased them for the formal parlor in our Victorian home. The antique lights that hung above the tables were the same ones we had selected to adorn our dining room years ago. There were family photos and memorabilia that brought to mind warm memories when I glimpsed them throughout my day. However, the miles between us couldn't withstand the simple march of time. The warmth of him lying beside me was a thing of the past, and the everyday reminders of him faded.

All the same things that were once a part of Phillip and me became part of a different world, one Phillip didn't inhabit. The twins and I had settled into a routine that didn't include him. We adapted and were thriving in the place we had thought of as home. We'd become members of a wonderful community, while Phillip was just a visitor.

I CHECKED the clock on the make-shift night stand to see if it was close to when I could leave for Jenny's. It was approaching six o'clock, so I still had an hour before I could reasonably leave for her house. I picked up Phillip's notebook but decided to avoid rereading his emails for a third and fourth time. Instead, I wandered downstairs to get a cold drink. Grabbing a can of club soda from the fridge, I glanced around the galley-style kitchen that had become my sanctuary. Away from Phillip's constant scrutiny, it was here that I found myself reawakening as my passion for cooking slowly reemerged.

Beginning to cook again had also caused me to realize how much of myself I'd abdicated to Phillip. Rediscovering my culinary flair gave me a sense of joy that had been smothered by the demands of churning out quick meals to feed my family. He always told me any meal that took more than a half-hour to make was a waste of time. Unchained from these demands, the luxury of watching the butter sizzle and brown in a pan to make a roux, and other mundane acts of cooking, became my elixir.

Standing there in the tiny kitchen, my anger boiled over as I acknowledged why moving back to the U.S. was so problematic.

I feared I would revert to the person I was when I had first arrived in Alexandria. The self-doubt and loathing faded only when Phillip wasn't there to present his image of me. I realized I had absorbed all the negative messages Phillip had sent me during our marriage when he attacked my character. In his absence, I had regained my confidence.

The bitterness swelled as I stood there, sipping my drink, wondering why he now wanted us to return to the States. I could only assume the worst because, for years, this arrangement had suited him just fine.

There was a part of me that wanted to go back in time. I yearned to retreat to the days before I had realized that none of the reasons Phillip initially gave me for his living six hours away made sense. I longed to erase the knowledge that he most likely had been lying to me for years. Now that I suspected why he wanted to be so far away; I couldn't shut out the thoughts that forced me to wonder why I didn't see it all along.

IN MARCH OF 2010, he'd taken a new job as a creative director for an ad firm in Albany, New York. I assumed he would happily continue our awkward arrangement of living separately. That wasn't the case. His attitude shifted dramatically, and he began overtly referring to the move north as a mistake and suggesting that it had been my idea. He complained bitterly that he was missing the twins' childhood and insinuated it was because the café wasn't making enough income to live on, so it forced him to get a job back in the States to support our family.

His comments alarmed me, but I only began piecing things together when he opened a separate bank account, one I didn't have access to. He said it was because I was "financially irresponsible" since I'd accidentally over-drafted our joint bank account one day. It didn't matter that I'd checked the balance before the withdrawal. We argued bitterly over whose fault it was. He'd made an unrecorded withdrawal which hadn't posted to the account, but he claimed it was my actions that resulted in the overdraft. Shortly after that, he closed our joint account because he claimed he needed to "put his foot down."

In April, he told me he would no longer contribute to paying any of the bills in Canada. He said it was a waste of "his money." The mortgage, taxes, and other building overhead, including all expenses related to his children, were now my sole responsibility. This made me furious, but it was another thing that opened my eyes. Now I knew he was hiding something—I just didn't know what.

When Phillip demanded the Beans and I move to the Albany area, I had to think that had been his plan all along. He made no mention of that before he took the job. He must have known that the property's overhead and expenses would drain any profit I made from operating the café. This would leave me with no funds of my own, giving him complete control over me once the Beans and I moved south.

At the end of June, I contacted an attorney in Alexandria who convinced me that if Phillip was planning to file for divorce, the only way to prevent a messy court battle was to go back south. Phillip was pleased that I wasn't resisting the move. Still, I was sure he wondered why I was so cooperative.

There were other things that struck me as significant signs of his intentions. One night, after he took the job in Albany, he called to tell me he'd found a place to live. He had moved into a single room in an expensive renovated mansion close to his job.

"My room is small, but it's close to work, so I don't have as long a commute anymore. You would love this place. There's a beautiful ballroom the owner converted into a common area for the tenants. I've been coming down here at night to play my guitar. Man, the acoustics are great."

I expressed concern when he mentioned how much it cost. It was twice the amount he'd spent on rent previously–and yet, he insisted money was tight.

"If it has no kitchen, what are you going to do about preparing meals? Aren't you going to have to eat out all the time?" I asked him.

"There are plenty of places to eat, and it was the closest place to work that I could find on short notice," he insisted.

"Okay. I get it. I'm just concerned because you told me your stomach acid is worse, not to mention the cost. It also worries me that the twins and I will have no place to stay when we come down there."

"I'll get up there again soon," he told me. "Look, I have to get up early. I'll talk to you tomorrow." He hung up abruptly without asking to speak to the kids.

By July, we began communicating mostly by email. Phillip's calls became less frequent, and when he did call, I put the kids on the phone immediately, or I let it go to voicemail. His tone of voice had changed. He was cold and business-like.

When the time came to look for an apartment to rent for the entire family, he suggested I look online at apartments forty-five minutes to an hour away from Albany, claiming the rents would be much cheaper. He was evasive when I asked why it was now okay to live that far away from work again.

AS I STOOD in the kitchen, I realized that for much of my marriage, I had taken Phillip at his word. He always seemed to have a reasonable explanation for spending time away from his family. However, when I began looking back at all the times he was away from us, I had to wonder what he was up to while we were apart.

It was hard enough to accept that our marriage might end, but all his actions made me assume the worst and more. My gut was telling me the miles between us were not the sole reason for his disengagement. I had begun to suspect there was another motive. I couldn't help but recall another time, years before, when we had broken up. His words back then echoed in my mind.

"I've met someone else, Kasey. I'm in love with her."

Chapter Two

DISTANT MEMORIES

I was astonished that I'd almost completely forgotten about Molly and the day Phillip announced he was ending our two-year relationship. The memories came flooding back to that miserable day in the fall of 1985. I had walked through the door of his apartment in Arlington, Massachusetts, a town close to Boston. I had just flopped on his sofa when I noticed the look on his face.

"I think somebody's had a rough day. You should have called me, honey. I would have stopped and picked up a nice bottle of wine. All I can offer you at the moment is a few Tic Tacs I found earlier at the bottom of my purse."

Phillip usually laughed at my attempts at humor, but my remarks did nothing to change the expression he wore.

"Phillip, what's wrong?"

He was silent for several moments.

"I've met someone else, Kasey. I'm in love with her."

I couldn't speak, my mind racing as it absorbed Phillip's explosive news. With heart pounding, I gathered my thoughts and waited some time before I trusted myself enough to say something civil.

"I see. Who is she?"

"The new receptionist at work. Her name is Molly."

Phillip had mentioned Molly's name several times since she'd started work a month earlier. I never picked up on anything more than a casual remark about a new colleague. I waited to hear more, but he said nothing.

"I'm assuming we're over?"

He nodded but refused to look at me.

I choked back tears as I walked towards the door. What he said next was beyond comprehension.

"Wait!"

I stopped, hoping he was going to tell me it was a horrible joke or that he couldn't bear to see me go. I turned back to face him.

"I don't want to lose you!" he said. "We can still be friends."

I didn't wait to hear more. I fled Phillip's apartment and drove to a nearby convenience store so I could compose myself enough to drive back to my apartment. As I sat in my car, I thought that was the end of my relationship with Phillip.

WHEN PHILLIP and I met in 1983, he was working as a producer in Boston. I'd scheduled a business meeting for my company, RSVP Communications, to introduce the work of a consortium of producers and directors that my partner Gerry and I represented. I was meeting with Phillip to learn more about the company he worked for, while I would be presenting highlights of RSVP's creative talent to the agency.

A handsome young man approached me when the elevator doors opened to the lobby of the ad agency. Phillip introduced himself and reached out to shake my hand. His engaging eyes and friendly demeanor left me taken aback.

During his presentation, he exuded confidence. I felt myself wanting to know more about him. My thoughts were no longer on my growing business as I focused on Phillip's crooked smile and authenticity.

Weeks later, I reached out to him about joining my company as one of our producer/directors. It was merely an excuse to contact him. We became fast friends and started to develop small film projects together.

My friends kept asking me if I was interested in him romantically. I insisted I wasn't, offering the explanation that he was several years younger than I was or, *he isn't my type*. But there was something about him that had me looking forward to seeing him. Our projects soon became an excuse to be with one another. He was so talented and funny, and we enjoyed spending much of our free time together.

WHAT I APPRECIATED MOST about Phillip initially was that he was different than many of the men I'd worked with in the past. I always seemed to work alongside this fraternal pack of grown boys who barely recognized their female colleagues as coworkers. Many of the women I worked with got smaller projects and lower salaries. Phillip, however, treated me more seriously, both personally and professionally.

One of the reasons I started my own business was I was sick to death of being just as skilled as my male counterparts without getting the credit for my work. It seemed like the only time I got positive feedback was when I wore something that showed off my figure. I'd hear the whispers and tried to laugh off the uncomfortable banter that my male co-workers referred to as *jokes*.

"Hey, where's your sense of humor?" was my least favorite comment from these colleagues.

As a single woman, I was often passed over for promotions in favor of male coworkers who, I was told, deserved the raise more since they had families to support.

I started my own business to get away from a company where men had the right to say and do despicable things, and I was expected to go along.

By the time I met Phillip, I found it so refreshing to work with a guy who never displayed these horrible, misogynistic tendencies

—at the time. Back then, he treated me like an equal, and I couldn't help but admire him.

As our working relationship grew, we pooled our financial resources in order to option the tv/film rights of a book by local writer, Art Meyers, called *Ghosts in America and Where to Find Them*. I was the producer, while Phillip directed, and we co-wrote the pilot episode, with Art acting as the pilot's narrator.

We had scheduled the film shoot for a weekend in early September of 1984. It was a cold and rainy day. We were shooting the film at two locations. First we set-up in a graveyard and next, at an inn that was supposedly haunted by the ghost of a woman.

Things went haywire all day. We had to end our graveyard shoot early because of heavy rain. Then, our fully-charged batteries failed when we tried to use them to power the camera to shoot a scene in the attic of the inn. While shooting a scene in a meeting room, Phillip tried to do a white balance on the video camera. He ended up recording a shadow between the camera and the wall that was only inches away. We were all spooked by the strange events of the day, and most of the footage we recorded was unusable.

The owner of the inn provided us with dinner at its in-house restaurant. Before our meals came, I hurried off to use the restroom, the one rumored to have ghostly sightings. Per usual, I was the only woman on the crew. I was apprehensive about going in by myself, but I couldn't wait, so I sucked it up and off I went. Shortly after I used the toilet, something startled me so much, I screamed.

The camera guy knocked on the bathroom door.

"Are you okay? We thought we heard a scream."

"I'm good. There was a huge spider. It scared me. Nasty creature. The size of a quarter," I fibbed. Embarrassed, I came out of the restroom, and sat down, convinced I had covered up the truth about what had occurred.

Phillip and I had driven to the shoot together, so he drove me back to my apartment after we wrapped for the day. When we arrived, he parked in the driveway and turned to me with a knowing smile.

"Okay, Kasey. What happened in there?" he quizzed me.

I hesitated for a moment before telling him.

"All right; busted. If you tell anyone about this, I'll kill you, got it? Well, I accidentally wrapped my underwear around the toilet seat. When I went to get up, the seat came up too, and as I pulled up my undies, it crashed onto the enamel bowl. I thought the noise was a ghost."

He started to laugh so hard, I had to laugh, too. At first, I thought he was making fun of me, but then he looked over and pulled me towards him.

"I've wanted to do this for a long time," he said, kissing me.

We went upstairs to my apartment and started a new chapter of our relationship.

AFTER WE BEGAN OFFICIALLY DATING, our romantic and creative goals became wholly intertwined. We talked about moving to New York City, where we planned to produce independent films together. I was working at a company near Boston at the time because my business had folded when my former partner and I had creative conflicts. I wasn't happy with the job, so we had decided I should look for work in Manhattan first, and Phillip would move down shortly after that. But before any of that happened, our relationship was abruptly over and he started dating Molly, a divorced woman with a young child.

I was heartbroken. Not only was I losing the man I'd fallen in love with, I was also losing one of my best friends and my writing partner. Gone, too, were our dreams of moving to New York City. I'd already started sending out my resumé so I could secure a job in advance of Phillip quitting his full-time position. When he ended our relationship, I felt like I'd lost my world. In many ways, I did.

I didn't realize until he broke up with me how much Phillip seemed to complete me. I couldn't console myself and felt as though my entire life was falling apart. I picked up the phone dozens of times to call him but didn't have the courage to dial his number. I found myself going to a second-run movie theatre in town so I had an excuse to cry, watching sad, romantic movies. I didn't realize, at the time, there was another reason for my fragile emotional state.

MORE THAN A MONTH PASSED WHEN, out of the blue, Phillip called me. I tried to control myself when I heard his voice. He told me he was in Los Angeles, where he'd gone on vacation. Just like that, he announced his relationship with Molly was over, claiming it was a huge mistake.

I didn't know what to think. I was overjoyed to hear from him, but skeptical of why he assumed I would be so willing to just accept him back into my life. I wasn't sure if he wanted to resume our romantic relationship or just reconnect as friends. I didn't ask the hard questions and, instead, we chatted about safe subjects like work and movies. But we talked for hours. By the time I got off the phone, I knew I still wanted to be with him.

When he came back from Los Angeles, he arrived at the door of my attic apartment with a bouquet of roses and asked me to forgive him. I let him in and made dinner, grappling with a way to tell him my big news.

"So, speaking of awkward timing, I have something to tell you," I started, trying to find the right words.

"Did you get that job in New York?"

"Not exactly." Finally, I blurted it out. "I don't know how this happened, but I'm pregnant. I mean, I know how it happened. Shit, you know what I mean."

Phillip was quiet for a long time.

"Say something, Phillip. I need to know what you're thinking."

"Well, it's not the news I expected. What happens here is your decision, but I am hoping you'll decide not to have an abortion. It's the whole Catholic thing. Other than that, Kasey, I don't know what to say about the situation."

I moved the food around on my plate. I knew it was a complete shock, so I didn't press him. I'd had weeks to process the news. He'd only had a few minutes, so I let him be. He left shortly after that without saying much. I cried endlessly over the next few days when I didn't hear from him. When he did finally call, he didn't even bring up the subject.

I was riddled with guilt, believing I was ruining Phillip's life. It didn't occur to me at the time that we were both responsible for the situation and this life-altering news affected me too. Regardless, humiliation overtook me. Clinging to the religious upbringing of my childhood made me believe the unplanned pregnancy made me a bad person and I felt ashamed that, even with taking birth control, it still happened.

Phillip seemed to disappear once again and, losing him a second time was even more devastating. The belief that I was completely at fault for the circumstances overtook my reasoning and I fell into a state of constant anxiety.

Deciding whether to keep the pregnancy kept me up at night. I assumed I would be raising the child on my own if I kept the pregnancy and struggled with the idea of what being a single mother would mean. I was never one of those women that dreamt of weddings or motherhood. I had wrestled control of my life away from my father. I couldn't see myself following the same path as my mother who had little control over the direction of her life.

Long before this happened, I had decided I didn't want to answer to a man. I cherished my independence and I was determined to avoid what I saw as the pitfalls most women face once they leave home. I even refused to learn how to type, fearing it would mean I would only be considered for secretarial positions or office work. I frequently joked that if I married, it would be in my eighties, and I'd have kids in my nineties. To me, marriage and children meant relinquishing control over my heart's desires.

As the youngest of seven children, I watched my mother struggle to gain her independence from my father, and it had a big impression on me as I was growing up. I didn't want to be overcome with the bitterness I saw in her. She had a total of eight pregnancies, which meant she was carrying a child for most of her twenties and thirties. She finally got her driver's license in her forties and got a part-time job as a cook in a nursing home when I was around ten. I feared marriage and children would make me dependent on a husband. I was unwilling to give up my cherished independence.

As I faced the decisions over what to do about the unplanned pregnancy, however, I found myself very conflicted. I couldn't see myself having an abortion because, deep inside, I kept imagining myself with the baby. Finally, I decided I wanted to keep the pregnancy, despite the circumstances, and was determined to raise the child on my own since Phillip seemed to have walked away from the relationship yet again.

WHEN HE CALLED WEEKS LATER, he seemed cold and distant. I was surprised when he asked me to go out to dinner on the weekend. I assumed he wanted to meet someplace neutral so he could break up.

We met at a steak house, not far from where I lived at the time. Shortly after we ordered dinner, he looked across the table. I held my breath, expecting the worst.

"Kasey, I've been thinking about asking you this for a while but—will you marry me?"

I was in shock. It was not at all what I expected.

"Gee, Phillip. I do love you, and I do want to marry you." It was true. I did want to marry him. "Honey, I don't want to start a marriage feeling like the only reason you want to marry me is that I'm pregnant. You broke up with me because of Molly, and now you're suddenly willing to commit to marriage? I have to think this is more about my being pregnant than it is about our relationship." And that was precisely how I felt. He reached across the table and took my hand in his. He looked me in the eyes and pleaded his case.

"Kasey, the fling with Molly was a terrible mistake. It happened. But when I went to L.A., the only one I thought about was you. I missed you. I didn't miss her. There was an attraction with her, but it's over. I called her before I called you that night because I had decided I wanted to be with you. That was before you even told me. We have a chance for a life together. I know that now. I've been thinking about asking you to marry me even before you told me. Honest. The pregnancy just hurried things along."

I wanted to believe him but, deep inside, I had doubts. We always talked about a life together, but not once could I recall ever hearing the word *marriage*. Still, that night, I accepted his proposal. We decided to get married after the New Year.

IN JANUARY OF 1986, we said our vows before a justice of the peace. I was several months pregnant at that point, and it seemed like he was happy about raising a child. He moved into my attic apartment and, we started our life together.

The cracks in the relationship started soon after that. The biggest one was that Phillip refused to tell anyone other than his sister Rachel that we were married. While he told his close friends and colleagues at work, he kept the rest of his family in the dark. Phillip wouldn't even tell them we were living together. Instead, he told layer upon layer of lies to conceal his secrets.

The awkwardness of this was detrimental. I'd told my friends and family members that we'd gotten married. I didn't tell them why but knew they'd figure that out soon enough. Our marriage was now a secret to some and public to others. I kept wondering if he had really been planning to ask me to marry him before he found out I was pregnant. I was having serious doubts.

My anxiety and guilt magnified as weeks passed. Phillip made excuse after excuse for keeping our marriage hidden. Whenever I brought up the subject, he acted like I was making a fuss over nothing.

In February, right before President's Day weekend, we were out buying a gift for his mother's and grandmother's birthdays. We were heading to his parents' for a big celebration since Phillip's birthday and my birthday were that weekend too. When we got in the car, I finally mustered the courage and asked him the looming question.

"Are you planning on telling your folks we got married?"

"You don't know my mother very well," he told me. "This news will ruin the weekend. I'm already the black sheep of the family. I'd rather not contribute to my already shocking reputation," he told me.

I reasoned that he knew them better than I did, but it bothered me.

MONTHS PASSED, and still Phillip refused to tell them. When I was almost five months along, I had a routine visit with my OB/GYN. I'd been feeling poorly and had little appetite. The doctor ordered an ultrasound, which revealed there was no longer any movement. He determined I had miscarried and did an emergency D and C procedure.

The day was a blur. I remember calling Phillip to come to get me at the hospital. We were both distraught. He took the next day off of work to stay with me. The shared experience didn't seem to move us closer together or, tear us apart. We seemed to ignore the emotional toll by moving past it without any discussion. This became a familiar pattern to our conflicts.

Whatever Phillip felt about the loss of the pregnancy, he kept it to himself. The whole matter became a dark moment in our relationship, one we never discussed. There was only one sign regarding his grief. The tiny booties my friend Dawn had knitted for me, the ones I'd kept on my dresser, disappeared one day. I never saw them again.

A new sense of guilt festered in me. I believed Phillip blamed me for miscarrying, or for the pregnancy itself. I blamed myself too. I wondered if I did, or didn't, do something that triggered the miscarriage. One moment, I was glad I didn't have to face the complexities of raising a child; the next, I was grief-stricken. I tried to reason that I was hardly ready for the responsibility; however, I was outright sorrowful, too.

AFTER THE MISCARRIAGE, our expectations for the future seemed to hang solely on the creative nature of our relationship. There were unspoken emotions that lived on in the tiny apartment. Moving to New York became even more of an urgent goal. All Phillip and I talked about was where, when, and how to move to Manhattan so we could further our careers in the film industry. It was a safe subject and one that raised few of the emotions we'd buried.

I happily agreed to pave the way for both of us since I'd lived for a short time in Brooklyn, years before, with my parents. We again discussed the idea that I should try to get a job in New York City first, and once I was established, Phillip would quit his job and move there.

In the fall of 1986, I landed a full-time job at an animation company in mid-town Manhattan and rented an apartment in Brooklyn. Phillip moved down months later. He continued to avoid telling his parents we got married and even told them we were living in separate places. The fact that he wouldn't even broach the truth that we were living together was hurtful.

Without much fanfare, I somehow went from being his *girl-friend* to being his *fiancé*. When we visited Marblehead, where his parents lived, I had to remove my wedding ring and put on my engagement ring.

In many ways, however, I didn't feel like we were married, either. Our relationship seemed almost like a "friends with bene-fits arrangement." We still had the same intense physical attraction, but we were much more reserved since the unplanned pregnancy. Trying to make sure I didn't get pregnant again, I not only kept using a diaphragm, but I started using the Pill, too. Still, he questioned me every time we made love.

"Is it safe?"

The question made me wonder if he thought I had a way of knowing exactly when I was ovulating. I was not inclined to subjects like biology and had to trust that my birth control methods were working. It angered me that he insinuated I should be able to assure him that I wouldn't get pregnant.

ANOTHER COMPLICATION EMERGED after we moved to Brooklyn. Phillip wasn't working. He was relying on his savings so he could "establish himself" as a film director. He always spoke of being the next Joel Coen or George Ramos, directors who started out making low budget films that catapulted their careers. He kept reliving his glory days as the young up-and-coming Boston director that created a commercial news insert series. The inserts his company created featured a prominent Boston actor that spoke of consumer and safety tips. After a disagreement with his partners, the company dissolved and he moved on to the ad agency where I had met him.

I couldn't understand why he wouldn't take any job to show off his skills to those who could help him move up the ladder.

"I'm not going to work as a production assistant, Kasey. Forget it. I'm sorry if you don't think I'm more talented than that."

"Phillip! No one believes in you more than I do! But you can't expect to get a job directing in New York right away. The markets are completely different. I see all these young guys your age working as producers or editors, making great money, so they can build their director's reel. It takes time to break into this market. You need contacts and a reputation."

"Yeah, I'll get right on that."

PHILLIP ALSO INSISTED we both keep separate bank accounts. Unlike most married couples, we kept all financial transactions both independent and private. While that changed over time, initially, it was the way we handled our expenses. It reinforced the notion that he wasn't planning for a long-term future together.

This also reinforced significant problems. Because he wasn't working, I was never comfortable asking him to reimburse me for the money I spent on his behalf. However, if he went grocery shopping, I was expected to fork over my share when we reconciled expenses at the end of the week or month. He kept track of all these things, while I rarely did. It seemed petty at the time.

As a married couple, he was covered under my health insurance, just as I was once covered under his with his job back in Boston. Those costs were deducted from my check with a family plan instead of the less expensive individual coverage. I never asked him to reimburse me for the difference because I never even knew if he was required by his employer to pay for the additional coverage at his old job. There were other expenses I paid over and above my share, but I was always reluctant to mention them.

I imagined that, outwardly, we appeared to be a *happy couple*. But the fact he continued to lie about our marriage gave me doubts about the true nature of his feelings. He said the words, "I love you," but what did that mean if he couldn't even tell his parents that we got married and why?

I started to believe he was somehow ashamed of me, which wreaked havoc on my self-confidence. I believed that, at any minute, he could decide it was over. Deep inside, I thought if I gave him a reason, he would end the relationship once again.

I didn't mind our awkward arrangement most of the time because I was utterly in love with Phillip. He made me laugh so much of the time. We had great fun together, exploring New York City and dreaming of the days ahead when we were both established in our creative careers.

WHEN HIS SAVINGS started to run out, I had to chip in more and more to keep us afloat. I started covering the rent so he didn't have to worry about that financial concern. I thought it was another way I was showing him my love.

Soon, work and our creative goals became a sore spot to discuss. Instead of compromising his dreams, he spent the last of his savings optioning the film rights to a screenplay. He found someone who promised to finance the project, only to have that fall apart, too.

Next, he began sending his reel to the directors who owned production companies in the City. When there were no bites, he asked me to bake cookies to send along with his reel and his resumé. Finally, he landed a job with a large entertainment company, but he only lasted about three weeks before quitting and sending a hot-headed letter to those he worked for, telling them how unprofessional they were.

IN THE MEANTIME, I kept working full-time at the animation company and continued to work on a musical I had started long before I met him. The more progress I made as a writer, however, the more Phillip seemed resentful that my work was getting noticed while his career had stalled.

When I came home from work one day, Phillip greeted me at the door with a smile on his face.

"Say, thank you," he joshed.

"Okay… thank you," I replied cautiously. "Now what exactly am I thanking you for?"

"I spent the whole day fixing your script," he told me, beaming.

"You did what?" I asked, unsure of what he meant.

"The expository writing in your libretto needed a lot of work, so I took the time to fix it," he told me, certain I'd be overjoyed.

"You saved my original script, didn't you?" I asked, panicking.

"Of course not," he told me. "You have a hard copy so I just wrote over the last draft on your disk."

I was beside myself. It was as if he took my child to a tattoo parlor and permanent ink now covered their body.

"Did I ask you to do that, Phillip?" I said, more sharply than intended.

"No, but…" he began to explain.

"The musical is my project. I didn't ask for your help because I want to do it on my own," I tried to explain while keeping my tone in check.

"Screw you, Kasey. I tried to help you because your work needs it," he said, his voice escalating.

"How would you feel if I did the same thing?" I asked him sharply.

"That's a joke. You would never have a reason to revise my work because you aren't skilled enough."

"Oh, is that so? That's not what you've said in the past. I seem to recall plenty of times you said you admired my writing. And if my work isn't up to par, why is it that any time you're working on a writing project, my ideas always end up in your scripts?"

"Don't make me laugh," he snarled, refusing to answer my question. "You'll never be a writer, Kasey, because you lack the education it requires to be successful. You don't even know how to type properly. Why don't you start by learning how to type, and then maybe you should consider going back to school if you want to be a real writer," he shouted as he stormed off to his office.

That was the first time I recall Phillip taking aim at my talent as a writer, but it wasn't the last. It stung because some of what he said was true. I was better at the large picture elements of writing, like character development, plot, and writing dialogue, while he was much more adept at expository writing. When we began working together, our strengths and weaknesses seemed to balance one another. Now, however, he seemed to imply I had no talent at all just because I lacked a college degree. For a while, I put my musical away. And for some time after that, if he asked me to look at his writing, I refused because I no longer had the confidence that he truly valued my input.

While I eventually got over his hurtful remarks and began working once again on my musical project, he'd learned something from this encounter: When he wanted to truly hurt me, he stoked the flames of my insecurities and they grew.

AS I WAITED to head to Jenny's, I finally realized I should have confronted Phillip long ago. However, as time went on, I was too afraid to hear the truth. Ignoring it was so much easier. I didn't know then that buried feelings would linger and color our relationship for years to come, leaving me assuming things about our relationship that would eventually haunt me.

Looking back, I realized that my inability to confront him about money established an imbalance in our relationship. Back then, I believed that he felt trapped and was staying with me because he needed my help to further his career. In the early days of our marriage, it made me try harder to please him. I thought if I proved I was worthy of his love that he'd love me the way I loved him.

My recent revelations made me realize that if we stayed married, I would either have to confront the issues that plagued our marriage or remain trapped in an unhealthy relationship. If we divorced, I would be presented with another set of problems. That was the reality of what life looked like both with and without Phillip.

Phillip wasn't going to make the process easy. I could already tell by what he'd written in his emails to friends and family that he was blaming me for much of our dysfunction and had portrayed himself as the injured party. Additionally, I knew that divorced women rarely recover financially. In my case, my lucrative career in New York was long over. Even if I was able to someday return to Alexandria and keep my restaurant, I knew that the expenses for the building were mounting, and repairs often exceeded the income I made from the business.

His refusal to contribute to these expenses left me with little in the bank at the end of each month. So, now, when I returned to the States, I would have no money of my own to reestablish myself or care for the Beans.

I finally understood my mother's decision not to leave my father decades ago. She was so unhappy about his decision to move the family to Western New York so he could attend Bible school. My mother complained bitterly about moving away from her family and friends, but my father made many of the decisions in their marriage.

I realized that when you leave a marriage, you're not just leaving a husband or wife. You're leaving all the entanglements marriage involves. It means giving up more than a spouse. You're giving up a way of life. The language of marriage is *we* and *us* and *ours*. Years of living together blends the boundaries of family, finances, and memories. There is little individuality anymore. Where one ends, the other starts. There is this homogenous creation that is difficult to separate, like the yolk from the egg white.

When my mother thought about leaving my father, she struggled because it meant leaving a large chunk of herself behind. So she stayed. For her, it turned out to be the right choice. She seemed to reconcile herself to this new experience and adjusted to the change. But unlike my mother, I was grappling with a host of different issues. My father loved my mother, and she never had to question his fidelity or commitment to their relationship.

However, I began to recognize that doubt plagued my marriage from the start. Phillip's concealment of our marital status from his family had meant keeping our two families apart. My family and friends became secondary in all matters related to things we did as a couple. It had set up a dynamic in our relationship that left me feeling erased. My traditions and experiences weren't a part of *us*. I assimilated into his world to accommodate his lie.

I realized I was just beginning to grasp the full extent of the impact the past had on my marriage to Phillip. In those early days of our marriage, I was offering Phillip reason after reason to stay in the relationship. While my intention was to be supportive, it fostered an unhealthy way to use money as a tool to get what I wanted: a husband that would love and appreciate the sacrifices I was making. My acts however, resulted in giving him even more control over me.

Suddenly, I realized that back then, the message he received, loud and clear, was that I was willing to work full-time while he spent time establishing his career. This left me wondering, for years, if he truly loved me.

I couldn't understand why telling his parents the truth had been so daunting. It didn't seem to bother him at all that for more than three years, he had to remove his wedding ring each time we went to visit his folks. During our more than twenty-five years together, he had kept secrets from those he loved the most. Now I had to wonder, what secrets Phillip might be keeping from me.

IT WAS FINALLY ALMOST seven o'clock. I opened a can of cat food and separated the contents into two bowls before placing them on the kitchen floor for our two Maine Coon cats, Duncan and Felicia. With that out of the way, I began to gather items I would be taking to Jenny's and placed them on a table by the front door.

I went upstairs to get my overnight bag, and Chubby tagged along. He patiently waited while I gathered my belongings so we could leave. The look on his face expressed his love for me: unwavering, complete and forgiving. I was so grateful for his company.

I didn't want to rush up and down the staircase, so I closed Chub in the office, knowing he'd be unmanageable once he sensed it was finally time to go. I could hear him frantically scratching at the door as I carried my bags downstairs. When I was finished getting everything together, I grabbed his leash off its hook and went back upstairs to open the door for him. He looked crushed, thinking that I'd left him behind.

As he rushed down the stairs, I dropped his leash. As I picked it up, I noticed the reflection in the window at the bottom of the stairs. I could see all three rooms that comprised my former business. To the right was the tiny galley-style kitchen, stripped of all the equipment. It looked naked now that the cupboards were bare. Ahead of me was the entrance to the café. Other than the counters that still held the cappuccino machine and coffee grinder, it, too, was now empty. To the left, the once elegant tearoom was piled high with boxes and bags of trash to be discarded. It was a reflection of my life, which was in a total state of disarray. I left for Jenny's feeling thankful I had something else to look forward to instead of the whole scene I was leaving behind.

Chapter Three

TIME FOR WINE AND WHINE

"Come on, Chub. Let's go."

I locked the door of the café and left for Jenny's, looking forward to the evening with friends, trusting it would lift my spirits. I put Chubby in the front seat, hoping he'd behave. He had a bad habit of trying to climb on my shoulders as I drove. The kids were usually there to prevent him from advancing towards me. When I was alone, however, he had a sneaky way of waiting until I wasn't looking, then he'd lunge towards me. The sudden movement was startling, and he'd almost caused me to go off the road more than once.

That had me thinking about the long drive I faced the next day. I would be dealing with transporting two angry cats and a devious dog for hours by myself. The van itself was barely roadworthy. The instrument panel was faulty, and I couldn't determine fuel levels or speed. I started thinking about whether I should see if my friend Jody would board Chubby for a few days at her kennel.

I drove down the gravel laneway to Jenny's house. Vast fields of grasses, wildflowers, and trees of various sizes lined either side of the drive. White balls of Queen Anne's Lace offset the deep pink flowers of the milkweed in bloom. Long, dusky green stems of mullein with delicate, yellow petals could be seen interspersed with the thin stragglers of miterwort poking out of the chaotic array. I took in the familiar scene, trying to remember every detail to use as a reminder of good times.

The small, brown, bi-level ranch was set about a quarter of a mile from the road. As I approached the house, Chubby tried to get out even before I stopped the car. Unable to climb over me, he retreated and hung his head out the window and barked at Lacy, Jenny's aging black lab. I opened the door, and he jumped over me, chasing Lacy down the expanse of the back yard. The place was a second home to Chubby, too.

The house sat on fifty acres of wooded land with large, lush lawns surrounding the house. The manicured areas were lined with towering blue spruce, dogwood, and eastern redbud trees. The magenta, heart-shaped leaves of the redbud would soon start to fade, but they created a lovely border. There was an aging barn with a small pond to the right of it. At the very back of the property, there was a large beaver pond.

The smell of fresh-cut grass filled the air. The dogs dodged Jenny's riding lawnmower parked near a storage shed. Seeing them disappear into the bushes made me smile. I left my overnight bag and laptop in the car but gathered the bag of food I'd brought for the occasion.

Climbing the steep, wide steps of the back porch, I found Jenny sitting there, talking with Carole. It was a familiar scene. Carole, Jenny's no-nonsense, snarky but brilliant neighbor spent as much time on Jenny's back porch as I did.

The expression on my face must have given away my mood. Jenny and Carole met me halfway up the steps. Carole took the bags and disappeared into the kitchen. Jenny walked over to the table, where there were several bottles of wine and alcohol. I needed no encouragement to join her. She gave me a gentle hug. I looked away, knowing that she understood the night would be difficult. Her wry smile was an unspoken acknowledgment that it was okay to be sad.

I knew the occasion would be fraught with a range of

emotion. I'd been through this same scenario too many times in my life. I used to believe it was possible to maintain friendships at a distance, but my past informed me not to be optimistic. There would be earnest promises to stay in touch and, for a while, those promises would be kept. But life has a way of filling in around us. The one leaving is soon replaced with new people or experiences. They are fondly remembered but forgotten over time. I'd learned it was best to write names in address books in pencil because even the closest of friendships don't weather distance easily.

"Looks like someone could use a big ole glass of wine!" she said, handing me a large glass of chardonnay without asking.

"Make it a bottle, and now we're talking," I said with a lame smile.

Over the last three years, Jenny and I had confided in one another about our marital woes. Having experienced the break-up of a marriage on multiple occasions, she was able to offer advice. She schooled me on how to handle the situation. I was grateful for her input because I was so sure my marriage was heading in that direction.

Jenny and I crossed the porch and took seats next to Carole. I caught them up on the events of the last few days, then began telling them about Phillip's notebook.

"I couldn't believe it. I wish he'd jotted down his bank account information. I don't even know how much he's making in this new job. Of course, he's hounding me about getting the packing done. He completely ignores the fact that I had the kids and a business to contend with up until a week ago. He's sitting in an air-conditioned office, writing advertising copy. He thinks it's nothing to pack in this heat."

"Has he offered to come up and help you?" Carole asked.

"Nope. He said he was coming up last weekend but then called me at the last minute and told me he had to work."

"Do you think that's true, or is he making excuses?" Jenny asked.

"Who knows? I don't know what the hell is going on down there. And I still have one last catering job tomorrow. Thank

God, Kate offered to do all the baking. He was furious that I agreed to take the job, but I need the money since he refuses to pay any bills up here."

"What? When did that happen?" Carole asked as she grabbed the crudités off a nearby table and offered me some.

"Jeez, he did that months ago. Yup. He opened up a separate bank account when he took the job in Albany." I gnawed on a carrot loaded with dip.

"Gee, Kase," Jenny cautioned. "That's not a good sign."

"I've only met him a few times, but he always seemed like such a nice guy," Carole added.

"I know. That's the problem. He is a nice guy. Or at least he can be. None of this adds up," I told them. "That's why I'm convinced he's decided to divorce me, and he's trying to get custody, too."

"Well, I agree he's up to something... but do you really think he wants custody?" Jenny added, frowning.

"It sure seems that way. Maybe I'm reading too much into things, but why would he be trying to make me look financially unstable and lying about where our savings went? Plus, he knows exactly how vulnerable I'll be without a job once I move back to the States. He doesn't want me back there because he misses me. The kids maybe, but not me. That's for sure."

"Well, we could always throw him in the beaver pond!" Jenny said with a smile.

"Why didn't I think of that? Problem solved!"

We raised our glasses.

"To the beaver pond!" we all cheered.

I pictured the acres of marshy wetlands and Jenny's beaver pond. Throwing someone in the beaver pond was the Canadian version of sending someone to sleep with the fishes. We all touched one another's glasses of wine and cheered again.

"Wait! Who's going in the beaver pond now?" Lisa asked as she came around the massive row of bushes that framed Jenny's back porch.

"Hi, Lisa. Phillip, of course!" I said jokingly. Like many of my customers and friends, she'd met Phillip. She climbed the steps carefully, holding a platter of lemon squares and brownies.

"What did I miss?" she asked. I made room for her platter on the table before responding to her question.

"Well, I'm pretty sure my marriage is over," I told her. "For some reason, Phillip seems to resent the life I've built here. He's convinced moving to Canada and opening a café was all my idea."

"But that's not true! It's all sour grapes. It's too bad it never worked out for him here, but he can't blame you."

"He can and does." I heard the gravel of Jenny's driveway crunching. Moments later, Betty poked her head around the corner. I grabbed the antipasto she was carrying, while Lisa took the bottle of wine.

"What did I miss? I heard you all talking!" she asked.

"Kasey was filling us in on her troubles with Phillip," Lisa said, looking my way.

"It's the same old story," I assured Betty as I turned to take the antipasto into the kitchen to place it in the fridge.

My cavalier attitude belied my deep concern. I shuddered at the thought Phillip would try to get custody of the Beans. He was a loving father, but I had grave doubts that he had any idea what it took to both work full-time and care for them. Once, when I told him it was hard to work all day and always be available to address the kid's needs, he scoffed. He'd told me repeatedly, in dozens of ways, that he didn't even consider owning and operating the café *work*.

And then there was another issue that was bothering me even more. What if Phillip was having an affair? Would he come clean and tell me he was leaving me for someone else? Would the twins be introduced into his new life? The Beans were so shy around new people. I couldn't imagine a scenario that would be good for them in any way. They already resented him for forcing us to move after we'd promised them, when we left the States, we were moving for the last time.

I returned to the porch carrying a bowl of hummus and a

platter full of naan bread I'd taken from the fridge. Lisa and Betty were talking, and looked at me intently, with questions that lingered from our earlier conversation. Lisa seemed a bit skeptical that my concerns about the custody issue were as serious as they were.

"So, do you really think he would try to get custody? They've lived with you, here in Canada, for what, three or four years?" She took a slice of naan bread and dipped it in the hummus.

"I honestly don't know. But I think that's why he's trying to guarantee I'll have no means of supporting the kids. And he's lying about things to his sister. You wouldn't believe the horse crap he's feeding to her in his emails. The man is up to no good."

"Wait! How do you know what he said in an email to his sister?" Betty asked. I smiled and let them speculate.

"Let's just say Phillip's not the only one who's up to no good."

"Hey, ladies! We're here to party. Betty doesn't even have a drink yet!" Jenny reminded us, pouring her a glass of wine.

Jenny and Carole approached the table and started chatting with Lisa and Betty. I ducked inside the house, pretending I needed to use the washroom. I really just wanted a moment to myself. I wanted to enjoy the night, but it was hard not to wonder what the future held for the Beans and me, knowing I would be trying to navigate life with no job and no money, and a husband I no longer trusted.

A few more of our friends joined us as the evening progressed. When we'd had enough of the appetizers, I went into Jenny's kitchen to make our main entree, my famous "Tuscan Chicken." I had no idea if this dish was Tuscan, never mind Italian. I called it that for lack of a better name when I served it at the café. Like many chefs, I hated to use recipes. I drew my culinary inspiration from what I found in the fridge or while cruising the aisles of the grocery store.

I knew Jenny's kitchen almost as well as my own. I grabbed a large skillet out of her pantry. I began to relax, away from conversations laden with heavy questions. I hummed to myself as I took the chicken breasts out of the fridge. The tension melted as I pounded each breast into thin medallions, seasoned each portion with generous amounts of salt and pepper, and then seared the medallions in olive oil before adding minced garlic.

Removing the nicely browned chicken, I turned up the heat, then added balsamic vinegar and honey to the hot pan. The flavorful bits of chicken and garlic loosened from the bottom of the pan and, soon, I had a thick brown sauce that smelled rich and fragrant. In small batches, I returned the chicken to the pan, coating each piece with the tangy mixture. As I turned each piece, the chicken became a mahogany brown. The tang of the vinegar and honey had almost an Asian flavor, making me wonder, now, why I called it "Tuscan Chicken" in the first place. I guess it was the balsamic vinegar that inspired the name. Plus, anything that sounds Italian was bound to sell at the café.

Standing over the stove, inhaling the savory scent of chicken, I thought again about my relationship with Phillip. I had to wonder why I never realized the scope of how bad it was because from the very beginning; there were so many signs along the way.

ABOUT A YEAR after we moved to Brooklyn, Phillip got a letter from his sister that got him to finally consider resolving the awkward situation about our semi-secret marriage. One day, when I got home from work, he came out of the office and told me about a letter he'd received from Rachel. She had grown frustrated because she and her boyfriend Dennis wanted to set a date for their wedding.

"Well, what are we going to do?" I asked him.

"I think the only way around this is for us to get a divorce, and then we can get remarried in the Church sometime after their wedding."

"What? Phillip, that's insane! Why can't you tell them we got married?"

"You don't understand my family dynamic. I'm the screw-up, Kasey. I didn't get a normal job and stay in Marblehead. I constantly live in my sister's shadow. I don't want to add to my parents' disappointment in me. Telling them we got married more than a year ago would add to their belief that I'm a failure."

I was furious.

"Well, first of all, I don't see that at all. Your folks love you and would have understood. But they're not my parents. You can tell them whatever makes you feel comfortable, but I'm not getting a divorce unless we're really getting divorced. It's a complete waste of money, so we're either staying married, or it's over."

"What do you recommend?"

"The same thing I've recommended for the last year, Phillip. Just tell them and get it over with."

That pissed him off, and he pouted for days.

He bought time by announcing on a visit that we were engaged. He said he wanted to wait before setting a date, so he wouldn't upstage his sister's wedding, so we were in limbo for another year.

It seemed like he would never resolve the matter. But, sometime after Rachel and Dennis got married, he offered a different suggestion.

"So what I'm thinking is, we go up to another county in Massachusetts and take out a marriage license."

"How can we do that? We're already married."

"I've done some research and I don't think they can check the records that easily. We just pretend it's our first marriage and, since we are already married to one another, it won't be illegal or anything."

Regardless of how ridiculous it all was, I relented because it was the only solution he could come up with to move forward and end the charade.

Phillip announced at Christmas of 1985 that we were planning to get married the following summer. By that June, we would already be married for three and a half years. We got a marriage license and reserved a date for a wedding at Saint Elizabeth's in Marblehead.

His parents generously offered to pay for the wedding, and Phillip accepted. He no longer had a savings account to pay his bills, never mind being able to contribute to the expenses of the wedding. That left me in an awkward position because, in many ways, it wasn't my wedding. I couldn't ask to do things the way I would have liked to since I wasn't paying for the wedding, and neither were my parents. The two of us had a massive fight when I complained about that to Phillip one day.

It started when I casually said, "I thought it would be nice to have something other than white tablecloths and napkins."

"Well, if that costs more than white linens, forget it. I'm not asking my parents to pay for anything more. You could ask your parents to chip in."

"Sure. I'll call them right now and ask them to pay for part of the wedding they know nothing about. Yeah, that will work, telling them that their thirty-three-year-old daughter is getting married to the man she's already married to. Should I send them an invitation to attend the wedding, too? How about my brothers and sisters? Are they all invited?"

"Screw you, Kasey. All I said was, I didn't want my parents paying for napkins."

"No, Phillip. You said I should ask my parents to chip in. Do you understand how insulting that is under the circumstances? I can only have a few of my most trusted friends attend our wedding because I know they will keep our secret. I'm not allowed to invite even one relative because that would mean revealing the lie we've been trying to maintain. So, no. This isn't about napkins. It's about you spending thousands of dollars of your parent's money because you don't have the balls to tell them the truth."

I left the apartment and didn't go home until late that night. It was the first of several nights that I stayed away because I refused to apologize. Eventually, the tension eased, and once again, we buried the root cause of the argument.

When the wedding day arrived, it was surreal. We played the part of the happy bride and groom. I gave my friends knowing glances, and they were troopers about going along with the charade. I was relieved it was over, but realized it didn't change anything. There was still a secret to be kept, and nothing we did would make that go away. We drove to Florida a few days later for our honeymoon. When we stopped to see my parents, I couldn't help but feel like I'd betrayed them.

GIVEN the current financial crisis I was facing in Canada, I realized how often similar situations had occurred earlier in our marriage. I'd relinquished control over the purse strings too often throughout our relationship. No wonder he was perfectly comfortable stripping me of all financial decisions regarding income and paying for expenses. I knew I had to regain my financial independence from him once I left Alexandria but, knew I had to figure out a way to address the problem immediately.

I heard my friends laughing out on Jenny's porch as the sunlight began to fade in her kitchen. I was just placing the last batch of chicken on the large serving platter when Jenny came in to see when the main course would be ready. She called to the others to come grab the side dishes that were in the fridge, and Betty held the door as I carried the hot chicken outside to the table and placed it on a trivet.

Conversations swirled around me as we all ate. I kept my mouth full so I wouldn't have to say too much. My problems had seemed to dominate the conversation earlier and I feared it was getting tedious. It kept me from enjoying myself, and I wondered if they knew I was a complete mess inside.

I gazed at the lovely and kind faces of the women around the table chatting with one another while I ate. I tried to absorb all the details, all the nuances, of what made them so important to me. I had had many close girlfriends in the past, and some friends that remained close even though distance prevented us from seeing one another frequently. What made these women different was that they had made me a part of their community. Because I had moved so often, it was something I'd only experienced as a child, that feeling of belonging. The love and support these women provided made me feel like I was a part of something, that I had contributed to something as a whole. That was what I'd missed, moving from place to place. The longing to belong somewhere, to feel like I mattered somehow. That was what made leaving Alexandria so painful.

BY 9:30 THAT EVENING, many of our friends had left, since it was a weeknight. Those that remained gathered dishes and brought the leftover food inside. "Anyone up for coffee?" Jenny asked. Murmurs of approval indicated we were.

"I am if you have anything to add to it!" Lisa quipped.

I still had to wash and dry my laundry, so I headed downstairs to go through the basement to grab my things from the van. As I came out of the basement door, the most beautiful magic was on display. Hundreds of fireflies lit up the night sky, twinkling like a gathering of magical faeries. The scene captured my feeling for this place. I stood in awe, unable to move, as I took in the dreamlike quality of this special quiet moment, bringing me a sense of peace and tranquility. I vowed to myself that, somehow, I'd figure out a way to come back to Alexandria with the Beans, the place we all thought of as home.

The spell was broken by the roar of laughter coming from inside. I smiled. The sound was an antidote to my angst. These were the women that believed in me when I failed to believe in myself. They knew I could be a total goof, and they would laugh with me and share my humor. They accepted me, warts and all.

I gathered my laundry from the van, loaded the washing machine, and then headed back upstairs, planning to tidy the kitchen. The aroma of the coffee wafted through the air. Jenny stood at the cabinet grabbing a few empty mugs. She handed them to me so I could take them into the living room.

"When you come back, can you get the Bailey's out of the fridge?" she asked, placing a pitcher for the cream next to the sugar bowl.

"That's why I love you," I turned to her and winked. "You know what I want before I do."

I poured a bit of the liquor into my mug and then settled into an overstuffed chair by the fireplace. I hardly needed another drink with all the wine I'd had earlier. I justified it, knowing it would be a long time before I would have another chance to be this carefree.

Betty took a seat on the couch, and coffees in hand, Jenny, Lisa, and Carole joined us in the living room. My mind wandered as I listened to snippets of conversation coming from around the room. After awhile I excused myself and went to check if the laundry was ready for the dryer.

As I passed the guest room, I looked longingly at the king-size bed and wished I could climb into it and go to sleep. Jenny's guest room was so much more comfortable than the mattress on the floor in the stuffy room above the café. I resisted the impulse and went to put the clothes in the dryer.

I had to check my email before I went back upstairs, so I went into the guest room with Chubby at my heels. While I arranged all the pillows at the head of the bed against the wall, Chubby jumped up onto the bed and promptly fell asleep. I grabbed my laptop off of the nightstand, hoping it would power on—a damaged input jack made that an iffy proposition.

My last official catering job was early the next morning, and then I would have to leave. My client Lise had responded with a headcount for breakfast, as promised. There was also an email from Phillip. I decided to wait to read that because I knew it would ruin my evening. Instead, I composed an email to Kate with the headcount so she could start baking in the morning.

Kate was one of my former employees, and a dear friend, who had worked with me over the last few years. Kate and Sharilyn had been my two longest employees, with Sharilyn starting with me shortly after I opened the business and Kate coming on board about a year later. The three of us were from very different backgrounds, but we got along famously. We seemed to bring out the best in one another, with each of us contributing different skills to the operation of the café.

Kate came from a large, middle-class, Irish family with strong connections to the community. She was lovely, with dark auburn hair, a flawless complexion, and deep-set green eyes. When she wasn't working at the café, she was a fitness instructor and her body reflected her commitment to a strict workout routine.

Sharilyn, on the other hand, was from a hard-working, blue-collar family, who married the love of her life at a young age. They raised two daughters, who were now adults. She was attractive with a pixyish haircut that framed her face. She was upbeat and fun, cheering me up even when I was in the worst mood. She wasn't as skilled at cooking or baking as Kate, but she was so good at everything else that she more than made up for her lack of culinary skills. I felt very fortunate these two women always had my back, especially now that life had become so complicated.

From the moment we assembled in the kitchen each morning, the three of us would chat as we prepared to open the restaurant. Music in a range of styles played in the background. We had a routine that allowed us to get our tasks done while chatting about whatever was going on in our lives. Once we opened, Kate waited on tables, Sharilyn assembled the previously prepared foods for each order, and I ran between them doing whatever needed to get done.

Kate had gone through a divorce shortly after we opened. She was so smart about the way she had carefully planned everything before making her move. She read books, talked to friends, and had a network of support by the time she filed for her divorce.

"Take the emotion out of it," she told me all the time when we discussed my situation with Phillip.

I heard the activity coming from above, so I knew it was time to rejoin Jenny and the others upstairs. I shut off my computer, ignoring Phillip's email. "Let him wonder what I'm doing for a change," I thought. Before I could get off the bed, Chubby snuggled closer to me. His gentle breathing made me smile. I wished I still believed I was married to someone just as faithful as my furry companion.

As I went back upstairs to join my friends, I was so thankful for the experience and my encounters with all these magnificent women. Suddenly, I realized I'd almost overlooked something. Each one of my friends had been through a divorce, except for Carole, who had never married. They had survived their ordeals and even thrived in the aftermath. As evidenced by the laughter and gaiety around me, they were through with the anger and bitterness of their dysfunctional relationships.

I began to feel better knowing someday, I would be able to look beyond these dark days. If I had known then what was to come, however, I'm not sure I would have had the courage to leave Alexandria the next day.

Chapter Four

OUT OF EXCUSES

Even though Jenny's guest room was much cooler and more comfortable than the room above the café, I'd found it difficult to sleep. I woke up early the next morning feeling drained. My almost daily routine of three years was to wake-up by seven so I could start preparing to open the restaurant. It was a hard routine to break.

The client wasn't expecting me to deliver the catering order until 10 am, but I decided to leave anyway since Jenny and I said our farewell the night before, knowing that it was for the best. I wrote her a note thanking her for a wonderful evening and left as quietly as I could.

I still had to purchase some fresh fruit and two large containers of yogurt. I couldn't help thinking about the fact, it was the last catering job I'd do for my business. Throughout the years, there had been weddings and Christmas parties, social events and office parties. It was the most profitable part of the café's services, but also the most demanding. I had gained an excellent reputation around town but had to compete against others who had developed their clientele over decades. I was glad I'd cultivated both small and large corporate clients.

When I got to the parking lot at the grocery store, I looked to see if anyone I knew was around. I didn't want to strike up a conversation with a former customer, or someone I knew from the kids' school, or one of the many friends I wouldn't have a chance to say goodbye to personally.

Then I realized it was impossible to know who was inside based on the vehicles in the lot because I had no idea what type of cars or trucks they drove. I knew my customers by the tea they drank or how they took their coffee. I would often bring a pot to their table before they even ordered. I made sure I had plenty of Jade Garden for Sharon and Earl Grey for Glen. Mrs. Spicer preferred Lemon Ginger, and if I had none on hand, she would most likely order the Orange Spice Black tea. Lisa always ordered a latte, and Mary drank her coffee black but her tea with milk.

I decided the grocery store was too much of an emotional landmine, so I headed to a farm stand that sold fresh fruit and produce in the small town south of Alexandria. I backed out of my parking space to head down the 34 towards Lancaster. I justified this as an act of emotional survival, reminding myself, by going to the farm stand, I didn't have to leave Chubby in the car while I shopped.

AS SOON AS I got back to the café, I turned on the aging Rancilio Espresso Machine. I could hear the water heating in the double boiler. I decided to make a cappuccino with an extra shot of espresso because I needed the caffeine boost to get me through the next few hours. I poured the remainder of my beans into the grinder. The angry sound of the beans being crushed by the blades matched my mood. I wished I was doing anything but packing to leave, as I tamped the freshly ground coffee into the portafilter. I didn't bother frothing the milk in the stainless steel cup but poured it directly into the largest mug warming on top of the machine.

"These will have to be packed, too," I thought, watching the foam building in the mug. In the early days, I struggled to get the milk to cooperate. Now I could do it in my sleep. I poured the espresso into the mug and wandered into the tearoom, followed by Chubby.

With a few hours to go before I had to deliver the catering, I started taking decorations off the wall, teapots off the shelves, and wrapping the glassware in bubble wrap. Every item had a story. The delicate teapot was one I had found at the thrift store, St. Vincent de Paul's, a block away from the café. It wasn't very practical, but I thought it would look nice on one of the shelves. One day, Kate ran out of the teapots we kept on top of the espresso machine. We kept them there because they stayed warm since pouring a hot beverage into a cold cup or pot was counter-productive. Kate grabbed this very teapot off the shelf and, without checking, she used it to make tea. I'd never thought of it as anything more than a decoration, so I'd never cleaned it prop-erly before setting it on the shelf. Kate delivered the pot of tea to the customer, only to have the woman she served call her over to the table moments later.

"Are you charging me extra for these flies?" she asked Kate. While Kate was mortified, we all had a big laugh. Almost all of my customers were so good-natured. This one appreciated my offer of lunch on the house!

Those were the types of memories I packed that day. There were so many laughable memories of things that had happened over the years. Each time I placed an item in a box, it seemed like I was burying a piece of myself in the depths of the stiff and unyielding cardboard.

I HAD CHANGED SO MUCH since I'd opened my restaurant. In Alexandria, I thrived on a pace and had a sense of well-being that had eluded me for so long. The work I did to establish my restaurant and reconnect with my artistic side brought out the best in me. I worked long hours and often struggled to balance the needs of my kids and myself. Yet, the experiences had restored a part of me that was lost before we moved to the north.

I knew I had to figure out how to remain strong. I feared that I could lose my sense of self once again.

With the morning sun streaming through the windows, I stopped packing and took a moment to call Jody about taking Chubby for a few days. Chub was so attached to me; I knew it would be hard on him to be left behind. But I also knew it was a necessary decision because of his habit of trying to climb on my shoulders. Of course the twins would be upset when they found out I'd left him behind. But, I would explain, it would also give the three of us the perfect excuse to head back to retrieve him and say good-bye to their friends. I was warming to the whole idea.

I tried to imagine my encounter with Phillip once I arrived at the new apartment in Cobleskill, New York. The trip was about a five hour drive from Alexandria, and I calculated that if I left before 8 p.m., Phillip might still be awake and I'd have to spend time alone with him. I started thinking more and more about leaving as late as possible so I could avoid interacting with him. The only way to manage this was to arrive late, then unpack the van the next morning after he left for work. Then I could head to Vermont to get the Beans before he got home from work, thus avoiding seeing him altogether.

I knew eventually we would have to come face to face, but having the Beans with me when that occurred would be more comfortable. I needed time to adjust to the situation and knew that when I spent time alone with him, I was the most vulnerable because he'd manage to find a way to push all my emotional buttons. But he couldn't sabotage me if I were a moving target.

I dialed Jody's number but the line was busy, so I went into the kitchen to make a light breakfast before I assembled the fruit platter. As I cut the strawberries, I thought of how much my daughter Lucy loved them. It was her favorite fruit. Jack seemed more partial to blueberries and watermelon. I hoped the twins were enjoying their time with Jake and Meredith.

Before I dropped them off, they had been having a rotten summer. All the talk of moving and leaving their friends behind was too much for them. Only three years ago, we'd torn them away from their home in the U.S., now we were making them move again. I worried that the instability wasn't good for them.

I knew how they felt all too well. The Beans still believed their close friends would remain close. They thought that when they came back to visit, everything would be the same. I hated the fact they were reliving the part of my childhood I'd vowed to avoid with them. Since selling our home in Blairstown, New Jersey, in 2006, we had moved three times. They were reluctant about moving to Canada when we'd made that decision years earlier, but they had adjusted and made friends. They were a part of the small community. It was hard to watch them being torn, once again, from the place they thought of as home.

I CAREFULLY CUT A SMALL WATERMELON, pineapple, and honeydew, then placed the neat slices into separate bowls before I washed the red and green grapes. I made decorative rosettes out of a pint of strawberries and used the leafy green top of the pineapple as the center of the platter. I placed the uniformly cut pieces of fruit around the pineapple leaves to form a colorful pattern before adding the grapes and strawberries, interspersed with the melons, to create an attractive arrangement. I was pleased with the way it all looked and knew it would be well received, especially with the basket of Kate's yummy baked goods to round out the presentation. I covered it with wrap and stuck it in the fridge until it was time to leave.

Looking at the clock on the stove, I saw that I still had a few hours before I needed to pick up the miniature coffee cakes and banana muffins Kate was baking, so I made use of the time and tried to reach Jody again. This time the call went through. Not only did she offer to take Chubby, but she also offered to let him stay in the house with her and Brice so he wouldn't be in the kennel with the other dogs. I was so thankful she made the offer, as it eased my guilt about leaving him behind.

When I went to pick up the baked goods from Kate, it unleashed a wave of emotions the moment she opened the door,

"I forgot the eggs at the café," I told her, holding back tears.

"Not to worry," she said, giving me a quick hug. "Do you have time for coffee?"

"Not really, but I'll make time. I'm already exhausted from packing."

I walked into the foyer of her home and saw that she'd hung the beautiful arched mirror that once hung in the tearoom. She'd bought from me when I was struggling to pay the bills the previous month. I'd begun to sell things because I needed the money. It looked as beautiful as it had in our tearoom. I was glad it went to her because it held so many good memories.

When I had told Phillip about it, I justified selling it to her, saying we couldn't fit everything in the apartment he'd rented in Cobleskill, New York. As it was, most of our belongings were going into storage. I didn't want to reveal to him how desperate I was for money since he seemed determined to keep financial matters secret from me, too. He hadn't said anything about the mirror but put his foot down over items like our antique sleigh bench and a stained-glass window that had once hung in our old Victorian home in Blairstown.

"How's the packing going?" Kate asked as I followed her into the kitchen.

"Argh! I've been at it for two straight days and feel like I could spend another month without finishing. Whatever I get done is going to have to be it until I come back again. I need to get to Cobleskill with the cats before I pick up the Beans in Vermont. I want them to have a chance to settle in before school starts. Most of what I'm packing is going upstairs in the office or into storage.

"Why wasn't Phillip here this weekend helping you?"

"He said he had to work, of course. Or that's what he claimed anyway. It's like he thinks I should be grateful he came up to help move all the heavy stuff."

"Don't let him off the hook. He should be here helping you," Kate reminded me.

"You're right. As of late, the only thing Phillip's good at is offering excuses."

I sat at her farmhouse-style table that stretched across her kitchen. I imagined her and her new husband Jason having meals there with their blended family. She pulled out a bag of 2Beans coffee from her cabinet. The familiar brown bag stamped with my business logo was easy to recognize.

"I think I wiped you out of the rest of your coffee. I don't know what I'm going to do once this is gone," she lamented.

The coffee was a specialty blend crafted just for the café by a local coffee roaster. I'd tasted various blends of coffee beans for days before deciding which one was right for my business. It was a smooth but dark blend of beans that had a velvety taste. It made excellent espresso, too.

"I'm sure Yves would be willing to roast some for you if you bought it in bulk. He's a good egg. I can give him a call before I leave if you want?"

"Would you? It's just one of the things that's hard about closing. You're going to be missed, you know," she said, measuring the coffee as we chatted.

"I know. I ran into four people at the grocery store while I was buying some cleaning supplies a few days ago. They were gobsmacked I'd closed. I could barely get out the door without sobbing. I don't want to go."

"I know. Maybe you can work it out and can come back?"

"You know I'd love to, but it might take a while. Phillip's putting me in a very precarious position financially. I've been selling everything I can to make ends meet. He won't contribute anything towards the bills up here now. He claims it's a waste of *his* money. I'm so broke I wouldn't have gas money to Cobleskill if it wasn't for this catering job. All of a sudden, the café, the building, and everything related to Canada is my responsibility."

"Have you pointed out to him that's abandonment?"

"I doubt he sees it that way. Right now, I'm playing nice. Or at least I'm trying to. I don't want him to realize how alarmed I am about what's been going on, or that I suspect he's going to try to divorce me. He's had more time to put a plan in place than I have. If we do end up in court, I can show them how I was completely responsible for the Beans, along with everything else, once he moved back to the States."

"Are you sure that's all it is? I know you've told me you hate confronting him."

"You're right, but that's not it. I'm trying to figure out what Phillip's up to before I take action. A good friend of mine taught me that."

She smiled and nodded.

"Well, Sharilyn and I have been talking, and we might have come up with a way for you to keep things going up here. What if she and I took over the healthy school lunch program?"

THE HEALTHY SCHOOL lunch program was something I started shortly after I opened the Café. Alexandria was a farming town, and the schools were built at a time when kids still went home for lunch. When my kids showed me the order form provided by their school to order lunch, I was dumbstruck at the lack of choices and the cost. That's when I learned that the five area elementary schools didn't have cafeterias so they ordered food from area restaurants.

At the school they attended, a bagel with cream cheese from Tim Horton's was considered a lunch, and it cost two dollars and fifty cents, with most of that money going to finance other programs at the school. I created a power-point presentation and sat before the boards of the French and English schools pitching my *healthy school lunch program*. Within a year, I was providing the five area elementary schools with lunches. It kept me afloat when business got slow, like the time the town spent two months tearing up the street in front of my business.

"YOU GUYS WOULD DO that for me?"

"Well, you'd have to pay us, of course, but maybe we can

figure out a way to do that. Did you send out the letters to the schools yet, telling them you were closing?"

"No. I haven't had a chance."

"Well, think about it. Maybe that will help keep the door open until you can come back."

"I will. The only hitch is Phillip's pressing me to sell the building, too. I could always rent a separate kitchen." I told Kate.

"That's an idea! It will all work out. You'll see," she assured me.

Kate poured the coffee, and we chatted for a while longer about more pleasant things before I left. Her suggestion gave me hope that maybe coming back wasn't such a crazy idea after all.

RETURNING FROM KATE'S, I picked-up the fruit platter and yogurt from the café before delivering the food to my client at the bank, only two blocks from the café. Lise met me at the back door with a cart to carry the food upstairs. She handed me an envelope with an enclosed check to pay for the catering and I tucked it in my purse and gave her a brief hug. Turning quickly away, I swallowed hard, knowing my last official catering duty as the owner of the café was over.

After depositing the check, I headed back to cram what remained of the life I'd built in Alexandria in cardboard liquor boxes. I had no more excuses to stay in Alexandria.

I TRIED to stay focused on packing, but the August heat was once again wearing me out. I decided to take a break and went up into the office to do a little snooping on the internet. Thinking about Molly and the time Phillip broke up with me decades earlier had me considering again that Phillip was having an affair.

Once online, I Googled "signs your spouse is having an affair." Several articles suggested the signs of a cheating spouse were staying out late, showering more frequently, losing weight, and an increasingly hostile attitude. Among a list of other clues,

Phillip had lost weight recently and was definitively hostile. But if he was having an extramarital affair, he didn't have to worry about staying out late or showering more often because I was never there to know what he was up to.

I spent some time trying to determine what possible steps I would need to take if Phillip made his move. Once I got to Cobleskill, I realized I might not have much time. I scanned sites like Barnes and Noble for books Kate recommended when she was going through her divorce, knowing I couldn't afford to buy them but could perhaps get them from the library. I realized I would have to hide them or just read them at the library without checking them out. It wouldn't be the first time I'd hidden things from Phillip.

IN 1990, Phillip wanted to move out of the New York City area and we began looking at property in Western New Jersey because properties were more affordable than areas surrounding Manhattan. Initially I balked because he was working from home much of the time, and I was the one commuting each day into the City. I finally agreed to give it a trial to see if I could cope with all the traveling and we rented an apartment in the town of Blairstown, leaving me to commute via bus or to drive the two and half hour trip each way into work each day. I made the most of it by working on writing the libretto of my musical on the long bus rides to and from Manhattan.

Three years later, when Phillip inherited a small sum of money, we decided to finally purchase a home. By that time, I was so used to the commute, I agreed to looking in that area. We purchased an old Victorian in 1993 and settled into a life that mostly revolved around renovating the property more than pursuing our creative goals.

Phillip and I had been married for more than a decade when I began doing things behind Phillip's back. It started with little things, like mostly buying something I wanted that I knew he wouldn't have approved of if I'd asked before purchasing it. The fact I had to get his permission was what set me off. I earned most of the money, but he got the final say in how it was spent.

We'd agreed early on to always discuss purchases over a hundred dollars. But that seemed only to apply to me. Whenever Phillip wanted a new piece of film equipment for his lackluster business or tools required for renovating the house, it was never discussed. Whatever he bought; he considered a necessity. Whatever I bought, was wasteful.

Per usual, I never had the guts to call him on it. I recall buying a comforter on sale and hiding it in the attic. When sufficient time passed, it magically appeared on our bed.

"Don't you remember when we bought this?" I asked him. He faked remembering and accepted the plausible explanation that it was a forgotten purchase.

I started getting bolder and bolder because he never caught on. Clothing and household items miraculously appeared. I even bought a new 9x12 rug for our bedroom. Since we were doing major renovations in areas of the house, I'd blend things into the piles that remained in unused rooms so when we got to unravel the mess in the room, things were there and he just assumed they were there all along. He never said a word, even when he helped to lay the rug on our bedroom floor.

This became a pattern, and I was emboldened by keeping things from him. For some reason, it made me resent him more because I had convinced myself that he made me do these things. But even though I knew it was wrong, I continued to go behind his back.

I found myself getting angry and annoyed with Phillip over other things, too. After more than ten years of marriage, rafting down the Delaware River, going to movies, antiquing, or dressing our cats up in hats to take funny pictures of them wasn't enough anymore. I was getting tired of the very insulated life the two of us had.

I tried varying our routine, but circumstances made it difficult. If I wanted to go out with my friends in Manhattan, it didn't make sense to have Phillip travel two and a half hours from the home in Blairstown, to join us for dinner or drinks. However, the only friends I had where I lived were casual acquaintances I chatted with on the bus, so I rarely socialized with anyone in the very place I lived. I was caught between two worlds, and neither one fulfilled me anymore. My life was so disjointed.

About the only thing I found fulfilling in those years was working on my musical. I'd been plugging away on the project for over a decade. I'd workshopped the show in Manhattan several times and had recorded a demo of the music in studio. I finally found a producer who wanted to produce it in his small theatrical venue in Soho. He brought a director/choreographer on board who loved the project. Everything seemed to be coming together. But shortly after we started raising money for the production, we learned the older actor we had cast as our leading man had cancer, and the funding that was already secured went out the window.

I was becoming more and more disillusioned with the whole theatre scene in New York City. Despite all the progress I'd made, I started to doubt my work would ever make it to the stage. After struggling for years, my dreams began to disappear.

Phillip, however, still clung to the idea that someday his career would be solidified, and financial success was right around the corner. He reinvested almost every dime he made from his company back into his business; however, success never came. It wasn't his talent that held him back. It was his lack of understanding how networking played a large part in who got hired for lucrative jobs in the film industry.

"I refuse to kowtow to morons," was his repeated lament. "They let their mommies and daddies buy their way into the industry and they don't know squat about how to direct or produce. And you want me to hang out with these people so they'll give me work? Fat chance."

.   .   .

SOMETIME AROUND 1996, he got a short gig with the production company I worked for in the City. For whatever reason, he didn't complain about using my connections. The scenario that played out thereafter led me to recognize one of the many underlying problems within our relationship.

When he got hired for the job, Phillip had to commute into the City each day instead of working from our home in New Jersey. He started looking for a room in Manhattan so he didn't have to deal with traveling by bus to the City, though I had commuted five hours each day, round trip, back and forth to our home in Blairstown, for ten years.

He rented an expensive room on the Upper West Side of Manhattan where he could stay each night he was required to be at work. I stayed there sometimes as well, but it was a tiny room and very uncomfortable for two people to share the twin bed.

The whole situation made me furious. I found myself glad I didn't have to see him when I got home or worry about making us dinner. Without him there, I had more time to think about the fact that it seemed like, in Phillip's mind, his time and needs were always so much more important than my own.

"Are you staying in the City tonight?" he asked me, one day, when he called me at work.

"No, someone has to go home and feed the cats."

"Well, I have an early day tomorrow, so call me when you get home."

"You bet."

He didn't even hear the sarcasm in my voice. He seemed utterly oblivious to the fact he was a complete prima donna. I hung up the phone, seething, but never mentioned that I, too, had an early day.

All this reinforced my belief that my needs would always be secondary. Phillip's double standard and my inability to broach the problem led to my mushrooming anger. My friends were tired of hearing about it and suggested I confront him. I balked but knew they were right. I grappled with hating myself for being too weak to do anything and hating him for being too blind to see how unhappy I was.

One day after that, I was having lunch with a friend from work who was pregnant. Sitting there, I realized the depth of my despair. For years, I had spent so much time focused on my career, I was able to ignore a growing desire to start a family.

As I approached forty years of age, my desire to have children became more urgent. However, Phillip wouldn't even talk about starting a family. Whenever I brought up the subject, he came up with one insane excuse after another. He even told me, once, it would be unfair of us to have a child since his sister Rachel and her husband were having difficulty conceiving. All this led to more arguing, and I found more excuses to spend time away from him.

Finally, I decided to try and approach the subject rationally, without blowing up like I usually did when my anger boiled over. I practiced what I wanted to say all the way home on the bus. When I got home, I delivered my speech.

"You know, honey, if we're going to start a family, we need to start thinking about that soon because the clock is ticking."

"I've had a long day and if you think we're going to discuss this, forget it," and with that, he left the room. I followed him into the dining room where he was pouring himself a scotch. He stopped and looked me.

"What don't you understand?" he asked, without waiting for a response. "If you think we're going to do a Dave and Beth, that is not happening." He ignored my gaping mouth and finished pouring his drink, then headed upstairs to his office, where I heard him slam the door.

I was gobsmacked. Beth was a close friend who had given up her teaching career to stay home and raise her three kids. Her husband, Dave, supported her decision, but Phillip refused to have children if it meant that I would be quitting my job to raise them. I went after him, storming up the stairs and pounded on the door.

"You know what, Phillip? Screw you."

"Back at you, Kasey."

This time, I left the house and, by the time I got back, I could hear him snoring on the couch. The following week, he stayed in the City. Whenever we talked on the phone, the tension was thick between us.

For months after that incident, I was a complete bitch any time we were together. So much so, he began making veiled threats.

"You know, if you don't change your attitude, you're going to see what happens."

"Yeah? What's going to happen, Phillip? Are you threatening to divorce me?" I scoffed at him.

"Don't think I haven't thought about it. You've been a complete asshole lately."

I turned and looked at him, calling his bluff.

"Just remember, Phillip. You have a lot more to lose than I do."

I walked out of the room, feeling smug. I'd finally given him something to think about. If we divorced back then, he would have been forced to get a full-time job if I was no longer around to cover all our expense. I relished the thought of him panicking as I had for years, afraid he was going to leave me.

Gone were the days I rushed home because I wanted to see him. At that moment, I no longer cared if he stayed. Those feelings became more deep-seated as months passed, and we avoided being in the same place at the same time.

After his gig in Manhattan was over, he gave up the rented room and had to be home more. On a rare Saturday morning when we were both home, I heard him come into the kitchen as I was making breakfast. I was tired of all the fighting, and when he seemed to be in a good mood, we started chatting casually about our plans for the day. I don't recall why, but I mentioned that I'd missed my period. This caused Phillip to fly off the handle.

"So you got pregnant anyway? Even though we talked about this months ago? This is how you get what you want, Kasey. You do things even if I say no."

"I never said I was pregnant, Phillip. I said I missed my period. That happens to women sometimes, especially those my age. But, gee, I'm so happy to know you think I would intentionally get pregnant," I said as caustically as I could.

"Well, it's not the first time you got pregnant on me."

His flash of anger revealed what I'd suspected all along. He thought I got pregnant on purpose. At that moment, I regretted ever trying to prove I was worthy of his love and commitment. I was done playing the martyr. For more than a decade, I had put his every desire before my own and, in that moment, I confronted the reality that my actions bolstered his belief that his heart's desires were, in all ways, more important than my own.

I'd been suppressing my longing to start a family for years because he said we had to wait until we were financially stable. So I waited, never asking the logical question of, "How much stability do we need?" When those words flew out of his mouth, I knew his excuses were about so much more than financial stability. It was all his need to maintain a lifestyle, one where he got to pursue his career goals without any interference.

I left the room without commenting because, really—there was nothing to say. He must have known I wasn't pregnant. We had barely had sex during the few times we were home at the same time. I had to believe he said that to hurt me. It did. All the feelings I'd pushed back came to the surface. This time, I didn't shrink back and shove them away. I realized that I was just as responsible for the situation as he was. He took full advantage of my insecurities, but I let him.

After that, I finally gave into my deepest longings and began exploring fertility options without him. If he was unwilling to even discuss having a family, I began considering a divorce and entertained trying to get pregnant through means of a fertility doctor or adopting a child on my own.

Knowing that the window for conceiving a baby was rapidly closing, I became frantic. I started looking into the subject of *in vitro* fertilization, especially since one of my colleagues, who was years younger than I was at the time, was going that route.

I began staying in Manhattan later and later, telling Phillip I had to work late. This was mostly true because I had changed jobs with the ad agency and went from working as a broadcast business manager to being the sole business manager of the agency's new interactive, or *new media*, department.

Because the internet was so new, it was an opportunity that came with a lot more responsibilities, so Phillip never questioned my revised schedule. But sometimes I stayed late to get information on all the ways older women were successfully getting pregnant. I read extensively on the subject and reviewed the success rates of a fertility specialist who had an office not far from Blairstown.

My boss at the time seemed to realize that my newly developed skills as an Interactive Business Manager made me a hot commodity. He must have heard I was being headhunted by other ad agencies looking to establish their own interactive departments. But, still, I was shocked when he offered me a twenty-thousand-dollar performance bonus that was contingent upon documenting the workflow of the agency's new interactive department.

I was thrilled because it seemed like fate had finally intervened in my favor. Once I got the bonus, I could actually afford to pursue fertility treatments, which were very expensive. But, more importantly, I was being offered a position on staff, which meant I would get health insurance as an employee instead of paying out the hefty monthly premiums for minimum coverage, like the insurance Phillip and I had at the time. Most ad agencies at the time hired staff as freelancers even though they worked in long-term positions. Having a staff position was a huge boon.

One weekend morning, I was in the kitchen making breakfast when Phillip came up behind me. He put his arms around my waist, which caused me to stiffen.

"What's wrong?" he asked me, trying to kiss my neck.

"What's right?" I replied as I shook him away.

"Not this again," he said in a teasing manner.

I wasn't going to allow him to make a joke of my feelings so I continued making my omelet, allowing the uncooked eggs to get firm as I looked down at the cast iron pan.

"So, you're going to ignore me?" he said, stroking my hair.

"I'm not ignoring you, Phillip. I'm making breakfast," I replied sharply.

"Are you making me some?" he asked, continuing to make light of the moment.

I ignored him. I finished making my breakfast, poured myself a cup of coffee, and headed into the dining room. He stood in the kitchen. I sensed he was watching me as I went and, a few minutes later, he followed me.

"Why?" he asked, taking a seat at the table.

"Why what, Phillip?" I said after swallowing the eggs in my mouth.

"Why do you want to have kids?"

I sat there, stunned, unable to think. Were we actually having a conversation without shouting at one another?

"I don't know. I just do."

"That's about the most honest answer you've ever given me, Kasey. Okay, what if we were to do this?"

I turned to face him.

"That's it? You're agreeing to start a family?"

"I guess I am. So now what?"

I felt like fainting.

By that time, I was forty-one years old. When we finally committed to try to conceive, I told Phillip we should immediately make an appointment with a fertility doctor because time was of the essence. He never asked why I already had names and information available, or why there wasn't a long wait to get into seeing one. But, it was because I'd already made an appointment.

Trying to get pregnant seemed to change everything. Suddenly we were this happy couple, totally in love and planning for the future. I couldn't wait to get home each day. All we talked about was our latest "production." It was like the old days, when we wrote screenplays together and talked endlessly about how to accomplish our goals.

During this time, Phillip was kind and loving, especially when he needed to stick me with needles containing the powerful drugs the doctor prescribed or when the effects of the large-scale hormones affected my moods.

We got pregnant in the first round of *in vitro*. We went for blood tests, and the results showed there was a good possibility we were having twins, or even triplets. We held our breath, waiting to hear back. When the doctor's office confirmed we were indeed having twins, we breathed a sigh of relief because the doctor had warned there was a chance of conceiving multiples with *in vitro*. We danced around our kitchen, singing and laughing. It seemed like every negative thing he had ever done or said was wiped away in the moment.

Even in those happy days, when our relationship seemed to be mending, we never took the time to deal with the dysfunction of our marriage. Once again, we buried all the issues. Our decision to try to have a baby made them magically disappear. Now I realize, none of it ever went away. It was still all there, hidden right below the surface.

Chapter Five

EMERGENCY ROOM

I was due to give birth at the beginning of May in 1998. I still traveled into Manhattan three times a week for work and was telecommuting the other two days. It became increasingly uncomfortable to sit on the bus for hours and get on a crowded subway for the trip to downtown Manhattan. Thankfully, my assistant Dana was able to carry on when I wasn't in the office. Working from home allowed me to get things done without the stress of traveling each day, but I felt it was essential to work as far as possible into my pregnancy.

Phillip had found a freelance job writing advertising copy for an agency in Morristown, New Jersey, an hour from Blairstown. He was offered a full-time staff position several months into the gig. We were both making good money and looked forward, with excitement, to this next chapter in our lives.

On the 24th of March, I was scheduled for a routine checkup. At the appointment, the doctor said the ultrasound revealed baby A (Lucy) was no longer thriving. Her weight was stagnant, and the doctor feared she might not make it to the end of my term. He told me it was time to deliver the twins even though they would be five weeks premature.

I called Phillip on his cellphone and gave him the news.

"Are you sitting down?"

"Yeah, what's up?"

"They want to induce labor and said I should report to the hospital tomorrow or Thursday."

"Woah! We don't even have cribs set up yet!"

"I know, but I don't want to risk losing another pregnancy, so I want to go in tomorrow, okay?"

"Sure. Whatever you want. I'll let my boss know as soon as I get off the phone."

They induced labor around seven o'clock the following evening. Phillip stayed with me the entire time. He held my hand and told me jokes and kept me calm through the whole nerve-wracking ordeal.

I didn't go into heavy labor until a full twenty-three hours later. I kept falling asleep after contractions and everyone thought I was fainting. But considering my age, my doctors told me I was doing well, and around 6:30 that night, the doctor on call told Phillip he might want to get dinner since I had only dilated five centimeters.

A new doctor came on duty shortly after he left.

"Let's have a quick look before I go have dinner," she said, lifting my hospital gown. "Well, this isn't what I expected! You're almost ready to deliver," she told me. "Unfortunately, now we don't have time for any medication or epidural. Let's get you to the emergency room."

Phillip came back into the room as they were wheeling me away. She told him what was happening and he turned gray. They allowed him to accompany me, and he held my hand as I delivered Lucy at 7:12 pm.

Activity whirled around me. I knew something was wrong. Then I learned that Jack was breech.

"You're not going to like me for this, but I'm going to reach up and try to turn him. Otherwise, we might have to take him by caesarian."

Tears fell while Phillip stood off to the side, trying to comfort me. We were so distraught with worry. For eleven very long minutes, everyone in the room worked furiously to aid the doctor in Jack's delivery. She was finally able to grab him by the legs and gently pulled him out. At 7:23, I heard him cry.

"Do you want to hold him?" she asked moments later, then placed him on my chest.

"Where's Lucy?" I questioned the nurse.

"Lucy's APGAR score is low. We took her to the Neonatal Intensive Care Unit as a precaution," she told me reassuringly.

"But I didn't even get a chance to say hello," I sobbed, frightened we were going to lose her.

Both Jack and Lucy were taken to the NICU. I too had to remain in the hospital. Phillip spent the night, reluctant to leave us behind. The next day, though, we were able to have Jack with us in my hospital room while Lucy had to stay behind in the NICU.

Phillip seemed like a new man. He was so attentive to both Jack and me during those first days. He held Jack tenderly and teared up when we left Lucy behind after each visit to the NICU. Although she was tiny, four days after the birth, she was well enough to join us in my hospital room.

Phillip and I took them home at the end of March. The temperature had reached an unusually high eighty-six degrees. It felt surreal to see people in shorts and tee shirts passing us in the hallways of the hospital. The only clothing I had for both the twins and me were heavy winter clothes.

I dressed them in tiny matching striped one-piece outfits that were too big for their bodies, and we placed them in car seats made just for preemies. Phillip and I barely spoke on the drive home, but it was a comfortable silence.

We walked up the front steps of our house, each carrying one of our Beans. Our neighbor saw us and called over to us.

"Getting prepared? It will be here before you know it!"

Phillip and I just looked at each other and laughed.

"Actually, they arrived earlier! Come take a look," I responded.

She climbed up the porch steps and looked at Jack and Lucy.

"They're beautiful!" she said.

"I know," I beamed.

AS EXPECTED, life changed dramatically over the next few years. I was still trucking into Manhattan three days a week, even though I'd left one agency to work for another. I was now an interactive business manager for J. Walter Thompson's new division. I was able to get my new boss to hire Dana, who worked with me at my previous employer, and together we established the business process for the department. Initially, I had a lot of responsibility and couldn't take much time off, but eventually, I was able to work from home several days a week, and then I cut back altogether. My skills were in high demand back then, and I was now making more money working three days a week than I had been working five.

But life was far from rosy. Even cutting back on the number of days I had to commute did little to keep me from being overwhelmed. The first year of the Beans' lives remains a blur. I remember almost nothing from those sleep-deprived months when I had little time to eat, sleep, or even shower. Jack had colic and I carried him in a sling. Lucy was very content and earned the nickname of *angel baby*. But while Jack was colicky and frequently cried, he was developing more rapidly than Lucy in most areas except speech.

Lucy said her first word at eight months and could count to twenty by the time she was thirteen months. She could recite full passages in books, which made her look like she was reading them. But she didn't start walking until she was eighteen months old. Jack, on the other hand, was hitting all his milestones right on time. Once he outgrew the colic, he, too, was wonderfully content, even though he still hated to be put down for a nap.

Watching the two babies grow and develop simultaneously enabled me to observe their many differences. Some of what I saw was just their burgeoning personalities. However, I became concerned about other observations. For example, Lucy cried whenever she heard loud noises, even laughter. She seemed to panic when she saw bright lights. She screamed when I put her on the changing table, so I had to change her on the floor. Jack exhibited none of these behaviors.

When I tried to discuss these matters with Phillip, his reaction was upsetting.

"It's in your head, Kasey. They're both fine. You're just a worrier," Phillip told me.

"But when I take them to playgroup, she's not even interested in playing with the other kids," I reported. "She is totally content playing by herself."

"So what? Maybe she doesn't want to play. Did you ever think of that? You create problems to get attention. What's wrong with you?" he fired back.

I couldn't even respond. Phillip came home each night long after the kids were in bed, yet believed he knew better than I did about what was happening. I knew I was right, so I kept exploring the issue and ignored him.

At a well-baby visit, I expressed my concerns to our family doctor. After observing her, the doctor also believed Lucy was experiencing developmental delays. When I told Phillip that the doctor suggested getting early intervention to help her, he acted as if I had forced the doctor to draw his conclusions.

As the Beans got a bit older, I observed more things that had me combing the internet. It wasn't just at playgroup sessions that social interactions were difficult for Lucy. At swim class or any other group activities, Jack would naturally interact with the other kids, but Lucy always stayed by herself. The only child Lucy would interact with was Jack, who would sweetly check on Lucy from time to time, but he was drawn to spending time with others. He would reassure himself she was okay and then run off to play with his pals.

While I was able to get Lucy some therapy to help increase her gross motor skills, that didn't help with the other things that alarmed me about her socialization skills. All these things made me more and more uncomfortable being two and a half hours away from my children. I knew that these years were critical in terms of their development. But any time I mentioned my concerns, they were rebuffed by Phillip.

Things came to a head when the Beans were about eighteen months old and I came back from Manhattan to find my usually happy son clinging to Lydia, his babysitter. He wasn't crying, but he was utterly listless. I looked at her questioningly.

"How long has he been like this?" I asked Lydia.

"All afternoon," she responded, handing Jack over. I took him in my arms and he was barely reacting to me.

"Why didn't you call me?"

"I tried to leave you a message, but your voicemail was full."

"Okay, sorry." I felt horrible.

I'd never seen Jack like this. He was always bubbly and energetic. I held him tightly, rocking him back and forth, and kissing his forehead to see if he was hot.

"You can take off," I told Lydia. "I'll see you tomorrow."

"Let's go upstairs, buddy," I said, trying to soothe him.

This was the third childcare arrangement we'd had. The first one was a childcare center that charged two hundred dollars a week, per child. The Beans got sick for the first three weeks and we still had to pay for the care they weren't getting. On top of that, it cost fifty dollars per half hour when a parent was late picking up a child. Since I commuted by bus, that was a frequent occurrence, and I had to pay double because the fee was per child.

The second babysitter was so inept, she fed them soy-milk that had been in a bottle on the kitchen counter and had fermented. She also threw away expensive cloth diapers because they were *too poopy*.

Lydia was a delightful woman and a former teacher, to boot. I was very comfortable leaving the Beans with her. But I hated the idea of them always being cared for by someone else.

I sat in the oversized chair in the twins' room for a moment, watching Lucy in the playpen. Jack clung to me and continued to be unresponsive. For some reason, I checked his diaper and noticed it was soiled. I carried him over to the changing table. I carefully unbuttoned the wool diaper cover for his cloth diapers. His diaper was full of a loose stool, and his bottom was a bright red. Phillip came upstairs and into their room a moment later.

"Don't get your coat off. We're taking Jack to the emergency room."

Somehow, Lydia had missed Jack's horrible diaper rash. His inflamed bottom was a scarlet red and he cried when I touched it. It might have occurred right after she changed his diaper earlier, or it was a simple oversight. Regardless, I was livid.

Until that moment, I had gone along with Phillip's reasoning that we needed two incomes. He saw nothing wrong with both of us being hours away from our children. That day, however, I realized I couldn't do it anymore. The next day, I gave notice at work.

THE CRACKS in our relationship became chasms overnight. "How could you do that?" Phillip yelled when I told him I'd quit.

"It was easy. I should have done it after the Beans were born. I'm not going to be two and a half hours away from our children anymore, especially when they're this little. They need a parent close by," I screamed.

"Oh, course, that parent is you."

"Are you saying it should be you? Are you kidding me? You have to call me three times if I leave them with you to go to the grocery store. Who was the one that noticed that Lucy was having issues? The only reason I was able to get her help was that I have the flexibility in my work schedule. Those appointments alone took months to get. If I had to pick and choose when I was available, I would never have been able to get an appointment. Don't worry, Phillip. I'll find a job out here so you don't have to support us alone."

"You're never going to earn the same money out here. You know that!"

"So that's what's important here? Not the welfare of our kids?

It's always my paycheck that matters most to you, isn't it?"

"You can manipulate this any way you want, Kasey, but not having the income to support them makes you the selfish one. I'm sure you've been planning to leave your job from the moment they were born. You do whatever you want and I'm the one that has to pick up the mess from your half-assed decisions."

"Really? How many failed businesses have I had?"

The moment those words came out of my mouth, I regretted saying them. I knew that when Phillip made insensitive comments to me, I was devastated. This was a low blow because his company folded years ago when his former partner embezzled all their money, on top of the film and office equipment. This led to a deep depression and he didn't work again for almost three years until he took the job as a copywriter at the agency in Morristown, NJ.

While I was glad I'd decided to quit my job, my anger was about the frustration of always being torn between caring for my kids and working. I tried to ease the tension.

"Look, I'll put out some resumés and get a job out here. You're making a good salary now. We have plenty of money saved, too." He was still furious with me, but I didn't back down, and wasn't surprised when he didn't speak to me for days.

AT FIRST, I didn't see just how unbalanced things had become once I stopped working full-time. I was too busy trying to work several part-time jobs and keeping up with the twins to notice how much had changed regarding the dynamic of our relationship.

The changes were subtle and seemed petty, and it was only upon reflection that I became aware of their manifestation. I was doing some housework before the kids got up, and Phillip wandered into the kitchen, asking if I'd made breakfast.

"Not yet. How about you make it for a change," I said half-jokingly.

"I'll wait until you're done, thank you," he said in a tone that reflected annoyance.

"Well, it's going to be awhile. It's hard to get housework done while the kids are awake," I told him.

"I'm going to run to grab something at Dunkin, then," he replied.

"Phillip, you eat something from there five days a week. Can't you wait for a little while so I can get the dishes done? I didn't say I wouldn't make you breakfast," I responded.

"I have stuff to do, so I don't feel like waiting," he told me.

"Well, this is my stuff to do. And while we're on the subject, why is that when you were home alone, we could afford a housekeeper, but now that I'm home alone with the Beans, that's off the table?"

"What housekeeper?"

"What do you mean, what housekeeper? Have you forgotten about Lynette? "

"No, I haven't forgotten. Look, Kasey. Don't blow this up. I can easily count the number of times Lynette came to clean."

"What are you talking about? She was here once a week for years!"

"I'm not doing this, Kasey. You exaggerate everything."

"How am I exaggerating?"

Soon the morning turned dark. He ignored my questions, so I pressed because I knew I wasn't the one exaggerating.

"So, she was only here occasionally? Really? And was that you who had meals on the table when I came home each night?" I said, becoming impatient. "You spent your time shopping for groceries and doing laundry on the weekends all those years? You emptied the litter boxes and paid the bills? That was you this whole time? Gee, I thought I was the one who did all that."

"There you go again. You're pretty pathetic. Why is this even an argument? I can't be expected to come home from work and do housework, so forget about Lynette. As it is, I spend all my time working to support you and my family."

"Need I remind you that you didn't even take one job for almost three years before the kids were born? Why was it okay to pay for someone to clean when you were home alone? And secondly, how can you forget that I supported you for years?"

"This is so typical. I worked my ass off renovating the house during that time and you're here complaining. What do you have to do all day? Oh, don't even bother to answer that because I know the answer. We're not discussing this anymore. You were the one who wanted to stay home. Deal with it." He left the house and didn't come back until noon.

ARGUMENTS LIKE THIS PERSISTED. Phillip claimed I exaggerated or outright lied about the past even when I had proof to the contrary. He used a common phrase, "I wish I had recorded what you said because I'd play it back so I could prove you're lying." Or sometimes it was, "You don't even hear what you just said."

There were times I started thinking it was all in my head. When he wasn't home, I'd dig through records to prove that I wasn't losing my mind. I had canceled checks to show that Lynette was there each week, and yet, his accusations made me question myself, always putting me on the defensive. I began to wonder if something was wrong with me. I started to think that I couldn't trust that the words I thought I spoke were the actual words that came out of my mouth.

Phillip tried to trip me up by instructing me to repeat exactly what I'd just said. According to Phillip, this would prove his point. When I couldn't recall the precise words I'd used previously, he claimed it showed I lied or had no idea what I was saying.

This became a source of anxiety when we argued. I would try and remember the exact words I used so Phillip couldn't make these accusations. It made me hesitant to engage him in any argument because I couldn't recall every word I'd uttered and then parrot them back to him. Even if I pointed out that he couldn't do it either, he turned the tables and said I was now trying to manipulate him.

I noticed when I got a part-time job designing and maintaining a website for a local realtor, he started to be kinder because he was hoping it would lead to a business we could develop together. While the income helped, it was nothing compared to the weekly paycheck I once made. Since I only had the most basic coding skills, I needed his help to do the more advanced coding. He was a natural coder. But, I stopped asking for his help after he told me I was faking not knowing how to program so he would have to do the work.

Once I wasn't contributing as much to the household income, Phillip was in charge of every dime we spent. But, at the time, I didn't care. I was frequently so exhausted I could barely manage to get through the day. I was scared because my energy levels had become so depleted that I began to suspect something was wrong health-wise.

I finally acknowledged to myself how bad it was when I couldn't find the strength to push the Beans' carriage home from a small park only two blocks away. I had to call my neighbor and ask for help. When I mentioned this to Phillip, he snapped.

"Don't tell me about tired. You're not the one who has to leave for work at 7 a.m."

"No, I don't. I just get up two or three times during the night to deal with the kids. Do you even remember that I got up each morning to be on the bus at 5:30 for twelve years?" He shook his head, insinuating that I was again exaggerating.

All the years I supported him so he could develop his career were erased or forgotten. So were the promises that, once he was established, I could relax and have time to pursue my career goals. I didn't even care about "my career" anymore. I just wanted him to support my decision to stay close to home to care for our children. Yet, he refused to acknowledge any of the contributions I'd made to his life, not just the financial ones.

To combat my fatigue, I began going to bed as soon as the Beans were asleep. If I heard Phillip come up the stairs, I pretended to be asleep because I knew he'd be angry with me for not waiting up. Sometimes, he sat down on the bed.

"Hey, what's up?" he asked one night.

"Not much, I just have a headache," I lied.

I knew if I told him again about my incredible fatigue, it would lead to an argument or an accusation. That was the all-too-familiar pattern.

"It's all in your head," Phillip told me repeatedly.

"I left some dinner in the fridge for you to microwave. I'm going to try and get some sleep."

I BEGAN SLIDING INTO DEPRESSION, thinking maybe Phillip was right. His snide comments that I was lazy or inept played over and over again in my mind. I was so full of self-doubt, I allowed him to take more and more control of our lives without questioning his decisions. I began seeing myself through his eyes, and what I saw wasn't pretty.

When I told my friend Shannon about feeling lethargic all the time and unable to focus, she convinced me that a trip to my doctor was warranted no matter what Phillip thought. I didn't tell Phillip I planned to see my doctor and almost canceled the appointment, feeling foolish. Once there, I recall feeling ashamed for even being there, as though I was taking her valuable time over something so insignificant.

"Maybe it's because I'm too old to be the mother of such young kids," I half laughed with embarrassment. "Phillip thinks it's all in my head." She rolled her eyes and asked me to describe how I felt.

"It's like every ounce of energy has been drained from my body," I told her and began to cry. "I'm a high energy person. At least I used to be. Now I can't function some days. I'll start out feeling fine, and then it's like a battery has died and there's no power left. I've started limiting what I do with the twins because, too often, I can't finish what I started. I think something is out of balance somehow. I think something is wrong."

"When did this start?" she asked while poking and prodding my neck.

"I don't recall exactly, but it's been over a year. The first time I remember it getting really bad was when I had to call someone to help me get the twins back home because I couldn't push their carriage."

She stopped and looked at me. As my regular physician who I'd seen for years, she must have noticed the change in my demeanor.

"This is not in your head. Without more tests, I can't say exactly what's wrong, but this isn't something imaginary. I'm going to have one of the nurses get you an appointment to see a specialist. We're going to figure this out," she assured me.

After seeing the specialist, tests revealed I had several benign tumors that were affecting my parathyroid glands. That caused my calcium levels to drop dangerously low, causing my severe fatigue. I was relieved to learn it wasn't all in my head, but angry that I was harangued and characterized negatively by Phillip over these real physical problems. Not once did he apologize for all the times he said I was just lazy or that it was my imagination. After surgery, I recovered with the help of some supplements to compensate for the lack of calcium.

The slow erosion of my confidence didn't bounce back just because I was feeling better. However, the experience made me realize just how much I conceded in my marriage now that I wasn't earning more money than Phillip. I had absorbed all the negativity Phillip spewed at me since leaving my job. A part of me even clung to Phillip's vision of who I was, or wasn't. I had relinquished so much of my control to him while I was suffering from unexplained exhaustion, it was hard to regain any measure of confidence.

Gone was any equality we had in the relationship. The man who I once thought treated me as an equal controlled almost every aspect of my life. I no longer had much, if any, input into the decisions within our marriage. Instead of calling him out on it, I did what my mother did. I adapted to the new dynamic of our relationship.

Chapter Six

WHAT TO DO ABOUT CHUBBY?

I t was one in the afternoon, but I couldn't force myself to continue packing. I decided that the best thing I could do was to get some sleep so I could make the trip to Cobleskill safely.

I was overtired but had a hard time drifting off. I tried to keep my thoughts on the Beans and wondered what they were doing, and if my brother was enjoying having them there. He was good at keeping them entertained. I imagined them playing some of the invented games Jake had played with his own two girls when they were young. Their favorite was something he called Louie Prima ball, a game his wife Meredith had played with her siblings, growing up in the house where they now lived. Jake convinced the Beans it was an official Olympic sport and that they were, in fact, world champs. He proved it by creating a homemade certificate, then printed and framed their award to present to them. They were still at an age where they believed anything an adult told them.

AS I DRIFTED OFF, I couldn't help but think about the startling events that had unfolded in recent years. Selling our home in

Blairstown was unsettling enough. I thought our old Victorian was where we would raise our children and, once they left home, Phillip and I would grow old in that home together.

Then I was reminded of the long conversations the kids and I had driving back and forth from Cobleskill to Alexandria. They pelted me with questions about why we had to move. There were things I didn't want them to know. I didn't want them to be in the middle of a tug-of-war between Phillip and me. I tried to be honest but left out as much as possible about the reasons we were moving yet again. It bothered me tremendously that I'd already broken my promise that if we moved to Alexandria, they wouldn't have to move again. I had believed it at the time. I never imagined things would take the turn they did.

THE SOUND of banging startled me. I woke abruptly from my nap. The noise was coming from downstairs. Someone was pounding on the café door. It took me a minute to realize where I was because I'd fallen asleep after I lay down for what I thought would be a few minutes. I stumbled to get dressed, then rushed down the stairs. But by the time I reached the door, no one was there. I saw a car pulling away but didn't know if it belonged to whomever had banged on my door.

Meandering into the kitchen, I looked at the clock on the stove and was shocked to see it was approaching five o'clock. I'd slept for hours, never even taking Chubby for his walk. I grabbed his leash from the hook near the door and locked up, hoping the black flies would be kinder than they usually were when we ventured out to one of the trails that surrounded the lake a block from the building.

When I returned from my walk with Chubby, I began packing the van in earnest. A little after seven o'clock, I returned inside and started hunting for Duncan and Felicia so I could get them into their crates. They were nowhere to be found. I searched everywhere. I shook the treat bag, opened a can of cat food, and did everything I usually did that brought them running. I didn't blame them for hiding because I wished I could hide too.

I went upstairs, thinking maybe they would wander out if I wasn't around. Chubby followed me up the stairs and jumped on the mattress. I noticed how matted and dirty he looked. It would have been embarrassing to hand him over to Jody looking so grubby.

"Hey, Bud! Come with me. I know a tub with your name on it." The amount of dirt and grime in the tub was pathetic after washing him.

By eight, I knew I had to make a decision whether to leave or head out in the morning. I was still exhausted but knew I couldn't delay the trip forever. Even though the thought of being out on the road by myself late at night was worrisome, I decided to head out as soon as I located the cats.

My growling stomach reminded me I hadn't eaten since breakfast. I reasoned that if I went to Tim Horton's to grab a bagel and cream cheese, the cats might come out of hiding. I brought the crates to the bathroom upstairs, so if I was able to locate them, I could close the door to prevent them from escaping. About ten minutes later, I headed to the local Tim Horton's Coffee Shop with Chubby in tow, hoping my elusive cats would make an appearance.

I finally got back about a half hour later and found the cat food in the kitchen gone. I headed upstairs, hoping for the best. Both cats were now asleep on the mattress. They looked up at me as though I were the enemy who had come to bring them before a firing squad. I corralled them into the bathroom and then into their crates.

They yowled and complained while I packed the last of my stuff into my suitcase, the same one I had brought to Jenny's the night before. I went over to the desk for the picture I kept of the Beans. I was finally ready to go.

Suddenly, I was overwhelmed. I knew it was best to have Chubby stay behind but, somehow, having him with me kept the loneliness at bay. Knowing he wouldn't be there on my trip south left me distraught, and I again considered calling Jody, to delay my trip by a day. But I thought it would be rude to change plans so late at night when she was up waiting for me. So, with all the pets in the van, off I went to hand over my faithful companion.

I arrived at Jody's a little after nine. She and her husband Brice had a farm in the countryside outside Alexandria. They bred small dogs and had a kennel that was right next to their house. Jody was originally from the U.S. but had moved to Canada decades before. She and Brice were a wonderful couple. I met them through the café, of course, just like almost everyone else I met in Alexandria.

Even though she'd offered to let Chubby stay in the house with her and Brice, I was reluctant to leave him. Internally, I reasoned that he would be in good, loving hands, but it was still a struggle to hand over his leash. I didn't realize just how attached I'd grown to him. He yipped and whined, accusing me of betrayal. I could hear his plaintiff yelps and howls as I climbed into the van. I almost turned back at the end of her laneway but kept going because I was embarrassed I was crying so hard. A profound loneliness crept into my heart as I headed towards the border.

As I drove south towards Cobleskill, I had hours to think about what the future held. I was tired of starting over every few years. I longed for a home and a place where I could feel settled. I wanted that place to be Alexandria. At one point, Phillip had wanted that, too.

I knew I would make new friends, but it was the constant upheaval, the starting over, that left me feeling defeated. Knowing that Phillip could soon exert even more control over my life than ever before was what made me so distraught.

Phillip believed my desire for friendships outside our marriage was a betrayal. The simple pleasure of an evening out with friends was something that he constantly discouraged, even before we had children. I struggled to understand why gatherings like the one at Jenny's upset him so much. I knew that this evening had only happened because he wasn't there. Once I moved to Cobleskill, all social activities would again be a point of contention..

What was so mystifying was that Phillip was outwardly a friendly and engaging person. He eagerly kept up with his former classmates and friends from high school. But he rarely interacted with those people regularly because they were so far away. What was also odd was, before we got married, he loved to socialize. We organized enormous parties at a local state park to play Capture the Flag, and had BBQs, or went with friends to listen to bands or hear comedy shows. But they were usually events shared with his friends. We saw my friends and family over the holidays, or not at all.

His attitude extended beyond going out and socializing. It extended to phone calls, too. Any time I made a call from home to a friend, it frequently became an issue after I got off the phone. Phillip told me my call to them had taken too much time. Depending on who I was speaking to, he even went so far as telling me my friends were using me somehow.

He told me it was "abnormal" to have these relationships and called them "selfish" and "harmful" to our marriage. He said I was immature for even wanting these friendships.

When I worked in New York, I got around it because he wasn't a part of that social life. However, as time went on, even events like an office Christmas party or joining another couple for dinner became problematic. After these evenings ended, a fight would ensue. He always framed his complaint the same way: "We have too much going on to spend time socializing." Phillip's to-do list was a revolving excuse to avoid spending time with anyone other than his friends or his family.

AFTER WE HAD CHILDREN, Phillip attempted to isolate me even more. It was easier to do that when I no longer had my life in New York City to shield me. Back in Blairstown, all the people I associated with were casual acquaintances, except for my friend and neighbor, Shannon. She was a godsend, especially when the twins were little. She came over frequently to help with the kids when I needed a break. As they grew, the twins called her Auntie Shannon and her husband, Uncle Vince.

Phillip liked Vincent but barely tolerated Shannon. He told me he found her too outspoken and opinionated. The longer we were married, the more I realized he felt that way about a lot of women, and that Phillip, the same man I once believed thought I was his equal, was quite the chauvinist. He repeatedly claimed his female colleagues only got where they did by "sleeping with the boss." I wondered how he thought I got ahead.

Other situations made me realize his attitude towards women was consistently negative. It was particularly hard to ignore after something happened one weekend while Phillip was away on a business trip. Shannon offered to help me paint our dining room. I thought it would be a lovely surprise for Phillip.

"How could you do this behind my back?" was the response I got.

"Phillip, I thought you'd be happy, for Christ's sake! It looks amazing. It's one less room you have to contend with doing. Why are you so mad?" I shouted back at him. He wouldn't speak to me for days after this happened.

Instead of being pleased, it had led to an ongoing battle about "priorities" and my friendship with Shannon. He was angry because we had painted it "without his permission." Anything related to the house was under his complete domain and done at his absolute discretion. Once, when I complained about an unsafe light fixture with exposed wiring right near a shower stall in the bathroom, he scoffed at my concern. It didn't get fixed for years, even though it would have taken less than a half hour to do. The fact it made me nervous seemed to please him. Even making a suggestion would lead to an argument, and he would get so angry, I wouldn't bring up the subject again.

When Shannon and I painted that room, his fury was over the fact I had taken control of something he considered his domain without consulting him. He said Shannon was "unqualified" to paint our dining room. This was absurd because she and Vince had renovated the bed-and-breakfast they operated in our historic neighborhood entirely on their own. She could paint without using painter's tape to prevent getting paint on the ceiling. But, in his mind, she wasn't qualified.

"Is that because she's a woman?" I asked him, point blank.

"Screw you and screw Shannon, too," he said, storming out of the house.

From that point on, he spoke ill of Shannon.

I believed his resistance was a fear that anyone from the outside could weaken his influence over me. While I did have friends, somehow, if they didn't meet his approval, socializing with them was a major flash point. It had become so commonplace; I didn't have the perspective necessary to see any of it until I moved to Alexandria and I no longer needed Phillip's approval.

I FINALLY PULLED into the driveway of the new apartment in Cobleskill about one o'clock in the morning. I stopped for a moment before heading in. The cats were yowling to be let out of their cages. I knew exactly how they felt.

Phillip was supposed to leave me a key in the ashtray of our Elantra. I grabbed it before carrying the cats, in their cages, to the back door of the apartment and hoped it would work in the lock. It was unsettling to be entering an apartment, that I'd never been to, after midnight. After opening the door, I put the cats inside, hoping they wouldn't wake Phillip, and grabbed my suitcase and their litter box from the van. The crunch of my footsteps on the gravel of the driveway unnerved me as I looked around to make sure I was alone. The noise seemed too loud for my small feet to be making. I hurried inside.

I could see a light ahead of me as I entered the mudroom,

passing a staircase that I discovered, the next day, led to the master bedroom on the second floor. I passed the bathroom and then went through another small room before I found myself in the kitchen. I returned to the bathroom and set up the cats' litter box before I let them out of their cages. They looked grateful to be out, and quickly disappeared into the night.

I looked for the smallest of signs of welcome to my new home. There were none. I found the living room and, without unpacking or even brushing my teeth, I lay down on the couch and quietly wept before sleep overtook me.

PHILLIP WAS GONE by the time I woke the next morning. I never heard him leave. After using the bathroom, I wandered around to get a closer look at the place. The layout was strange because it was advertised as a three-bedroom, but there was only one minuscule bedroom on the first floor and a larger bedroom, accessed by a staircase to the second floor. What they called the third bedroom was a room that was between the kitchen and mudroom. Anyone who needed to use the bathroom would have to travel through the room, making it awkward to use as a bedroom.

I determined that Phillip was using the small bedroom because there was a pillow and a light blanket on Jack's twin bed. A small TV had been placed on top of a dresser. A pair of his jeans also hung on a hook on the back of the door.

The kitchen cabinets were bare. I desperately wanted some coffee. I was even willing to drink instant if that was all there was available, but the only things I saw were some Tastykake Powdered Mini Donuts, a jar of peanut butter, and a loaf of Wonder Bread on the counter. There was a pint of milk in the fridge, an open bottle of red wine, and a half-eaten burger and fries in a to-go container.

"Welcome to your new home!" I thought and wondered why it surprised me. I knew Phillip had a habit of stopping at the closest Dunkin Donuts for his coffee and breakfast each morning, so I assumed his habits hadn't changed.

I was famished, but there was nothing available to eat. I thought about picking up a few groceries before unloading the van, then leaving to pick up Jack and Lucy. Suddenly I realized I had no money to spend on groceries. This made my new reality abundantly clear.

OUR AGREEMENT TO move to Canada was the result of several unforeseen events in our lives. In 2005, Phillip came home from work and headed straight for the liquor cabinet before he delivered the bad news.

"They let go of a few more people today. I might have to start sending out resumés."

"What positions are they cutting?"

"It seems across the board. I think I'm safe for a while, but the risk is that if I wait, there's less of a chance of finding any positions open at another agency. You know, you could send out resumés, too," Phillip told me.

"Not this again!" I replied and went into the kitchen to fix dinner.

I was always on the defensive about wanting to remain close to home. I stubbornly resisted his attempts to make me feel guilty for quitting my job in Manhattan.

However, I worried when he would come home, unable to eat due to his persistent acid stomach and his self-diagnosed IBS. He managed his symptoms with over-the-counter medicines and some changes to his diet.

"Honey, can you pick up some Tums?"

"Are you out of them already? Do you think you should see Dr. Powers?"

"I can't take time off right now. Can you buy me more Tums or Rolaids?"

"Sure. I'll run out now. Is Mexican food okay for dinner? I picked up some stuff to make burritos."

"Yeah, did you get the mild salsa? I can't handle the medium anymore."

With his hectic schedule, he ate an enormous amount of fast food. I often suspected his diet contributed to his stomach problems. He would get angry if I offered to prepare lunches because, somehow, he thought it was lame to bring lunch from home.

EVERYTHING FELL APART in the beginning of February.

"Hey, what's up?" I asked when he called my cellphone.

"I just got escorted out of the building. It was the most humiliating thing I've ever experienced. I'm on my way home."

"I'm so sorry, Honey… drive safe. Love you."

When he came home that evening, devastated, I just held him for a long time. For weeks they'd been laying off more and more personnel. He thought if he worked harder, stayed later, took work home, he would magically escape the layoff.

"Well, I guess I can pour myself a double scotch tonight because I don't have to work in the morning."

"Look, it stinks. But we'll be okay. Something will turn up."

It didn't. Soon the fighting began again, as we tried to hang on to our very different solutions to this urgent problem.

BY THE SPRING OF 2006, we had blown through most of our savings, trying to stay afloat. We had two mortgages for the rental properties on top of our personal expenses. Our monthly COBRA payment alone was more than our monthly mortgage: over twelve hundred dollars each month just for healthcare insurance.

We discussed selling the two rental properties we owned in the city of Scranton, about a forty-five minute drive from our home in Blairstown. I thought this would be best because they were losing money. Phillip said we should keep those and sell the Victorian we had lovingly restored. I disagreed vehemently. By that time, however, he had grown accustomed to having the final say in decisions. The financial stress led to long, extended arguments.

"Why can't we sell the income properties?"

"That's my retirement."

"Don't you mean *our* retirement?"

"Yeah, whatever. We'll get a lot more money for this than we'll get in Scranton. Those places still need work."

"Exactly. We should sell one and cut our losses. This is our home, Phillip."

"If we sold this, we'd have money to invest there and have rental income."

"But what about school? Where are we going to live if we sell this?"

"Well, if you would start looking for a job in New York again, we wouldn't have to have this conversation."

"No."

"Why not?"

"We have discussed this, Phillip. Asking me repeatedly won't change my answer. I don't have the same connections in the business to secure the type of job I once had. When I left Interactive Production, Netscape was still around. The industry has changed, Phillip. Why do you keep pressing this issue?"

"You're just stubborn. You could find something."

"And so could you."

We each dug in on our positions. I understood all too well why Phillip didn't want to commute each day, but he was the one who wanted to buy the properties that left him busy on the weekends. He'd already missed so much of the kids' lives. If he got another job, it would take him away from them each day, again. In the seven years since they were born, he had rarely had time to spend with them.

There was the practical side of the issue, too. Phillip had little interest in the day-to-day tasks of operating a household. Whenever I stepped out, he'd call my cellphone so frequently, I'd come home much sooner than I'd planned. He seemed so helpless that I rarely asked him to watch the kids.

Whenever he had to perform housework, he complained that he had other things to do. Or he did the chore so poorly, I'd stupidly jump in. I fell right into the trap of doing it all myself, unwilling to confront the angry mood that chores inspired in Phillip.

My various part-time jobs weren't enough to sustain us, and we finally ran out of options. While I was reluctant, we put our house on the market and it sold six months later.

WE RENTED an apartment in a town a short drive to the kids' school, where I taught computer skills two days a week. They were now in the third grade and flourishing in every way. They both had friends, and I hung out with some women I worked with at the school. It wasn't a perfect life, but it was far from horrible either. Phillip spent so much time away, completing the renovations on the properties in Scranton, I didn't have to contend with his unpredictable moods.

He stayed home on weekends and played with the Beans. We'd crawl into bed and speak about our more modest dreams of running a business or doing something that would provide both financial security and the freedom to be independent of the corporate world. Long gone were our creative ambitions. Now our shared dream was to leave it all behind so we could enjoy our time with the twins. It was a modest dream and one that I learned, when we moved to Alexandria, was also an illusion.

Chapter Seven

OH, CANADA

Our decision to move north began with what I thought was a casual conversation. One weekend when Phillip was back home, he confessed that he'd been looking online at real estate. As we sat on the couch after the kids were in bed, he said, "Hey, look what I found online."

"Where is it?"

"Alexandria,"

"Virginia?"

"No. Ontario."

"Oh, too bad it's so far away! It's lovely! How much are they asking?" I stared at the pictures of a brick heritage building. The wrap-around porch and Victorian features piqued my curiosity. We had owned a condo in the Eastern Townships in Quebec years earlier but had sold it and reinvested the money in the Scranton rental properties. We'd always discussed the idea of buying another vacation property in Quebec one day. I looked over at him and I could tell this wasn't the end of the conversation. Phillip didn't respond to my question about the price of the building, so I looked up to see why he was silent. The expression on his face revealed he was waiting to tell me something.

"Okay, confess! What are you thinking?"

He then delivered a speech that sounded like he'd rehearsed it a thousand times. "Well, it's no surprise that I'd like to consider moving north." I took a deep breath because he had talked about this many times.

"I know it was impossible before, but we always said we'd buy another place after we sold our condo in Quebec." I let him continue.

"Remember the place we stopped to eat when we were on our way to Ottawa last summer? The restaurant in that old mill?"

"Yeah, how could I forget? The food was excellent, and I spilled my wine all over the waiter."

"You've always been a klutz," he said, taking my hand. "Well, this place is right near the same lake and on the Main Street of town. I want to go up and look at this. I have a good feeling about the place."

"But when would we do this?"

"Maybe we can look when they have spring break? I know I still have loads of work to do in Scranton, but I want to do this. What do you think?"

"I don't know, Phillip. It's an odd location for a vacation property, even with the lake. Besides, we can't afford this right now."

"I'm not talking about using it for vacations, Kasey. Let's move there."

"What? Are you serious?"

"I am. This property is in Ontario, so the French language requirements wouldn't be as much of an issue for the Beans in school. Plus, the Ontario government still funds Catholic schools. We wouldn't have to worry about health insurance because they have universal health. So, instead of flushing our money down the drain every month on health insurance, we buy a property like this. Think about it. We could start our own business and do something that would build a future for the Beans. They could learn to work alongside us, and we wouldn't have to deal with other people fucking up our lives to save a buck or two on a salary. I'm serious about this. I think it would be a marvelous opportunity."

"Holy shit, Phillip. This would be an enormous step." My mind raced as he sprung this on me.

"Well, if it works out, not only would we be able to run some small business, it would give us time to do some of our creative projects. Kasey, I'm tired of missing the kids' lives. I don't want to go back into Morristown either. I don't mind writing copy for a living, but the commute is brutal. I could see about freelancing from up there. A lot of companies need content writers, and I could help with the business while doing some writing on the side. It makes sense to me. Don't you think it's worth looking into?" He reached over and stroked my hair.

"If you're going to convince me, you'll have to do a lot more than stroke my hair." We snuck upstairs as quietly as we could and got in bed.

OVER THE NEXT FEW MONTHS, our discussions continued. I came around to Phillip's idea for several reasons. Phillip kept reiterating that there were many reasons it made sense to move to Canada. He was adamant about the kids attending a parochial school. I had to agree that it would be a plus that we wouldn't have to pay tuition. I also liked the fact that the school they would attend was similar in size to the one they were attending now. This was definitely one of the factors in why his argument was so persuasive. However, nothing Phillip said weighed more heavily in influencing my decision than my concerns about the financial stability of the real estate market in the U.S.

One of my jobs at the time was working as a part-time mobile notary. This involved going to people's houses to witness borrowers signing second mortgage loan documents. My job was to watch the homeowners sign forms on all the lines before sending them back to the lender. Washington Mutual, Citibank, and Chase were just a few of the banks I worked for under the auspices of firms that used notaries who belonged to The National Notary Association.

While working with this organization, I kept seeing a pattern to the loan documents. The income-to-debt ratio of the individuals taking out second, and even third, mortgages didn't add up. These people didn't make enough income to be securing the loans they were approved for by these large financial institutions. I'm no financial genius, but long before sub-prime loans alarmed economists, I was unnerved.

"Phillip, these banks are giving people money like candy. I swear some of these numbers make no sense. These are people who have little to no equity in their homes, and yet, they are taking out second mortgages for swimming pools and heated driveways." Phillip just scoffed at me, saying I was ridiculous.

So what eventually convinced me wasn't anything Phillip said about saving on insurance or tuition. I thought it made sense to put the remaining money we had from selling our house into a Canadian bank, because Canadian banks are far more regulated than banks in the U.S. and are more solvent. Years earlier, when the U.S. had suffered because of the Savings and Loan Crisis, Canadians didn't suffer the same fate. Besides the limited number of banks in their country, their financial institutions are also more diversified. I thought it might be good to have our money in a bank that didn't need to get bailed out.

I also knew that the Canadian dollar was weak against the U.S. dollar. That meant we'd have a lot more Canadian dollars to buy a property. I checked the currency exchange rate daily and the more favorable the rates got, the more I was finally in agreement with Phillip about taking a trip to look at properties. My gut was telling me to get our money out of Dodge because what we had left over from the sale of our house would go a lot further. The biggest bonus, however, was that Phillip agreed to sell the rental properties in Scranton.

"Let's take a trip to Alexandria," I told Phillip one night when he was home. He was over the moon.

The eventual plan was to purchase a property and move

there, then apply for permanent residence status. We learned, after the fact, that it wasn't the most expedient way to immigrate, and we had to hire an attorney to help us navigate the paperwork.

The building Phillip had zeroed in on was the same brick "heritage building" in Alexandria he'd shown me months earlier. Before visiting Alexandria, it was hard to imagine the building's configuration from the listing information. But once we saw the place, it seemed ideal for a business.

There were three units in the main building, and someone had built an additional two-bedroom apartment off the rear of the building. On the first floor, there was already a large commercial space, that was once a bookstore. We imagined that space would be ideal for our tearoom. The one-bedroom apartment had a kitchen and living room on the first floor, and a bedroom and bathroom on the second floor.

We eventually turned that space into the kitchen for the café and the entryway for the business. We used the upstairs bedroom for an office for the business. We opened up a door that had been plastered over to connect the three first-floor rooms of the business. There was a long-term tenant living in that space but we moved her into the vacant rear apartment and kept the small two-bedroom apartment above the newly configured café and tearoom for our living quarters. It wasn't nearly as elegant and spacious as our former home, but it was a chance to start over. Eventually we planned on breaking through the wall to the other side of the building so the space we would be using as an office would become part of our personal living space.

"It'll take time, but I think if we were living over whatever business we have, it would be easier on the Beans because they could see us even when we were working," he reasoned.

"We could even put a balcony off the rear of the building so we could have a view of the lake."

Weeks after our visit, the owners accepted our offer, and Phillip and I purchased the property.

"Let's wait until school is over before telling the Beans and the rest of our friends about our plans to move north," I told him.

AT THE TIME, we still weren't sure exactly what type of business would be suitable for the building and didn't want to duplicate a more successful venture in such a small town. We crossed off bowling alley and curling club, right off the bat. There were already a few gift shops, a pet store, and plenty of restaurants.

Phillip was pushing for the latter because I loved to cook. That, too, was a frequent source of arguments because I liked to make things from scratch and could spend hours making a meal. He would open a box, dump it in a pan, and call it a day. I told him the space wasn't suitable for a restaurant because the kitchen on the first floor was minuscule, a galley-style kitchen with barely any counter space. The electric stove and refrigerator were in rough shape and not the type of equipment found in any of the restaurants I'd worked in while waiting tables in college and beyond.

One day, as we worked on touching up the paint in the building's front, a woman named Gail, who owned a used bookstore down the road, approached us. Like everyone we'd met so far, she was friendly and warm and asked us loads of questions that we politely answered.

"Is it true you're opening up a tearoom?" she asked.

I looked at Phillip and said, "That's the plan for now."

"Well, that is just lovely!" she exclaimed, thrilled her news was accurate. "I've always thought that a tearoom would do well in a town so rich with Scottish heritage!"

When she left, Phillip looked at me and laughed. "Well, that was interesting! So, this town needs a tearoom? I guess we have to figure out what it takes to open one."

Thinking back, it seemed like buying the building and working to turn it into an income property was the last time I recall that our goals were aligned. We worked all summer to make the place suitable for the business. Once we transformed the room that was once a bookstore into the tearoom, everything fell into place. We adorned it with our best antiques from our former home. We hung our beautiful authentic gasoliers from the ceiling, and we covered the industrial-looking green wall-to-wall carpeting with our colorful oriental rugs. We left the bookshelves. They were a deep cranberry color and coordinated with the rugs, and would give us a place to put items for sale like teapots, coffee mugs, and other related items on their shelves. We chose a rich tan to paint the walls, and placed plants and greenery around the room to give it a homey feel. I even scored six solid granite tables with wrought iron bases for eighty percent off at the local Giant Tiger. They made the room look more contemporary while blending in with the surrounding antique tables and chairs.

By mid-August of 2007, we finalized some decisions about the business. I handled all the details, such as getting our vendor licenses and other necessary paperwork together, to make the business compliant with both local and regional regulations. Everything seemed like it was coming together. For the first time since the birth of our twins, I was truly happy and fulfilled. Phillip and I appeared entirely in sync again.

The apartment above the tearoom was small but it held our huge dreams. Enclosed within the walls were joint ambitions of starting over and having a business we could run as a family. When Phillip and I bought the property in Alexandria, we were happier than we'd been in a while. We were once again a "team," each bringing our unique set of skills to the table. We discussed things and made decisions together. Now Phillip was willing to listen to my ideas and suggestions, something that had abruptly stopped once he gained control over our finances.

"What kind of food should we serve?" he asked when we got closer to opening.

"It's got to be simple with such a compact kitchen. I think mostly homemade soups, salads, and sandwiches. We should also have plenty of desserts. I want to look into the cost of an espresso machine so we can serve cappuccino and lattes. Those will turn a tidy profit."

"Why don't we get everything from one of those food supply companies? Wouldn't that be easier?" Phillip asked earnestly.

"Phillip! The restaurant right across the street does that. Why would anyone come here if we're doing the same thing? They sell everything from pizza to Chinese food. I see the Sysco® truck delivering prepackaged foods several times a week. We can't compete with a restaurant that's been around for forty years unless we're not only better but different."

"Well, I still think it would be easier just to get things pre-made, but, whatever," he said.

We still disagreed over things that summer but it felt different. I felt like I was being heard. I found I wasn't as defensive as I'd been in the past, when nothing I said seemed to matter and my thoughts and suggestions were shoved aside. Phillip always had an equal say in everything, even when he wasn't bringing in an income. In our new life, I was once again a valued member of a team instead of being his faithful sidekick.

"This paint looks fantastic. It was a brilliant choice." He complimented my selection, wrapping his arms around me as we admired our handiwork.

"It goes so well with the rugs, don't you think? I love the granite tables, too. They make it feel more like a café instead of someone's dining room. They're so practical, too." In those moments, it seemed like nothing could tear us apart.

Without friends or any family close by, Phillip once again became my sole companion. He seemed to relish the added attention and not having to fight me over going out occasionally with my girlfriends. We were more intimate than we had been for years. We laughed more easily and enjoyed spending time together. We seemed to fall in love all over again. He was once again my best friend.

As we got closer to opening the café, I stayed focused. I desperately wanted to make the 2Beans Café into a successful enterprise. I had lots of ideas on how to get quickly established. I told Phillip we could offer catering and to-go services. Everything was on course until late that summer.

"I created a sample catering menu," I told him when he came down from the office above the café kitchen one day in late August. "I did some research, and most of the local companies offer some pretty basic stuff. I think I can win over some corporate clients with this menu."

Phillip said nothing, so I looked at him and saw he had an odd expression on his face.

"You will never believe who I just got off the phone with!" Phillip told me, excitedly.

"Well, I hope it was our lawyer because we still haven't heard back from him," I teased.

"Marco called. He's opening a new company in New Jersey and he's offered me a job. Isn't that great?"

"That's fantastic! Congrats, honey! He knows you'll have to work remotely?"

"Well, not exactly. He wants me to be in the office. I already told him I'd accept the position."

This stunned me. "Is he willing to pay for the costs of moving back?" I asked him incredulously.

That's when Phillip told me that none of his former colleagues knew we'd moved to Canada. It was the whole secret marriage situation all over again. I realized Marco had no idea that Phillip had jumped at the opportunity to leave his wife and kids in a foreign country to take a job back in the States. This blew my mind.

"You told me that a restaurant could be a tremendous gamble. I'm nervous that if this doesn't work out, we'll have no income," he maintained. "We're spending a lot to get this going."

"Phillip, I told you that *before* we bought the property. You said we should do it. It was our chance to turn our lives around. Now we've invested our time and money into opening the business."

"We can still run the business. I can help develop marketing from anywhere, and I'll come home on weekends," he assured me.

"So, I'm supposed to stay here and care for the kids and run a new business on my own? Aren't you the same man who wanted to spend time with his family? Didn't you say you hated the fact you've missed such a sizable chunk of the Beans' lives? How could you tell him 'yes' without even discussing it with me? You get upset if I use the bathroom without telling you that's where I'm going. The whole point of moving here was to be together as a family, Phillip. What is the point of doing any of this if we will not be together?" I asked him through tears.

"I just don't think I should turn down this position. I'll be making more than you can make here at the café, and I can still visit. Don't make me feel guilty for wanting to provide for my family, Kasey."

I left the room because Phillip hated it when I cried. He claimed I was trying to make him feel guilty whenever tears flowed. I tried to control my emotions but I was utterly distraught. On the one hand, I, too, was afraid of relying solely on the income from a new business, especially a restaurant. The failure rate was not on our side. But the whole point to starting over was to reinvent our lives.

When I got myself together, I told him, "This is insane, Phillip. The cost of maintaining two separate residences will eat into whatever you're making. We haven't opened yet. The kids haven't even started school. Why don't we rent this place and all move back together?" He wouldn't hear of it.

The day before Phillip left to resume his life back in the States, he said something that, over time, bothered me more and more. The Beans were sitting at a table in our newly decorated tearoom, eating dessert. I was clearing the dishes and when I brought them into the kitchen, Phillip followed me and grabbed me from behind. I spun around so he could hold me. I was completely despondent over his leaving. Tears welled up but I choked them back.

"I'll miss you, you know," he whispered to me, holding me close to him.

"Me, too," I said, trying to keep my emotions in check.

"If Marco's company takes off, I'll let you and the Beans move back to the States, I promise," he assured me.

"Why can't we come back now? We still have plenty of money in the bank. I don't want to do this alone," I pleaded with him.

"Look, that's not a smart thing to do. This is a new venture and who knows if it will take off. If it doesn't, we'll be in the same boat but without the money to start over again." Then, with little emotion, he added, "Promise me one thing? Don't start making friends up here because we need this business to fly and, I know you, you'll end up blowing it because you'll be spending time with your new pals."

I was too caught up in thoughts of him leaving to process what he'd just said. Instead, I just nodded and told him, "Sure."

The next day, he called me from his hotel room and said he was looking for apartments around Blairstown instead of finding an apartment in Morristown, close to where he would be working.

"But, Phillip, didn't you say you hated the commute? Wasn't that a big reason for moving to Canada?"

"The apartments in Morristown are too expensive," he told me.

He ignored me when I pointed out that the money he spent on gas and the wear and tear on the car negated any savings he might have had by taking an apartment right back where we had just moved from months earlier.

AS I SAT on the couch in Cobleskill, all these thoughts left me unsettled. It was now three years after we had moved to Alexandria and here I was back in the States once again. The café was now closed, and the life I had created in Alexandria had ended. All the time and effort was for naught.

I knew that we were never that "perfect" couple. No family is ever what they seem to be on the outside. But now I questioned the most basic assumptions of our relationship. Were we ever really working together to create a fresh start? Or was the move to Canada part of some plan he had developed so he could lead a double life? He was the one who had introduced the idea of moving north. I accepted everything he told me at face value. The goal was to work together and build a family business. I envisioned us working side-by-side and watching the Beans grow into adulthood. It was a vision I thought we shared.

I was grateful for my time in Alexandria because I realized that owning and operating the café became a part of my healing. My time there enabled me to rediscover parts of myself that had been erased ever so slowly. The erosion of my self-esteem happened so gradually; I didn't even realize it had happened until he could no longer scrutinize my every move.

The overarching message from Phillip back then was that I was a deeply flawed person, but he tolerated, and even loved me, despite my failings. I internalized his perception of me. But while I was in Alexandria, I finally realized how deeply insecure I'd become.

I couldn't remain married to someone who inspired so much mental and emotional anguish. Phillip seemed to delight in sucking the life out of me. Based on all that had happened recently, I knew in my heart, I had to figure out a way to leave the marriage and, if possible, return home to Alexandria.

Part Two

OUR NEW REALITY

Do not just slay your demons.
Dissect them and find out
what they've been feeding on.

~ The Man Frozen in Time

Chapter Eight

OUR LOST BOY

September 1st Cobleskill, New York

I was all set to head to Vermont to get the Beans when I decided to check my email before I made the trip. My brief life in Cobleskill was turned upside down within moments. Jenny had sent an urgent message asking me to call her right away. I used the last of the airtime I had available on my Canadian data plan and called her, only to learn that Chubby was missing. He had gotten loose when Jody took him out for a quick pee before heading into the house the night before. Chub was determined to follow me and strained on his harness so hard, it broke. He took off into the night, and into the acres of woods and fields that surrounded her property. I was miles away by then. I was grief stricken after talking with Jenny and immediately called my brother Jake.

"What's wrong?" Jake asked me when I called. I could hardly speak, I was so upset.

"It's Chubby!" I told him haltingly. "He got away from Jody and is missing," I sobbed, recounting the events for him.

"I didn't even have his tags on," I told him. "What am I going to tell the kids?"

"Calm down. Where are you now?"

"I'm in Cobleskill. I left Jody's late last night. She couldn't reach me because I turned off my cellphone so I wouldn't get roaming charges. My friend Jenny sent me an email because Jody called her to see if she had a way to get in touch with me. It happened just after I left. They've all been looking for him, and there's no sign of him anywhere. Poor Jody is beside herself."

"The kids can stay with us longer if you need them to. Just let us know what your plans are. I won't say anything just yet," Jake said and hung up.

TWO OTHER FARMS bordered Jody's property, and hundreds of acres of corn surrounded her house. To the rear were miles of dense woods filled with predators that would love a tiny dog as a snack. I was sick with worry. Now my kids not only had to contend with leaving their friends and school behind, but they would also have to cope with a lost dog. It seemed like a terrible omen.

"Please don't blame yourself!" I told Jody. "I'm the one that forgot to put on his collar after I bathed him!" I told her through tears. "I'll call you in a bit when we figure out what the game plan is, and you'll be the first to know, okay?"

The Labor Day weekend was approaching. The original plan for the holiday was to have the Beans spend the weekend with Phillip while I traveled to Alexandria one more time to fetch more of our belongings. But I'd revised my plans several times, and with Chubby missing, I wanted to return to Alexandria to find him as soon as I could. I called Phillip at work to tell him the news. He was kind and concerned, as he should have been.

All the travel, packing, and unpacking left me exhausted. I needed some time to get more sleep, but I couldn't stop thinking about our sweet dog. My imagination was working overtime.

∾

CHUBBY WAS THE BEANS' tenth birthday present from Phillip and me. We'd looked at Labrador and Retriever puppies, since that's what Lucy had always wanted. But the cost was out of reach, and it felt wrong to buy a full-bred puppy when so many other dogs needed rescuing. I was also concerned about having a gigantic dog in our tiny apartment above the tearoom.

One day I was talking with Glen, the man who owned the antique shop next door to the café. His wife, Loretta, bred small dogs as a side business. They had ten dogs of various tiny mixed breeds. Whenever I took the twins to play with their two boys, one dog stood out over the rest. His name was Chubby Checkers and he was a Bichon-Lhasa mix. He weighed about ten pounds and was the sweetest of their entire lot. When Glen was in for tea one afternoon, he mentioned that Loretta planned to sell him because he was "too big" to breed with her other dogs. I called and asked her to stop by the next time she was at Glen's, and she came by later that afternoon.

"So, how much do you want for Chubby?" I asked while serving her a cup of tea and a slice of lemon pound cake. Loretta was smart and sassy and Glen's perfect foil. I related to her because she held everything together so Glen could open his antique business while she traveled into work each day.

"I'm looking for two hundred," she told me. I gulped. I wasn't sure if this was a fair price but didn't have that kind of money available regardless.

She got up from the table and looked around at the various items I had for sale on the shelves. Along with an assortment of coffee- and tea-related items, I also had some handcrafted items, paintings, and jewelry, all crafted by local artists. I had made most of the jewelry when I lived in the States. There were beaded bracelets, necklaces, and earrings on display.

"How about we barter?" Loretta asked.

"Sure!" I agreed. "What are you interested in?" I'd priced the earrings at ten dollars a pair. She selected twenty pairs and turned to me and said, "Sold!" That's how I paid for Chubby.

Jack and Lucy loved him. So did Phillip and I. Loretta was brilliant at training her dogs, and he was so well-behaved. He immediately became an integral part of our family and went everywhere with us. I especially loved bringing him to Jenny's, where he could be off his leash and run with Lacy. The two would bound down the mowed part of her back lawn at incredible speeds, with Lacy outpacing Chubby and his short legs. A quick shout or whistle, and they would reappear, begging for a treat or to get a drink of water.

MY HEART WAS SO heavy just thinking about what might happen to our puppy-boy. I knew I would have to do everything I could to find him, and that meant alerting everyone I knew in Canada to enlist their help in our search for him. I emailed all my friends and customers on the café email list and asked if they could look out for our Chubby. I was so happy my friends and former customers responded, reporting their efforts to assist us.

That day, Phillip offered to meet Jake halfway between his home in Vermont and our new apartment in Cobleskill so we could get the twins before heading back to Canada the next day.

The twins and I went up on Thursday with the van, and Phillip came up on Friday after work. We had agreed that the kids and I would pack more of our belongings in our Dodge Caravan, and Phillip would take the van back to Cobleskill and unpack it when he arrived at our apartment. He would leave me with the Elantra so Lucy, Jack, and I could spend time looking for our lost pup over the weekend. In the meantime, we made up flyers to post when we got there. Chubby had now been missing for a day. I didn't want to think about what he was doing to survive.

When we were about ten miles from Alexandria, I pulled over when I saw a woman who was walking her dog so I could give her a flyer.

"Excuse me. We're looking for our dog, who's missing. Could I give you a flyer?" I asked her.

"Are you searching for Chubby?" she asked.

"Yes!" I replied eagerly.

"My friend Natalie called me, and I'll keep an eye out for him," she said with a smile.

The same thing occurred when I stopped to speak to another two people we saw. They all were searching for him already. My friends, colleagues, and the whole community seemed to be there to help find our pup. I was so moved by each interaction I had with these strangers who were willing to help us.

One of Jack's close friends came over to keep the kids company while I searched for Chubby. When I got back to the building later that day, I saw a tiny gray kitten in the parking lot. It had startling green eyes and couldn't have been over six weeks old. I'd seen many cats dodging cars along the main street of Alexandria. I was determined the same fate wouldn't happen to this little thing.

I brought the kitten to the kids, who were playing upstairs in the office. The kitten was an instant hit. She was feisty and kept them amused for the remainder of day. When we left, I thought I could bring the kitten over to Carole, since she fed several strays. It was better than it being up against the traffic on Main Street.

WHEN PHILLIP ARRIVED, he helped us search for a few hours but felt it was a lost cause so we went back and continued packing.

"What are you going to do with that cat?" he asked as I was carrying a heavy box to the van.

"I don't know; I haven't thought about it," I replied in my distraction.

"That's so typical. You never think ahead about anything," he scolded me.

I shoved the box inside the van and stormed off, trying to avoid yet another fight. We barely spoke for the rest of the day. It was as though I'd run over to an animal shelter and grabbed a kitten to annoy him. He was livid. I was beyond caring.

Call after call came in from people asking if I'd found Chubby. Each time the phone rang, I jumped. But it also made me realize why I was so adamant about not leaving Alexandria behind. I felt like I belonged there.

The disaster underscored what I was losing in the community of people who embraced me enough to look for our dog. The emails I got, the calls I received, and the help from strangers touched me deeply. It was what I had longed for, this sense of belonging. And now I was leaving it all behind.

When Phillip left to return to Cobleskill, I could breathe again. Lucy, Jack, and I were again free to roam the back roads searching for our dog. We hunted for hours, but no one had seen him. Jody and her neighbor helped us explore the property around her house. But Chubby was still missing.

When the weekend ended, we had to return to Cobleskill so the Beans could start seventh grade. We were all crushed that our little guy with curly white fur wasn't with us. But I made sure one little gray kitten was coming along.

Chapter Nine

SWITCHING GEARS

I pulled into the parking lot at Sacred Heart Academy early on Tuesday with the Beans sulking in the back. The small Catholic school looked more like a modern church than a place for education. They shuffled across the driveway and up the stairs to the school's office. Jack held the door for Lucy and me. I knew he wasn't being polite. He didn't want to be the first to go in. I put on a fake smile as I approached the principal's office. I was anything but happy. I delivered the twins, like the sacrificial lambs they were, to Tammy MacKay, a small woman with an engaging smile. She exuded warmth, but the kids weren't having it. They stood like statues in the school office, waiting to be told where to go next.

The office secretary took Lucy and Jack to their class while I spoke with Tammy. She was very understanding of the fragility of the kids' emotions, especially having just lost their dog, who was now missing for almost a week. She expressed how happy she was they were attending the small, family-oriented school.

The place had a different feel to it than other Catholic schools I'd visited. Sacred Heart had more of an unpretentious feel than the previous school my children attended. While there were religious symbols throughout the building, it didn't reek of the antiquated hallways with children lined up with stifled smiles and curiosity. The modern building had a chapel at the center, classrooms and other offices on the first floor. There were additional classrooms, the kitchen, and the cafeteria on the ground floor. It also seemed less formal because the students didn't have identical uniforms.

I spoke to Tammy about doing some volunteer work at the school since I wasn't employed yet, and she informed me they needed help to serve lunches each day. I knew this opportunity could help me get to know other people and develop a support network immediately, which was the key to finding employment. When I told her my background, Tammy also asked if I would be interested in teaching a film class in exchange for tuition. I jumped at the chance. I had to start somewhere, and it would allow me to further connect with members of the school community.

My next mission was to get a phone. It pissed me off that no one could contact me in the States when Chubby first got lost. Phillip was refusing to install a landline at the apartment. He was trying to isolate me again from my friends and family, and I vowed I wasn't going to let it happen anymore.

I dug through every crevice I could in the apartment and van until I had about fifty dollars in quarters, nickels, and dimes. I left the pennies at home and hid them for an emergency. With that, I walked into a local credit union.

"I'd like to open an account," I told the clerk.

"Someone can help you with that in a minute. Have a seat." I felt like I'd asked them to be my co-conspirators in a crime because I had already anticipated a negative reaction from Phillip. I held the bag of change close, embarrassed that my life had come to this.

"May I help you?" a woman in a bright red pantsuit asked, approaching me.

"I hope so. I've recently moved here and don't have a lot of available cash. I want to open a bank account with the change I have here and a check I have from my business account in Canada. Is that possible?"

"Yes. Are you a U.S. citizen?"

"Yes."

"The check might take some time to clear, but the change can be deposited and withdrawn immediately," she assured me.

Once the check cleared, I would have about one hundred dollars in the account, give or take a bit because of the exchange rate. But, more importantly, I would have enough money from all the change I'd collected to buy a computer device called a "magicJack®," that allows a user to receive or make calls on a computer with an internet connection. I walked over to the Radio Shack in the same plaza.

"Hi, there. Do you have something called a magicJack?"

"Sure do."

"And I can use it to make phone calls through my computer?"

"You sure can."

"How much?"

When my older brother Will mentioned he used this device to make long-distance calls, I wrote the name down, thinking that, at some point, it could come in handy. Though part of the appeal was that calls to Canada wouldn't cost me a dime, the most important issue was that Phillip couldn't thwart my efforts to stay in touch with my friends up north. Now, however, I was most concerned about getting calls about Chubby.

When I got back home, I set up the device and emailed Jenny with the new number. I opted to unpack and do a little housework before heading to the school to help serve lunches. I was about to leave for school when I checked my computer one more time. I received an email from Jenny to call. My hands were shaking as I tried dialing her phone number.

"Your boy is back!" she told me.

"What? Where was he?" I asked Jenny when she told me her news.

"He just strolled up to the porch of Jody's neighbor's house. He's messy and thinner but, otherwise, he seems ok!" I was overwhelmed with joy.

As soon as I arrived back at the school, I went to the office and asked Tammy if she would let the Beans know that Chubby had been found. She was more than willing to oblige. Then she asked me if I would cater a dinner for a fundraiser the following week. I agreed without a moment's hesitation.

When I brought the kids home that day, the fact that our Chubby had been found erased the horrible day of navigating a new school.

"I think we should celebrate!" I told them. I pulled out a bottle of ginger ale from the fridge and put it in two water glasses. I poured some club soda for myself, and we raised our glasses.

"Here's to Chubby!" They laughed, as we clinked our glasses, through happy tears.

I emailed Phillip. That was how we communicated these days.

"Chubby has been found. He is at Jody's, and I am going to get him Friday as soon as the kids get out of school. He seems to be fine but needs grooming. Tonight, there is a meeting at Sacred Heart and I would like to attend as some of the meeting concerns the fundraiser that I have agreed to cater next week. If you get this email, please let me know what time you are planning to get home. If I know the kids are going to only be alone for a short time, I will leave them here. The meeting should be less than an hour."

I relished the thought of him reading his email. I'd only been in town for a few days and already I was making connections. While he was happy they had found Chubby, my catering job didn't seem to register and it surprised me he didn't react to my news.

After the meeting at school, I called Jenny through the

computer to let her know I'd be heading to Canada Friday afternoon. I heard Phillip come in, so I ended my conversation.

"Who were you talking to?" he asked.

"Jenny. I told her the kids and I would be going to fetch Chubby tomorrow. She offered to let us stay with her."

"I thought you couldn't call Canada on your cell?"

"I can, but it eats up my minutes in roaming charges. I ran out of airtime calling Jody, anyway. Besides, I wasn't using my cell. I bought a device for my computer. It's called a magicJack. It works over the Internet."

He went ballistic. Phillip's face turned red, and he stormed out of the room. I thought he was going off to sulk but, moments later, he came back and screamed at me.

"Where did you get the money for that?"

"I used some change."

"What change?"

"It was just loose change I found."

"My change? You're a thief, Kasey!"

"What are you talking about? That's not stealing. I used the loose change I had and more that I found around the apartment. Most of it was mine, and I had every right to use it."

That wasn't exactly true. I used the change I found in the van, in the closet, in the mudroom, and other places. But his response indicated that he believed it all belonged to him.

"You're such a liar, Kasey. Just wait."

He stormed off and shut himself in Jack's room. The twins were sitting on the couch and looked at me when I passed them and pounded on the bedroom door. I was about to scream at him but when I saw the look on their faces, I stopped. My need to express my anger wasn't worth putting them through this.

I started dinner in a rage. There was very little food in the fridge so I made pancakes for dinner. The only spice on hand was some cinnamon. I added some to the batter. I watched intently as the pancakes cooked. I flipped them when the bubbles formed onto the uncooked side. When they were nice and golden brown, I removed them from the pan and placed them on a cookie sheet in the oven to stay warm. I made an enormous platter so everyone could have some for breakfast, too.

"Dinner is ready," I hollered. Jack and Lucy came into the kitchen and sat down to eat. I was no longer hungry but was reluctant to leave them alone so I took a seat at the table.

Phillip came into the kitchen as if nothing had happened. He grabbed a plate, helped himself to the pancakes, spreading butter and pancake syrup on each. He asked Jack and Lucy about their day. They mumbled something about hating the math teacher, and I left the room so I wouldn't hit him on the head with the frying pan.

THE ANTIQUE VICTORIAN bed Phillip and I once shared was in the bedroom on the second floor, and I began sleeping there instead of on the uncomfortable couch. Phillip continued to sleep in the room designated as "Jack's room." To me, this indicated he wasn't interested in rekindling any aspects of our relationship. I was mostly relieved. But it also made me wonder why. It convinced me even more that he was aiming for a divorce, and also reinforced the notion he was having an affair.

When we set up the apartment, we put a twin bed for Lucy in the small alcove between the kitchen and back hallway. However, both of the kids came upstairs each night and ended up sleeping in "my" room. So I placed a twin mattress on the floor for Jack, and Lucy slept with me.

Phillip complained about this, too, but didn't seem willing to change the arrangements. I should have asked him why he thought Jack would be comfortable kicking his father out of his room at bedtime? I discovered he'd even mentioned the situation to Rachel.

"Per usual," he wrote her, *"Kasey is doing whatever the hell she wants to. She even has the kids sleeping upstairs with her."*

He never mentioned that he camped out in Jack's room each

night with the door closed. But that was how he presented it to her, and this arrangement suited me just fine.

THERE WAS no homework that night so, after dinner, Lucy, Jack, and I went upstairs and we began reading a book called *The Absolutely True Diary of a Part-Time Indian* by Sherman Alexie. It was absolutely what we needed to distract us from the emotional upheaval we all experienced that day. The sorrowful nature of Alexi's protagonist, Junior, and all his troubles made us forget our worries. We laughed and were entertained by this young man who was determined to attend *the white school* some thirty miles from the reservation where he lived. All Junior wanted was the same opportunities for a good education others take for granted. He walked or hitchhiked to school each day from his home on the Spokane Indian Reservation. Despite all the trauma he experienced, the story had us in fits of laughter. It took our minds off of the world around us.

As I read to them, I heard a creaking noise on the stairs. Phillip came up to join us. He made Lucy move over and sat on the bed between the Beans. I continued to read, but held onto my anger. I wasn't about to let him off the hook for his ridiculous outburst about buying the magicJack.

When it was close to the kids' bedtime, he told them to get dressed for bed. He said he needed to "talk with Mommy."

I held my breath. "Have you started applying for a real job?" he asked me.

"Are you talking about doing some catering for the school? That is a real job," I retorted.

"No. I mean the film class you offered to teach," he responded.

"Teaching that class will help us financially because we don't have to pay tuition. If it doesn't work out, I'll let it go after a semester."

"Why can't you apply at Walmart? I'm sure they're hiring," he asked.

That was Phillip's solution to everything. I'd make more money in one evening as a caterer than I would in a week at Walmart. It seemed like he wanted me to find work that paid minimum wage so I could contribute to the household income without giving me the ability to do anything more.

"I'm doing this, Phillip. You might not understand about networking, but I do. Most of the women I'm working with have lived in this area all their lives. They'll know who is hiring and about any possible catering jobs, or any other jobs, that pay better than minimum wage. If I end up quitting Sacred Heart, so be it. But, for now, I'm going to teach this class." He left, saying nothing more while I continued to stew.

Before leaving for Canada the next day to pick up Chubby, I checked my email.

He wrote,

"What is the phone number you got with the magicJack?"

Suddenly, he saw the value of the device and decided he wanted to use it, too.

Chapter Ten

CHUBBY RETURNS

When we returned to Cobleskill with Chubby, the Beans were happier, but not by much. They didn't like the school at all and they were having a hard time adjusting. I tried talking with their teachers to see how they were in class, and everyone said the same thing: They sat quietly and didn't take part unless the teacher called upon them.

Their unhappiness added to the dismal atmosphere at home, and the next few weeks were fraught with more tension. Phillip insisted I was using the Sacred Heart catering job as an excuse to avoid *working*. Catering was not *work* to him. Nothing I did was *work*. Teaching wasn't *work*. Running the café wasn't *work*. I had to wonder if any job I'd held in our twenty-four years of marriage amounted to *work* to him.

Another big issue we fought over was getting phone service. I was having more issues with my laptop because the port to plug in the AC adapter was getting worse. The pin was loose and rarely allowed me to charge the computer. I could only make calls or use the computer when it was charged, which became less and less frequent.

When I asked Phillip about installing a landline, he balked. He said we couldn't afford it. I wondered where all the money was going but had no way of knowing. He must have kept the checkbook and any records with him because I couldn't find them, regardless of where I looked.

It kept me imagining the worst. I reasoned that if our new monthly rent was half of what he was paying for his studio, where was that extra money? Did he keep the place in Albany so he could use it to have an affair? Was he working late all those nights he came home after eight? I searched for clues but couldn't find a scintilla of concrete evidence. Still, it made no sense to me that there was no money left in the budget for a telephone when the most basic service was less than $15 a month without long-distance service.

"It's too expensive," Phillip told me one night when I asked again about getting a phone. Then he asked, "Why can't you use that gadget you bought with my money?" There were times he left me biting my tongue so hard, I thought it would bleed.

"I've tried that, but it only works when my computer is charged. I've explained to you I'm having issues with it charging. And please don't suggest I use my Canadian cellphone because I've run out of airtime. If you want me to find work, what phone number do I put on the application, Phillip? I have to beg you for money to pay for gas, and the instrument panel on the van is still faulty, so I never know how much gas there is in the fuel tank. But, somehow, I'm supposed to get a job without a working computer, phone-line, or vehicle."

"We're not getting a phone, Kasey, so forget it," he said and left the room.

ALL FURTHER ATTEMPTS to reason with him failed. The impact of not being able to receive calls to find work or use a computer weren't actually obstacles to him. He insisted it was my resistance to finding work that was the problem. Anything I countered with was an excuse.

One day, Jack was home from school sick. Leaving him home

without a way to reach me left me conflicted about going out. I carefully worded an email;

"Phillip-

I would like to order phone service here today. I believe this is a basic need, and it is not good to be without a landline. I cannot rely on the magicJack because of the computer problems I constantly face, and I now have to either choose between leaving Jack by himself without emergency communication, as he is not in school, or go off and do the things I had hoped to accomplish regarding work, etc.

Please respond to this as the installation will take time and I want to start the process. ~ Kasey"

He responded tersely;

"I am swamped with work, so I do not have time to fully address the "logic" or what is insinuated in this email - "I now have to either choose between leaving Jack by himself without emergency communication."

If you are truly concerned about our children's safety, concentrate on getting a job that helps to pay for these "basic needs" and not spending time on opening another food business. Short answer...Do not order anything in my name that I will bear the responsibility for paying unless I am fully agreed to it. You purchased the magicJack with money "you found" without any input from me. Once again, I was told after the fact. Send me the information for a landline with a phone number that I can call so I can verify costs, etc. We are not generating enough money to cover our basic monthly expenses. It's no fun being poor, but that's the reality of our situation.

BTW...Have you put together your list of discussion items for our mediators yet?

As I have mentioned before, regarding your computer, call Computer Solutions using the magicJack. Tell them (using these words) "the power input on my laptop is loose and needs to be re-soldered. It only works when I hold the plug in a certain position. Could you give me an approximate estimate as to what this costs to fix?"

After reading his email, my contempt for him had reached a new level.

NOT LONG AFTER he moved back to the States, Phillip suggested to me we might need help to resolve our marital issues. He didn't mean professional help, however. He planned to present our grievances to a friend or family member so they could judge who was *at fault* for the deteriorating situation. He determined I couldn't request one of my Canadian or Blairstown friends as a mediator while he was free to use whomever he chose.

Resisting this request while I was in Canada was easy because the distance made his suggestion unworkable. But now that we were both in the States, he returned to this idea as a way to solve the problems within our marriage.

Knowing the kinds of things he was saying to his sister about what I supposedly did or didn't do left me in a precarious situation. I could use this knowledge to my advantage and prove he was lying. However, being too prepared might tip my hand and raise questions about my knowledge of positions he didn't raise in his "list of grievances." For Phillip, all our problems stemmed from my not having a job, the number of pets we now had, and the fact Jack and Lucy were sleeping upstairs in my room. I'd been in Cobleskill for a little more than a week, but he told Rachel that this was what was to blame for all the mayhem in our relationship.

There was another thing that bothered me about agreeing to a meeting with any third party. I knew I'd be terrible under pressure. Phillip knew this, too. I was not capable of presenting my side of the issues calmly and coherently. No matter how well I prepared, I knew I would get defensive and blow it. I didn't know if I could hold it all together when confronted with all the pent-up anger and frustration I was carrying around.

"Jen, you know me!" I complained when she called later that

day. "I'll break down in tears, yell, or act like a complete idiot if we discuss this with someone. He will sit there calmly and present his side of the situation with relish. Don't you think that's why he's pushed this for months?" I asked her.

"Well, I don't think it's about healing the relationship. Sounds to me like he's trying to prove his points. Don't tip your hand and let him know you're aware he's been lying. You need to keep that information to yourself just in case you do end up in court," she warned me.

When I got off the phone with Jenny, I responded to Phillip's email, carefully wording my reply.

"Phillip-

You can read anything you want into my email. It would not matter how I put it; it is never correctly worded for you. I am concerned about getting work and feel conflicted about leaving Jack at home. But, for some reason, this statement makes you think I am making a statement about you. Well, I'm not. It's a fact. It is also very frustrating trying to find work, making phone calls when people can't hear you. YOU TRY IT.

I am concentrating on getting a job plus making the type of income that could provide enough for all of us if you are out of work again, as you have told me you might be. I will not be put in a situation where I have no prospects for a meaningful employment. While I am willing to take just about anything, I will not be put in a situation that, because I make less than you do, you feel you can dictate everything to me. Once again, I am put on the defensive about everything. I am trying to find work with record unemployment, here less than two weeks and back and forth on the weekends to Canada, have no working phone, a computer that constantly craps out, but I am not trying hard enough to find a job. Once again, Phillip, it is stuff like this that makes me wonder why I bother. You get mad at me because you think I have insinuated something in an email but I am not supposed to respond to blatant put-downs?

IF YOU ARE TRULY CONCERNED ABOUT THE CHILDREN...." HOW DARE YOU!

I used change to purchase the magicJack, that I brought to the bank. This is exactly the type of situation that I cannot tolerate. I didn't have a phone for emergencies, no cell phone that works locally, and we had a lost dog in Canada that people were trying to communicate with me about. But you can't begin to comprehend the impact this has, not having a phone, because, well, it wasn't you. The difference between you and me, Phillip, is, I want you to take care of yourself and do what you think needs to be done. You are more concerned about a jar of change and the way I spent it rather than my having a basic necessity.

BTW- No. I have not put a list together for our "mediators." I would like to address issues that are important to me without being accused of insinuating things, just like you have here. I want to address the issues that matter TO ME. How do you expect me to detail things that are matters of the heart, that outline the conflicts I have with our relationship, when I can't be assured an email about getting a phone installed isn't going to be blown-up? So, no, Phillip. I haven't.

I went to a computer place on Monday. They don't do this repair. They said it doesn't last and people get angry, so they stopped doing it. Ask the kids. They were with me. They referred me to a place in New Hartford and said I was looking at about $300. If you doubt this, call, yourself, and verify."

I provided him with the phone number and address to the computer store and pushed the send button. I realized that, from that point on, I had to make plans to leave him much sooner than I initially thought. I also called Verizon and ordered a telephone.

Chapter Eleven

THE IMPORTANCE OF NETWORKING

My instincts about finding a network of women through Sacred Heart turned out to be a godsend. Within weeks, I was finding out more about the area and what options were available regarding possible work opportunities. I even made a friend named Maryanne Cahill. She, too, helped with the school lunches each day. Despite the fact she was having personal difficulties of her own, she took the time to reach out to me and helped me in ways that made my upheaval bearable.

Maryanne was raising her granddaughter Meg, who was in ninth grade at Sacred Heart. She was a no-nonsense kind of gal, and why she took to me, I'll never know. She'd owned a bed-and-breakfast in Idaho for years and, somehow, she ended up living in St. Johnsville, New York, a good forty-five-minute drive to Sacred Heart.

One day, after lunch was over and everything was clean and put away, we went out to get coffee. We both loved to cook and food was the most immediate connection between us. But soon she was spilling her guts about life's difficulties, and I was spilling mine.

Maryanne was planning on moving down to the Cornell area

of New York so she could live with her daughter Mary Jane and granddaughter instead of trying to raise Meg on her own. She was of retirement age and all the traveling to and from St. Johnsville was wreaking havoc on her aging body.

The expenses of maintaining two separate households impacted her ability to make ends meet. That was something I understood completely. Maryanne had placed her home on the market and, as soon as it sold, she and Meg would be moving to Cornell.

My new friendship with her reminded me of something I hadn't thought of in quite a while. It had to do with the first real friend I had in Alexandria, a woman named Diane. She, too, had come to my rescue, when Phillip took the job with Marco three years earlier.

DIANE ARRIVED at my doorstep one day, completely unannounced. It was the day before the Beans were to start fourth grade. I noticed Lucy had small inflamed, red welts on her back, and she said she wasn't feeling well. I soon discovered the same red bumps on Jack, and they both had low-grade fevers.

"Honey, call me when you get this message! I think the kids have chickenpox!" I was frantic.

I didn't have a pediatrician or a family doctor to consult. I had nothing to ease their fevers or a way to relieve the itching. I didn't want to leave them alone, and they were too miserable to come with me if I went to the store. Phillip was now living five hours away. When he finally returned my call, he doubted my assessment of the situation and seemed annoyed with me.

"I'm sure that's not the case. When would they have been exposed to someone with chickenpox?" he questioned.

"Well, how do you explain the fever and the itchy, puss-filled blistering rash all over their bodies?" I asked him impatiently. "Besides, there's an incubation period of several weeks."

I got off the phone, furious with him. I realized he had just started a new job, and it was late at night. He was tired and usually wasn't the one to deal with their colds, bumps, and bruises. But I was alone and frightened. I didn't know what to do to soothe them, and I felt like a horrible mother. I hung up the phone that night in utter misery. I went down to the kitchen and hunted for some oatmeal, thinking maybe an oatmeal bath would help.

Early the next morning, I heard a knock on the door downstairs. I opened the door to see a tall, beautiful woman standing in front of me.

"Can I help you?" I asked her.

"Are you Kasey?" the woman asked in a southern drawl.

"Yeah...," I responded incredulously.

This woman was Diana Manson. She explained that she was talking to someone in Alexandria, and they mentioned "an American couple" was opening a restaurant. I might have cried, I was so relieved to see her. Within minutes of explaining that the Beans had the chickenpox, she was off to the pharmacy, getting Tylenol and whatever sundries that were needed.

Diana was from Georgia. Before they moved to Montreal, her husband's hometown, Diana and hubby, George, were doing quite well financially. Diana was a professional decorator and George was a contractor. The two took advantage of the booming real estate market in the suburbs outside of Atlanta, buying properties to flip, and turning a profit or holding onto them for the rental income. When the real estate market started going downhill, they were left with properties they couldn't sell or rent. It ultimately destroyed their finances. They moved to Quebec for much the same reasons Phillip and I moved: they needed to start over.

This made it complicated for their son, who was, then, in his senior year of high school. For him to graduate from a high school in Quebec, he needed to be proficient in French. Since this would be wildly challenging for someone without even the basic knowledge of the language, they rented a house in Ontario so he could enroll in the local high school for his senior year.

They didn't spend much time at the rental property but used the address for the paperwork for enrollment purposes. Most days, she drove her son and daughter round trip to their actual home in Montreal, over an hour away. With nothing to do while they were in school each day, she was excited to hear there was "another American" in town and wanted to meet me.

From that day on, she came to the café to help with the remaining renovations and decorating. We worked with another local woman named Crystal to finalize the menu and come up with ideas for foods that would appeal to the local clientele. With Phillip gone, I hired a friend of Crystal's to assist completing with the kitchen renovation while Diana and I put the finishing touches on the tearoom.

Initially, I hired Crystal to be in the kitchen, and Diana agreed to wait on tables. I floated between the kitchen and tearoom, covered the takeout, and did whatever was needed. The arrangement worked for a while, mainly because Crystal was an excellent cook and a fabulous baker. But she kept forgetting it was my business.

"I think you're going to have a hard time selling a bowl of soup for five dollars," Crystal told me.

"That's because you've never tasted my soup," I assured her.

When we finally opened in early December, I greeted our new customers while Diana waited on tables, laying on the good old-fashioned Southern charm. I knew that wonderful food is only one challenge of a successful restaurant. Crystal and I had that covered, while Diana's stunning looks and charisma provided the other part. Soon there was a waitlist for lunch each day.

A few months after we opened, I heard through Glen, from the antique shop next door, that rumors were going around town about the owners of the new café. Apparently, because Phillip was never around, people assumed Diana was one of the owners and, because I referred to her as my "partner," people thought Diana and I were a couple. Adding to the confusion was another coincidence. One of my customers told me that, in Gaelic, the word "beans" roughly translated into "wives." I didn't know whether it was true, but maybe the "two beans" made people predisposed to thinking there was another meaning behind the name of the café.

When Phillip came north, he enjoyed teasing Diana about being his other wife. He even seemed to enjoy the way it made me uncomfortable. Diana was a gorgeous woman, and I was no longer the slim, attractive woman he married. I thought my discomfort hinged on a tad of jealousy. But I realized now, what made me so uncomfortable about how flirtatious Phillip was with Diane was that, years earlier, he begged me to take part in a threesome.

Like many couples, our sex life became predictable after our kids were born. When we managed to have time alone, Phillip frequently asked me to talk dirty to him and I discovered it was a fun way to spice up our intimacy. It seemed harmless and Phillip got extremely excited when I did, especially when I created scenarios that involved multiple partners.

This worked for a while but then Phillip suggested we take our intimate moments to another level and he began talking about taking his fantasy of having a threesome into a reality.

"What do you say, we put an ad in the paper? Scranton's far enough away and we don't know anyone there. We could fix up one of our empty apartments there," he asked me casually one night, in bed.

"You can fantasize all you want, Phillip, but that will never happen, so drop it."

He rolled over after accusing me of leading him on. Moments later, he turned back, expressing his full anger.

"You've talked about your fantasies for years, Kasey."

"That's the whole point, Phillip. They're fantasies. Nothing more." But watching the way he looked at Diana, I had to wonder if he pursued his desires for engaging in sex with multiple partners without me when he was alone in Scranton.

Diana left after her son graduated, as she no longer needed to come to Alexandria. Then Crystal and I had a falling out over a blueberry pie. By the time Sharilyn and Kate came on board, the influx of personnel stopped, and I had the ideal situation of working with two women that I loved and admired. So, even though Diana was sorely missed, and until recently, I never thought much about that uncomfortable feeling I had had back then.

TALKING WITH MARYANNE, however, brought up those memories. It reinforced my belief that Phillip was cheating on me and may have been for a long time. Maryanne suggested if that was indeed the case, I had to do more to uncover the truth.

I thought about what Maryanne said, and two things became apparent. The first thing was, I had frequently ignored signs that Phillip was most likely having an affair. His reaction to Diana was uncomfortable but I never doubted he would remain faithful back then. But for much of our marriage, he had the perfect set-up to "swing" all he wanted since I was miles away. Secondly, if he was planning to divorce me, I had to continue to look for evidence of his affair, or affairs. If he wanted to gain custody of the Beans, I figured this could be my only way to stop him.

Chapter Twelve

MOVING ALONG

As September moved into October, Maryanne offered to help me leave Phillip by slowly removing things from our apartment that I couldn't just take outright without him noticing. She had an enormous house with many spare bedrooms in which to store my belongings. I was afraid Phillip would catch on if I used too much gas, so she suggested I bring things to her at school, and she and I could transport them to her home while he was at work.

It was almost my old habit of introducing new items to our household in reverse. Gradually, I took clothing, books, photographs, and other items I might need to start a new life, one without my husband. Because we once had two households, many of the items we owned were duplicates. I took nothing of Phillip's, but I took things that were ours jointly. Mostly it amounted to older equipment that was still useable even though it was outdated.

I knew it would take time to get plans in place, but at least I felt like I had someone in the area that cared about my well-being. I was beyond grateful for her help. We worked together to do some catering, too. But we had to admit before long that life was pulling us in different directions. She was thinking of taking

Meg out of Sacred Heart altogether. The tuition cost, on top of the price of gas, was eating through her meager income.

We spoke almost daily once she pulled Meg from school. She would tell me about her trials over selling her house, and I would tell her what was happening with Phillip. Having Maryanne to bounce ideas off of was what kept me sane.

I told her about my growing concerns about Phillip's stress levels and the fact he frequently made comments that left me very unsettled. Of major concern, however, was one incident in particular that rattled her, too.

It started when I told him we had to address the issues we were having with the van. I'd already broken down several times and, without a cellphone, I was always putting myself at risk of being stuck somewhere, with or without the kids.

"We can't afford that right now."

"If you were driving it back and forth to work, it would get fixed, alright. Well, on Monday, I'm going to take it in and see how much it's going to cost. There's a guy from school that owns a repair shop and I'm calling him to get an appointment. Don't worry. I'll pay for the expense on my own."

"Kasey, first of all, I told you 'no.' Secondly, how will you pay for it on your own?" he asked me in a mocking tone.

"I'll borrow the money or put it on a credit card. Phillip, you may not be aware of this, but I have every right to do this. And guess what? I will. I know you think that just because you're the only one bringing in an income right now that gives you the right to dictate everything to me. But it doesn't. I can and will get the van fixed. And if you don't like it, go screw yourself."

I was so mad, I stormed upstairs, where the Beans were reading, and forgot to bring my laptop with me.

When I got up the next morning, my computer wasn't where I left it. I hightailed it into the living room where I found Phillip with my laptop apart and a soldering gun. He said he was trying to fix the input jack since he knew we couldn't have it fixed at the local computer repair place.

"What do you think you're doing?" I shouted at him.

"I'm trying to fix your computer."

"Did I ask you to do that?"

"I was trying to be nice."

"I don't believe that for one second. You've been trying to control my every move since the day I got here, and this is just another example of the despicable things you've done to me. Put it back the way you found it and don't touch it again."

"I don't care what you believe me, Kasey," he screamed at me, turning red in the face. "I was trying to help. You're just a bitch, like you always are, and, one day, you'll see what will happen to you."

"Oh, gee, Phillip. I'm terrified," I taunted him.

Again, I stormed off in a fury. The argument woke the kids up, and they asked if I was okay when I got back upstairs. I wasn't. I was trembling. The tone of his voice was thoroughly menacing. I'd never seen him so angry. His threat seemed serious, and even though I'd pretended I wasn't frightened, I felt like I had crossed a line.

My strong reaction to his working on my computer came because Phillip had no idea I was still doing the school lunch program in Alexandria. Kate and I had worked out a way she and Sharilyn could continue even though I was no longer in Canada. I'd planned on working on a new menu that very morning so I could send it to the five schools I'd previously serviced. I also had payroll to submit to the accountant. Kate agreed to collect payments and deposit them in my Canadian account. Not having a reliable computer added to the difficulty of conducting business long distance.

But I was so angry I had left it downstairs, assuming it would be okay until the morning. I couldn't assume anything at this point and should have recognized this. Even though I'd added a long password to access any files, seeing Phillip working on my computer sent me into panic mode. But hearing the tone of his voice and the ambiguous threat frightened me more.

Later, I took the kids to the library to do their homework since they didn't have a computer at home. I decided it was time to seek outside help, and while the kids were doing their assignments, I began looking through phone books to see what options might be available to me.

The rage Phillip leveled at me was new. In the past, we'd scream at one another, but I trusted that it would never cross the line physically. More and more, I wasn't so sure. For the remaining weekend, I stayed out of Phillip's way as much as possible.

When I called Maryanne and told her about the incident, she, too, was alarmed. "He's never struck you, has he?"

"No. He's threatened to in the past, but he's never raised a hand to me. But, Maryanne, there was something different about this argument. The look in his eye, the sheer hatred that emanated from his entire body, is something that I've never seen before. He keeps saying things like, 'One day, you'll be sorry.' Or sometimes he says, 'You're going to regret being such a bitch all the time.' I'm frightened that he will snap one day," I told her.

"I wish you could just come and live with me for a while," she said with a hitch in her voice.

"Me, too."

"Something is eating away at Phillip," I continued. "He is tense and stressed out all the time. He treats me like I am the enemy, and he won't talk to me about anything. All I know is, he hates his new job. He tells me that people are being let go without warning. I get that he's had some horrible experiences with his past employers. That alone is probably causing him a lot of anxiety. But his bursts of rage are terrifying. There are times I'm convinced he's going to do something horrible."

As I spoke these words, I wondered if I was getting worked up over nothing. I had a bad habit of burying my instincts. When I experienced his full wrath, I felt the fear. But when I described the situation to my friend and confidant, I began convincing myself that I was maybe exaggerating the situation. Surely Phillip would never come to hurt me.

I began to backpedal and softened my concern by telling her that, almost every night, Phillip stayed holed up in Jack's room, working on freelance projects. He'd agreed to do some copy-writing for Marco again, on the side. He said it was because we needed to bring in extra income.

"Do you need the money? Is he telling the truth?" Maryanne asked.

"I don't know. I have no idea how much he is making or how the money is being spent. Whenever we need food or something, I have to email him a list, and he goes shopping because he refuses to give me access to much cash or his debit card. Whenever I need gas, I have to ask him for money. And he expects a receipt and change if there is any. I hate the amount of control he's exerting over me financially," I explained.

After I got off the phone, my conversation with Maryanne had me stewing whenever it came to mind. I couldn't help but think of the fact that, not once, did I think of my hefty agency paychecks as my money versus his money. When I worked in advertising and made a six-figure income, he always had access to every dime I made. Now, my lack of independent resources left me feeling humiliated.

On more than one occasion, Maryanne suggested it was time to seriously consider leaving the marriage. When I told her, in another conversation, that I learned he was again misrepresenting facts to Rachel, she told me she believed I was right about his plans for a divorce.

In the latest version of blaming me for all our woes, he claimed that I had stolen "his" money and I was the cause of all our financial difficulties. What he was referring to was the money spent from the sale of our home in Blairstown after we moved to Canada. The business didn't open for months after he moved back to the States, and I used some of those funds for both business and living expenses until the café got going and I had an income. He seemed to have forgotten he spent far more of that money on renovating the properties in Scranton, which were still on the market. I couldn't comprehend how he expected us to live up there without spending money.

Meantime, even though I was back in the States, I was still

handling all the expenses in Canada on my own. Not once did Phillip ask how the bills were being paid. It was as if he'd completely forgotten about the place. The only time he addressed the matter was in terms of selling the Alexandria property. I was sure, however, when the property in Canada sold, he would expect half, or more, of the proceeds, even though it was my work that kept it afloat.

I explained to Maryanne that I was growing nervous about covering utility costs and being confronted with all the tenant issues in Canada on my own. As winter approached, it would be more expensive, since two of the three rental units were heated by electric and sometimes the monthly cost exceeded what the tenant paid in rent. With Sharilyn and Kate's help, I was still making an income in Canada with the school lunch program and I was hoping those receipts would be enough to cover both the business and building expenses.

I kept going back and forth over what to do. I couldn't reach out to friends or relatives over the phone, because I couldn't make long-distance calls. Emails were also problematic because I feared he might have my password and was reading them. If I changed them, it could alarm him, so I was cautious about communicating with others online. He'd already been caught twice in our marriage, reading my private letters or journals. Since divorce is an adversarial situation, it wasn't outside the realm of possibility he, too, was snooping around to find proof to support whatever claims he imagined he could make against me.

Chapter Thirteen

WHAT THE COUNSELOR SAW

As the weeks passed, I started having second thoughts about leaving my marriage. One moment, I spoke firmly about wanting and needing to leave, and the next, doubt crept in. It wasn't so much that I wanted to stay. I just didn't know how I could afford to leave with no money or place to live. In either case, I decided to seek the advice of a family counselor before finalizing plans because I wanted to make sure I was thinking straight. I locked myself in the bathroom at the library and used the last minutes I had on my renewed Canadian data plan to make an appointment.

I don't recall how I arrived at the name of the man I spoke to that day. It could have been a recommendation from Maryanne, but I remember he was somehow connected to a family services organization related to the Catholic Church. It was a service provided for those without means. I had no means. I was still waiting on payments from my school clients in Canada so I could deposit a check from that account into the one I'd opened at the credit union. I was so paranoid about Phillip finding out I even had those funds coming in, I was in a constant state of anxiety.

A week later, I climbed the steps of a large brick building and walked along a windowed corridor. I arrived at a small corner office and stared at the closed door. Just then, a man who I assumed was the counselor peeked his head out and let me know he was running late. As I sat waiting, I could hear a tearful conversation. The hushed voices caused me to review my circumstances as I sat in that empty lobby. I almost left several times, but the tightness of my chest kept me locked in place.

By the time I arrived at the counselor's door, I'd been living with increasing fear of Phillip's vague but ominous threats. He wanted to punish me, I could tell. Somehow, every breath I took defied him. There was a quiet rage about him, even when we weren't fighting. He seemed distracted and agitated all the time. He had been growing even more distant towards me for some time but, now, he was noticeably different with the twins, as well. In the past, he did his best to engage them as we sat around the dinner table. Now, he not only ignored me but was less patient with them, too.

While I waited for the counselor, I tried to figure out how I could condense the complicated history of my relationship with Phillip into the forty-five minutes allotted for the appointment. The door to the office opened and a woman hurried out, her head bent, avoiding my gaze. The counselor ushered me inside his office. He had the confidence of someone who spent hours untangling the lives of people who couldn't navigate the choppy waters of marriage and family. I sat down, feeling like I was about to be scolded, wondering if I was at fault for allowing my marriage to crumble.

"Have a seat," he said pointing to a chair. "What brings you here?"

I sat down as directed and crossed my arms over my body. I stalled for a minute because I didn't have the slightest idea where to begin.

"I'm having a hard time trying to figure out what to do about my marriage. I'm so unhappy and, frankly, I've become frightened over some things my husband has been saying. I don't know how serious I need to take his threats."

"How long have you been married?"

"Almost twenty-five years."

"Do you have children?"

"Yes, we have twelve-year-old twins."

"Boys? Girls?"

"One of each."

"Does your husband hit you?"

"Oh, no! He's not that kind of man."

"But you said you've become frightened of him. What makes you say that?"

"Well, he says things like, 'Just you wait to see what's going to happen to you.' He's said it more than once, and in several emails. I have this unsettled feeling because he seems like he's in a rage all the time."

"Why do you think he is saying these things?"

"He's mad at me. He blames me for all our problems. We've had several financial setbacks and he's stressed about money all the time. He wants me to find a job, but I've only been here for a short while. I have no money of my own. He only gives me enough money for gas, and I have to provide him with receipts to show him what I've spent. I don't have a reliable car—or computer, for that matter—to do a job search. I took a job teaching at Sacred Heart because they offered me free tuition for the Beans—that's what we call the twins. So I am helping, but he doesn't see it that way."

"What do you mean, you've only been here a few months? Where were you before, then?"

As I related the circumstances of our move to Canada and my return to the States, it sounded so convoluted. I told the counselor about the details of my last few months.

"When we incurred an overdraft fee on our bank account, he claimed I was financially irresponsible. I honestly don't even know if he made that up, because he was in the States and all the bank records came to him. But even if I did overdraft the account, he seems to have a very short and convenient memory of the main issues surrounding our finances."

"Give me an example."

"Well, I agreed to move to Canada if he was willing to sell some rental properties we owned. He wanted to finish renovating them prior to putting them on the market, and I was fine with that. But, while I was in Canada, he ran up our credit cards. He spent so much money repairing the rental properties, we had to file for bankruptcy. Even though I was hundreds of miles away and the expenses were almost exclusively related to costs related to the repairs on the those properties, somehow, he believes I'm financially irresponsible. I didn't blame him and tell him he was irresponsible when that went down. He wasn't buying luxury items, or anything. I knew he was working hard to make things work. He just invested too much into them before the market fell apart. But, now, every dime I spend is scrutinized. He's even told others I am at fault for all our financial problems. Now, he's told me that even getting a phone at the house or a working computer is an unnecessary expense. I have no idea if we can afford these things because he doesn't allow me access to the bank account."

"Has this financial dynamic between you always existed? Has he always taken such a tight rein on the finances?"

"No. When I was working full time, we both had equal access to our funds. Wait a minute. Here's the thing. Phillip doesn't count what he spends on business-related items as personal expenses. So, while he was operating his film business, whatever equipment he felt he needed, he bought and I had no say in the matter. The same thing for costs regarding the rental properties.

"It isn't just a money issue. We fight over everything. One day, when I was home alone, I moved some furniture around in the living room. He was furious with me when he came home. He said, since he was paying the bills, it was his right to determine the furniture arrangement. I put it back and didn't even argue about it because he's under so much pressure right now. I'm afraid something will make him snap."

"Why do you think he wants to prevent you from having money?"

"I'm not sure." I stopped to think.

"I think you know why."

"No. I don't understand it. I've never withheld money from him. He seems pleased to have stripped me of my autonomy."

"If you had the financial resources to leave, would you?"

"Yes."

"That's your answer. He's controlling you. All his actions show this is the source of his anger and resentment. Abuse is about power and control."

"I told you he's never laid a hand on me."

"He doesn't need to. Abuse isn't always about violence. When a person is trying to control someone, it often takes the form of emotional abuse or financial abuse. Even gaslighting a partner is a form of abusive behavior because those are ways someone takes control of another individual. Not all abusers strike their victims. But let me be clear. If he is exerting the extent of financial control you describe, that is abuse. He's trying to prevent you from communicating with others by limiting your access to a phone and transportation. Isolating someone is another way to gain control. You pointed out that's something he's done for years."

"I think he's just really stressed about making sure he's providing for his family, don't you think?"

"That might be an enormous part of it, but he's not providing for your emotional well-being. He isn't thinking about that aspect of his behavior. I'm sure much of this is also affecting your twins." The thought made me want to heave.

"Do you think, if I found a job, he would change?"

"No. I think your husband would find another way to control you."

"But if I found a job, he wouldn't be able to control me, right?"

He glanced up at the clock on the wall. The forty-five minutes had already evaporated.

"What do you think I need to do?" I heard my voice pleading for a resolution to the anguish I felt.

"You need to leave and protect your kids. This is not a safe situation. Would you like to make another appointment?" he asked.

I made an appointment for the following week but never went back.

On the way back to the apartment, everything should have come into focus. In forty-five minutes, the counselor figured out what was right in front of me, and yet, I refused to see it. The word *abuse* sounded ridiculous to me. It didn't apply to Phillip.

"His need for control wasn't abuse," I reasoned. It was just the way he dealt with this stress. Neither was his desire for power over me, his dismissive attitude, and constant humiliations over the simplest things. They weren't really abuse. I wasn't even sure what the counselor meant by "gaslighting." I had to look it up. I convinced myself that the counselor's assessment was based on one session and I was sure that, if we'd talked at length, he'd understand I wasn't abused. We just had significant marital issues because of difficult circumstances.

My awareness of an abusive marriage was stuck in the buried memories of our next-door neighbor Mrs. White, who lived in the other side of the duplex my father and mother rented while they attended Bible school. I still recalled the screams that could be heard through the shared walls when her husband beat her.

Instead, I convinced myself I could handle the situation. I reasoned that I was more familiar with Phillip than anyone else. I thought I just needed to be more careful not to provoke him. If I had admitted the truth, even to myself, it would have been devastating to my fragile self-esteem. I never kept that second appointment.

I had no choice but to wait it out until I could get a job that paid enough so I could support myself and the Beans. I even began convincing myself I was somehow at fault. I told myself that if I could just control my emotions, Phillip wouldn't have a reason to be angry with me.

"Don't you see," I told Maryanne one day. "Maybe I'm responsible for his terrible behavior."

"If that's what you need to tell yourself, go ahead. We do

what we have to do to get through it." When I hung up, I realized she was right and was thankful she had called me out on my nonsense.

In the days that followed, I grew even more anxious, not knowing what state of anger he would be in whenever he walked through the door. Sometimes, he was genuinely pleasant. But, more often than not, he was tense and irritable when he arrived back in Cobleskill. Sometimes, he seemed like he could snap any minute. After weeks of trying, I admitted to myself that being on my best behavior didn't help much.

Phillip's erratic behavior fed my unease. So much so, that one day, I called Phillip at work and asked him to buy a can of wasp spray on his way home. I was grateful he didn't ask why. He must have assumed I'd found some even though it was too late in the season for the pests to be around. I told him I'd take care of killing them the following day. Instead, I hid the can upstairs, next to the bed. I didn't want it to kill wasps. I wanted to use the can of spray as a means of protection in case Phillip came at the kids and me in a sudden rage.

Chapter Fourteen

TRYING TO STAY SAFE

For weeks, I had fluctuated between challenging Phillip's need for authority and keeping my mouth shut. Sometimes, my determination to avoid being treated like a doormat kept me from remaining silent. At other times, I realized I wasn't doing myself any favors by continually arguing with him. After I saw the counselor, however, I was too afraid to provoke Phillip, especially because our dysfunctional marriage was affecting the twins. I feared that he was going off the deep end. I struggled with the thought that by arguing with him, I was putting them in danger.

Since it was almost impossible not to piss him off, I minimized my interaction with Phillip more and more by taking the kids to the library to use the computers for their homework after dinner. I also used this time to look for work and keep the lunch program going in Canada.

By the time we got home, it was time for the kids to get ready for bed, so the lack of interaction between Phillip and me meant we argued less. But there was this undercurrent of hostility that kept me alarmed. I never knew what would set him off. Maryanne suggested I couldn't wait much longer to leave.

In early November, I got a call that the heat on the right side of the building in Alexandria was out. I arranged to travel north once again and planned to take Lucy and Jack with me as soon as they got out of school, as Phillip had no time or inclination to deal with the Beans for an entire weekend. They were delighted with the idea.

Before I picked them up, however, I wanted to make another attempt to find evidence of Phillip's possible affair while everyone was away from the apartment. I was still convinced he was hiding something—and that something was his infidelity. As I looked back on our history, I grew more and more suspicious, but still had no proof. Nevertheless, I couldn't imagine what else could be contributing to his hostility.

Maryanne reminded me that the only way I would ever know what Phillip was up to would be to locate irrefutable evidence. I no longer cared about his possible infidelity; I only wanted to substantiate my theories in order to provide leverage in a custody battle if he started divorce proceedings. So, whenever possible, I snooped.

Because I was taking a risk, I was careful. I took pictures on a digital camera we owned, so I could make sure everything looked exactly like it did before I began moving things that belonged to him. Then I deleted the photos and removed the SIM card, replacing it with one that was full but benign.

I hunted through the room where he slept to see if he might have jotted something down that would reveal a clue. There was nothing to suggest anything unusual. I came up empty-handed everywhere I searched.

I assumed that if he was communicating via email, then he must have a separate email account, or even a cellphone, to use to communicate with her. I also wondered if he could be hiding something else altogether.

The only thing I found was another email he sent to Rachel. In it, he was again saying something that suggested he was framing an argument to hurt my credibility.

"Kasey doesn't care, anyway," he wrote in this email, telling her I never even asked about the results from some tests he'd had regarding his persistent acid reflux. It floored me since I was the one who sent him the information, over the summer, about a medical practice in Albany that specialized in gastric issues. I even offered to make an appointment for him to see a doctor about his persistent problem. His response to me at that time was that he couldn't take time off of work right then, and he would handle his health issues on his own. The reason I didn't ask him about the test results was because he never told me about seeing the doctor or having tests.

THE EMAIL REMINDED me of a time when the Beans and I visited Phillip in the Blairstown area after he moved back to work for Marco's new company. He casually mentioned he was spitting up a white foamy liquid from time-to-time.

"Well, shouldn't you see Dr. Powers?"

"I will deal with this, Kasey. I can't afford to see the doctor."

"I thought you said Marco was providing health insurance."

"He is. It's just that if something turns up, the cost of treatment could bankrupt us. We only have eighty percent coverage with my new policy."

"If you're sick, Phillip, you need to get treated. The cost is not the important issue here."

"Kasey, you're only here for a day. Let's stop this so I can enjoy time with my kids."

PHILLIP WROTE copy for many healthcare and pharmaceutical companies, and he was hyper-aware of anything related to these fields. But it also made him think he could diagnose his own medical ailments. His self-diagnosis frequently went awry. Time and again, he made assumptions about either his or my medical issues that turned out wrong. But, I let it drop because I noticed any time I brought up seeing someone about his stomach acid there was always a reason why he couldn't, or wouldn't, be seen by his doctor.

In the same email, Phillip also told Rachel he still planned to push forward with mediation. He let her know he would set "strict parameters" on who could be my mediator since he wanted "someone unbiased." I thought that was a joke, since he was asking his sister.

While I loved and respected her, I thought Rachel would hardly provide an unbiased opinion. If the only information I had was what Phillip said in those emails, I would have a hard time being unbiased too. I couldn't point any of this out though, unless I was prepared to reveal I had read his emails. That would open yet another can of worms.

By the time I got offline, I realized none of it mattered anymore. I was wasting my time trying to get the goods on him. I had to stop wasting my energy on the state of our marriage and start focusing on moving forward without him. I was about to shut off my laptop, but, instead, got to work creating the next month's lunch menus to send to Kate and redoing my resumé.

THE TRIP to Alexandria was harrowing. Phillip offered to let me use the Elantra because it was better on gas, but it didn't have snow tires, I slid several times on the icy roads, making me tense and irritable.

Jenny's husband was home, so the twins and I were staying in the old office above the café kitchen. When we arrived, it felt strange when I unlocked the café door. Even though only a few months had passed, the scene was disorienting. Kate and Sharilyn had moved things to accommodate assembling the school lunches more efficiently. I felt as though I wasn't a part of my previous life in Alexandria anymore.

After we all settled in upstairs, I came down and wandered into the tearoom. It was now filled with antiques. Glen was renting the space for his on-again, off-again antique business. His friend Roberto was there, minding his store. After a brief chat, I took time to call the plumber, who agreed to come in the morning.

I RECOGNIZED, then, I was ill-equipped to handle these types of maintenance issues I might face again in the future, and that my only recourse was to figure out a way to sell the building. The only consolation was the money would provide the funds to start over once Phillip and I divorced. With little to do, I went upstairs to grab Chubby's leash so the twins and I could take him for a quick walk and grab some groceries.

It felt like such a relief to have access to my Canadian Bank account and the money from the school lunch program. Even though I needed to watch every penny, it left me feeling better, knowing, once again, I had some funds of my own.

When I tried to fall asleep that night, my mind raced from one issue to the next. For some reason, I started thinking about a horrendous argument I had with Phillip years earlier. It was in the late spring of 2009, shortly after Marco's new company in Morristown, New Jersey, had folded. Phillip had finally moved north again to live with the Beans and me in Alexandria.

THE ARGUMENT BEGAN SHORTLY after I'd climbed the stairs to the office above the café, feeling like I was entering Phillip's private domain. I was frustrated because I was running back and forth, trying to bake desserts for the next day and, simultaneously, helping the twins with their homework.

It angered me that Phillip never offered to help. It also occurred to me that he always managed to carve out a spot, wherever we lived, to call his own. He had taken over the room I had been using for years as an office for the café and, without asking, he had put my business records in the closet, making them difficult to access.

I entered the room without knocking and he looked up from

a program he was watching on a small, portable television with a built-in VCR.

"Phillip, the twins have some math homework tonight. Would you see if you can help? I've got some desserts in the oven and I'm afraid I'll burn them if I keep going back and forth to help them."

"Sure, I'll come down in a while. My show is over soon."

"Can't you watch that later? You've seen it a million times."

He turned to look at me as though I were asking him to leave a patient in the middle of surgery.

"I told you, I'll go when it's over. They can wait a while."

"But I asked them to do their homework now so they'll have time after dinner for other things. It wouldn't kill you to spend some time with them."

His body stiffened.

"I will go to help them when I'm ready."

"Well, they need help now, not later."

"I'm getting my resumé together."

"Oh, and you're consulting with Captain Picard?"

"I can have the TV on and work, Kasey. I'm trying to find a job and love the fact you can't even allow me a bit of peace and quiet while I update my resumé," he snarled. "Spending time with the twins is a luxury for me."

"That takes the cake."

"What's that supposed to mean?"

"It means the only time you spend time with them is to watch TV shows they hate. It means that you spend more time away from them and offer excuse after excuse about why you'd rather stay here in this stupid office than be with your own kids. It means you were the one who decided to leave your wife and kids behind when you took the job with Marco," I screamed.

"I had no choice," he yelled back.

"Don't rewrite history, Phillip. You were the one who decided to take the job with Marco back then. You never even discussed it with me. And you were the one who wanted those damn rental properties."

"So, now being away from my kids is all my fault? Is that what you're telling me?"

"I didn't say that, Phillip. Stop putting words into my mouth."

"Someone had to provide for our family, and that someone is always me."

"Really? Did you once stop to think about how much that decision cost us? It took me months longer to open the business and I had to hire people to do things you weren't here to do. And while we're on the subject, did you even once add up all the expenses you incurred living down in New Jersey? Those costs plus our additional expenses here gave us a net gain of practically zero. You never even stopped to think if it was worth living apart!"

"You loved being without me. The only reason you want me here is to run errands for you."

"Help me? Please! Is that what you call it when you refuse to do anything except shop for groceries?"

"And what have you ever done for me? The fact is, Kasey, I will have to support you and the twins for the rest of my life."

"Oh? Are you forgetting that I worked full-time for years while you got to freelance or work to build your company? And how about the three years you stayed at home, working on the house after your business partner emptied your joint bank account? With the exception of that one small job you got from my employer, you didn't work because you said you were too busy working on our house. But somehow, during that time, you magically wrote a play."

"Well, at least my play was worth producing."

"Of course it was, because I was out there, working every day, to support you pal!"

"You've never worked at anything more than an admin job."

I walked over to the office closet where my café records were being stored. While trying to locate something earlier in the week, I had found a box of old invoices from my time at one of the ad agencies where I worked before the babies were born. I pulled it out of the closet and began throwing the papers at Phillip. The invoices were for $5,550.00 each.

"They don't pay a person this much for an admin job, even in Manhattan, Phillip. You can lie to yourself all you want, but I have the physical proof right here."

He wouldn't look at them. It was all right there in black and white, and yet, he denied it. How was that possible? I left the room, disgusted, and shouted over my shoulder,

"You left us in Canada, just like you're planning to do again. If you want to blame someone for not having time with your kids, look in the mirror."

With that, I hurried downstairs, hoping what I had in the oven hadn't burned. I stayed in the kitchen to see if he'd leave the office or ignore me. He chose to ignore me. Looking back at the night years earlier, I realize that was probably when he decided to divorce me.

Chapter Fifteen

ONCE AGAIN A STRANGER

The Beans and I left Canada two days later and arrived late at night back in Cobleskill, exhausted and unkempt. I sent Tammy at Sacred Heart an email outlining the situation, explaining why the twins were going to miss yet another day of classes. There was no way I could send them to school without getting some more rest and showering. As it was, they were feeling ostracized and I didn't need to give them any more anxiety about attending school.

The lengthy drive back from Canada allowed me to talk with the twins alone. The kids told me how miserable they were at school, and I wasn't convinced that it was the right place for either of them. Their grades were slipping, and they were each regressing socially.

It didn't matter what I did, I couldn't find the right balance of the kids' needs, my needs, and Phillip's. But after that first weekend in November, I believed it was imperative to get a plan in place.

Later that day, I called Maryanne to tell her about my trip. During our conversation, I expressed how I found it strange that when I now thought of Alexandria and the café, instead of it being my sanctuary, it was now the place where my relationship with my husband had gone off the rails. I told her I'd finally decided to let go of our property in Canada.

What I needed to do was to figure out how to safely leave without Phillip's knowledge of my plans, to avoid incurring his wrath. I called my brother Jake and asked him if the Beans and I could come for the weekend. I was very candid with him about the state of my marriage and told him that I planned to leave Phillip. He discussed it with Meredith and they agreed to let us come.

Because one of the tenants emailed me about a problem with her water heater, I told Phillip that was the reason for yet another trip north. That was partially true. I informed him that once the plumber resolved the issue I planned to head to Vermont to spend time with my brother on the first anniversary of my father's death. That was also partly true. He questioned nothing. I wondered if he would be relieved that we would be gone.

Veteran's Day was on a Thursday and was a school holiday. I calculated that if we left on Wednesday after school, I'd have Thursday to handle the plumbing issue and purchase the supplies needed for the lunch program. Afterward, I would head to my brother's home in Vermont. Once there, I could evaluate my options and determine if Jack, Lucy, and I could live there until we could find a better arrangement.

Since Jake had said we could stay for a while, I was hoping I would have time to work out the rest. Admittedly, it wasn't a brilliant plan, but until I could sell the property and split the proceeds of the sale with Phillip, it was the only thing I could think of that would allow us to begin a new life somewhere.

There was a lot to remedy on both fronts; however, anything was better than our current circumstances. I reasoned that Phillip had been perfectly happy seeing our children every other weekend, on and off, while the Beans and I were in Canada and he was living in New Jersey. For that matter, he was happy with a weekend arrangement when we were in Blairstown and he spent much of his time in Scranton. I kept reminding myself that even when he was under the same roof, he rarely chose to hang out with them.

Knowing I was ending my marriage before he did it for me allowed me to be kinder to Phillip. I knew he loved our kids and he would be hurt when we left. Even when he wasn't always there with them, I had no doubt he cared for them deeply. For whatever reason, he connected with them differently than I did. I tried to understand and believe it didn't mean he loved them less than I did. He just loved them differently.

I recognized that the pain of ending our relationship would affect both of us emotionally. I cared about his well-being. I even admitted to myself that, to a great extent, I still loved him very much. Leaving him wasn't about love. It wasn't about getting even or seeking revenge, either. I honestly had no desire to hurt him or cause needless suffering. I was just so tired of the heartache of knowing how little he thought of me. He never seemed to appreciate the contributions I made to his life and to our marriage. I couldn't understand how he was able to erase all of the years I supported him, for a version of our lives where he single-handedly played the role of sole provider. It was as if all those years I traveled to and from New York each day so he could establish his film career were all a figment of my imagination. There were days I sought out physical reminders of the truth because he got into my head in a way that caused me to doubt myself again.

His inability to recognize I wasn't the only one contributing to the problems in the marriage made me wonder about something else. I spent hours leading up to our trip on Wednesday trying to untangle the events of the past.

Did Phillip truly believe I was baggage to him? He told me I was in so many ways. After all, he said scores of hurtful things about my character, often leaving me emotionally wounded. It wasn't just my character, though. It was everything about me. The music I liked was wrong. The way I fixed my coffee was wrong. I laughed too loud and too often. If I sent a meal back at a restaurant, I was a bitch. My family, my tastes, my whole being, somehow were a target of his insults. What it all amounted to was, I was unacceptable because I was not Phillip.

But I wondered if so much of what he said was about his own insecurities and his inability to achieve his goals. In his mind, I was an *uneducated* woman, yet my successes eclipsed his own. He was far more qualified to work in a business that I'd managed to navigate. I'd established a career in the commercial film industry, while his business fell apart. I had to believe he was jealous.

Phillip frequently expressed his feelings of being overshadowed by his sister's accomplishments and told me, when we first met, that he was the black sheep of his family. He wasn't. It was, however, how he perceived his family dynamics. It was that very perception that skewed the truth and allowed him to ignore reality. He was blind to anything that made him feel inferior, and that covered just about every aspect of his life. The unfortunate part was that much of it was in his head and heart because, in reality, he was one of the most brilliant, charming, and talented people I've ever met.

It appeared to me that much of his insecurity was connected with this idea that he was competing for his parents' love. It was as if he could earn their love and respect by accomplishing more than Rachel, who was a very high achiever. But throughout our marriage, nothing ever indicated that his parents loved him any more or less than they did his sister.

They had a different relationship with him because he wasn't five minutes away, like she was. So, naturally, they spent more time with Rachel and Dennis. Whenever we visited, it was clear he tried to make up for his time away by trying to repair anything that needed it. Instead of enjoying their company, he often found ways to make himself useful. He often commented about his perception of our visits in terms of successes or failures, as though their love could be measured by his sense of accomplishment.

And while perception is a truly powerful thing, it is not, in fact, a reality. Phillip frequently made comments about our visits to his parents' house after we returned home. His view of what happened, or didn't happen, never matched my own. He somehow always managed to feel slighted. I'd begun to realize Phillip seemed to have his own reality—it just wasn't real.

As I moved forward to end our marriage, I thought about all this endlessly because it helped me to understand how we got to where we were and why it was necessary to empathize with him, even if I didn't accept his actions and, most assuredly, his reasoning. Somehow, by invalidating me, Phillip was able to validate himself. By telling himself I was at fault for all our problems, he was able to absolve himself of the self-loathing he had for his decisions. He was unable to love me because, essentially, he didn't love himself. The lengths to which I strived to comprehend what was at the heart of his actions weren't entirely acts of kindness. They were acts of survival so I could be at peace with my decision.

Once I arrived at the conclusion that it was best for all of us, it was easier to accept what I had to do. I had no reason to believe anything would change now that we were living back in the States, and I had no desire to continue going along the same path, fighting over the same issues repeatedly. In the days leading up to my planned departure, this understanding allowed me to be more civil and less defensive with him. He seemed to think I was relinquishing control to him. The irony wasn't lost on me.

Because he was still having so many gastric issues, I cooked several meals so Phillip wouldn't have to contend with preparing dinner for himself over the long weekend. I made a few of his favorite dinners, put things in the freezer, and baked some chocolate chip oatmeal cookies and a loaf of banana bread, before leaving to fetch the Beans from school. I emailed him to let him know what I did. He responded with a "thank you," and he offered to give me some cash for our trip. I was dumbstruck. It was easy to leave when he was unjust. When he was kind and offered to help, it made me pause. But only for a minute.

When I stopped by his office in Albany to pick up the money, I started to feel like a villain. Phillip had no idea I was not only going to Jake and Meredith's to honor my father, this time, when I left, I didn't plan on coming back.

Chapter Sixteen

A BITTER NOVEMBER

The Beans and I were staying with Jenny on this trip to Alexandria. When we arrived, her gentle hug and knowing smile restored my faith that, somehow, life would go on. It was the antidote I needed for my gloomy outlook after days of being immersed in the complexities of my marriage.

While she chatted with the kids, I went downstairs to her guest room and composed an email to Phillip. After reporting on the progress with the maintenance issues, I wrote:

"If I stayed here tomorrow and left for Vermont from here, would you be able to come on Saturday?

I have been struggling with dealing with the loss of my father. I had a difficult relationship with him, as you know, and letting go of him has been much different than letting go of my mother. But I think part of why it has made me so very sad is that, in many ways, I feel I lost you, too, at the same time.

Things simply cannot stay as they have been between us. We are all suffering from the dysfunction in our relationship, and we have to talk about that. We have tried talking before and things always end up in a screaming match, or worse. I think you're right that talking away from the stresses of our lives with two people who love us and want the best for everyone concerned is the way to go.

We have been talking about trying to mediate some of the issues between us with Jake and Rachel helping us, so this weekend, I believe, is a good opportunity. I had given Jake Rachel's phone number and he is going to contact her to see if she is available. (This may already have taken place, I am not certain.)

I am hoping we can put our anger aside and work towards a relationship that serves the best interest of the kids and allows us to heal some of the pain we have both been suffering.

I will let you know where things stand as far as a plumber is concerned. I just called the guy who worked on Tracy's basement. I am hoping that connection will get him to call back. ~ Kasey"

I never heard from him that evening. I started to worry.

THE TWO OR three glasses of wine I had with dinner made me sleepy and even though I wanted to head to bed, I kept going to check my email. I was struggling with the idea of Phillip reading it and wondering how he would respond. I had an uneasy feeling and tried to remind myself of all the reasons why I was more than justified in leaving him.

Later that evening, Jack and Lucy went downstairs to play on their Game Boys while Jenny and I talked. It was really helpful to hear her perceptions on the series of events that led up to this moment because she genuinely liked Phillip. She reminded me that, while he was "a nice guy," it didn't mean that he couldn't be a controlling asshole, too. Being married was far more intimate than being a friend. It wasn't okay for him to treat me the way he had for much of our relationship.

Eventually, I recognized how unkind I was being keeping her up, and I said good night and headed downstairs. But, as tired as I was, I still couldn't sleep. My mind bounced between seeing Phillip waving to us as we pulled out of the parking lot earlier that day and a playlist of our petty fights to major arguments. I kept forcing myself to recall all the things that brought me to that point, to justify leaving.

In recalling all the things that had transpired, I realized that the move to Canada, the move that was supposed to bring us together, was the beginning of the end of our marriage. All the conflicts of the past paled in comparison to some of the blowout fights we'd had before he left again, once he took the job in Albany.

AFTER MARCO'S COMPANY FOLDED, and Phillip began living with us full-time again, it became clear he was uncomfortable with the change in the dynamic of our relationship. We had constant fights over how to run the business and he subverted any authority I had over the operation.

One of our most frequent arguments was his insistence we wouldn't need employees if I ordered all our food from a company like Sysco. He seemed to think that was the solution to cutting back on expenses but could never explain how that would work because he never presented any facts or figures. Instead, he expected me to change the business model without presenting a reason to do so. To drive his point home, he acted out and, one day, he even put on a childish display.

He came down from the office and asked me, "What's for lunch?"

Kate, Sharilyn, and I were busy preparing to open so I offered to heat up the leftovers from our dinner the night before. Phillip, however, wasn't interested in leftovers so I took the time to rattle off our menu. Standing in the middle of the tiny kitchen, he said, "That's not lunch. That's a list of ingredients," and stormed out. I was completely humiliated. Kate just looked at me and said, "Well, let's not tell our customers we only have ingredients for lunch today, shall we?"

Shortly after Kate placed the 'open' sign on the door, several customers arrived and she began seating them in the tearoom while others waited in the foyer to be escorted to their tables. Suddenly, Phillip arrived back to the café, carrying a bag full of groceries. He announced, "I just bought myself something to eat. I'll need the stove for a few minutes," and then he walked into the kitchen, where Sharilyn was, and asked her to open and heat up a can of soup.

I was mortified. He knew I wouldn't say anything in front of my employees and customers. He relished inserting himself into our daily routine and showing Kate and Sharilyn that he, too, was their *boss*. What he didn't seem to understand was that he was also leveling an accusation regarding the quality of the food at the café. Soup was our specialty. I had customers drive all the way from Montreal, which was an hour away, to have a bowl of our soup. He was determined to make a statement and what he was saying to me was, "screw you."

When we closed that day, I told Kate and Sharilyn I would finish up, because I was seething by then. I climbed the stairs and let Phillip have it.

"What do you think you were doing with your little stunt this morning? It's not enough that you refuse to help me, but now you want to sabotage my business?"

"That just it, Kasey. This is your business. It's always about you and what you want."

"What I want? You think this is about what I want? You were the one who wanted to move here. Did you think I was going to just step aside because you're here now? I've worked in restaurants on and off for years, but I'm supposed to let you tell me how to run this place just because you worked at a Friendly's for a few weeks?"

"All I wanted was some lunch. But that was too much to ask. What was I supposed to do today, Kasey? You won't even let me use the kitchen for a few minutes," Phillip told me.

"Did it ever occur to you that we have a kitchen up in our apartment? This had nothing to do with you wanting lunch, Phillip. You wanted to show who is in charge." I left him, slamming the office door shut and, per usual, we didn't talk for days.

After that, he spent more and more of his time in the office. He even slept and ate his meals up there. The only time Phillip came over to our apartment was to watch videotapes with Jack and Lucy.

I could tell, from that point on, that Phillip hated being there. He resented everything about living in Alexandria and said so. I'd made friends and carved out a life that didn't center around him. I knew how unhappy he was but, by that point, my own resentment had grown to the point where I was relieved when he started putting together his resumé to apply for jobs back in the U.S.

There was, however, a short period of time I thought things were turning around, and we'd found a way to make the business work for both of us by expanding into areas of entertainment. It was something that reached back to our beginnings as a couple. I hoped we'd, once again, find our marriage on a more solid footing if we weren't competing because we each had an area of of the business we could control.

It began when I was approached by Shaun and Marie Gagney, a couple who were involved in the local entertainment scene. Shaun had a band that was quite popular in the area, and Marie promoted his band and ran a small business out of their home. Somehow, they'd assumed that Phillip and I owned a property that we were actually renting. The property had a large barn that had once been used as a venue for classical music concerts. They suggested doing a co-production of some kind at the venue.

We'd rented the property the previous summer after the windows on the van were smashed twice. At that time, Phillip was still living in the States and I became nervous about living above the café because, not only had our vehicle been vandalized, but someone also kept ringing our doorbell after midnight.

The farmhouse owned by Andrea Rabe, a concert pianist from Montreal. She and her husband Saul had a friend of theirs put a stage in the barn, surrounded by hardwood floors. The rustic setting was where they held free concerts for decades, until they moved to another venue. The farmhouse and music barn had been vacant for years when a friend of Andrea's came into the café one day, asking if I would be interested in buying the place.

Purchasing the property was not something we could even consider, but I suggested we would be interested in renting it since I could rent out our apartment above the café to cover the monthly expense. Phillip was completely on board with the idea initially because the kids would have an enormous yard to play in. On weekends, we all had a place to relax away from the business. The only drawback was that Chubby often had to remain by himself all day.

The first winter the kids and I stayed there informed me of why no one had lived there for years. Despite what I had been told, I learned the house wasn't insulated, and the pipes froze constantly. While I loved it in the summer, the frigid temperatures made the place miserable to come home to in the winter.

By the time Phillip moved back to Alexandria, the kids and I had moved back into our apartment above the café. The farmhouse was now sitting idle and Phillip was pissed that we were paying rent and not using the place. It was another source of friction between us because he said he never agreed to rent the place, even though I had emails that contradicted this claim.

After the Gagneys approached me about a co-production there, I suggested the three of us meet with Phillip, whom they'd never met. We all sat around a table in the tearoom and decided we would work together to produce the event. Phillip suggested the name, *Glengarry Music Festival*, and everyone agreed with my suggestion that we call the venue *2Beans in the Barn*.

Because Phillip could take on a more active role in the business, the friction between us was buried for a while. He designed an elegant website to advertise the upcoming festival, and Marie booked the talent for our summer line up. Shaun providing his band for an opening act and I catered the themed meals to match the music featured. For a while, everything was on track.

We had sold out for every performance we had booked, when

things fell apart. Shortly after the first two concerts, Phillip began complaining constantly about Marie. He hated working with her. Instead of approaching her with the problems he had with what she was doing or the way she was doing it, he complained to me and said he thought she was deliberately doing things to piss him off. In reality, I believe he was threatened by Marie's assertiveness. Everything she did was wrong, according to him. Yet, when the Gagneys pulled out of the festival, Phillip was shocked.

Even though my responsibilities only extended to catering for the performances, I was somehow to blame for the failure, and he claimed I talked him into doing the festival in the first place. He conveniently forgot all about sitting down and discussing the idea with the Gagneys and agreeing to the co-production. When I reminded him of that, he said he "just went along" to appease me.

As frustrating as those arguments were, they were nothing in comparison to what happened later that year. On a night in mid-November, I got a call from my brother Ray who told me my father had passed away. Phillip was up in the office. I trudged upstairs and delivered the news, ignoring the TV monitor playing a video of one of his favorite sci-fi shows. His reaction devastated me.

After I told Phillip my dad passed, he flatly said, "That's too bad," and he turned back to watching his program.

I was shocked at his lack of a response. He never cared for my father, and I understood he had reasons. But this lack of understanding of how it affected me was cruel, even given the state of our dysfunction. I turned and went downstairs without further comment. He came down moments later and offered to send flowers.

"Who would you send flowers to? My brother Ray?" I asked him, puzzled.

"I don't know. I'm trying to help," Phillip said sharply.

"I'm calling Sharilyn and Kate to let them know I need to close the café tomorrow," I said, exasperated.

"You can't do that! We can't risk losing that business," he yelled across the room.

"We," I thought bitterly. There was never a 'we' in running the café. After the music festival fell apart, the only task Phillip offered to do was to occasionally shop for groceries. Otherwise, he spent his days sending out resumés or watching TV programs.

I let my tears flow freely as I crossed the tearoom and opened the door connected to the foyer so I could make my way upstairs to our tiny apartment. Phillip followed me. By the time I reached the bottom of the staircase, he grabbed the back of my arm and stopped me before I climbed them. I faced him, throwing his hand off my arm.

"This is what it means to have a business," he ranted. "You don't get to close up shop because something happens." It was as if I said I was closing to have my nails done or have a day at the spa. In the three-plus years that we owned the place, I rarely took time off, missing many holidays or special occasions with family and friends. He even threw a tantrum when I wanted to attend Jenny's sixtieth birthday celebration, so I didn't go.

"I'm going to call them to cover for me or close for the day," I insisted.

"We can't afford it," he replied to my back as I walked up the stairs.

I turned back to look at him.

"Of course not. It doesn't matter, because it's my family. If this were your father, you would have been heading home within minutes of getting the call." I continued into the apartment and locked the door behind me, fuming. I knew what it took to run a business. The Beans came out of their room when they heard me come in. They came to me and we sat on the couch. I couldn't fathom what had just happened. I held them as tightly as they held me, and we all cried together when I told them of their grandfather's passing.

≈

I HELD ONTO THESE MEMORIES, reliving them, so I could steel myself for whatever was to come. I replayed the scenes over and over again, trying to rekindle my anger, to justify leaving Phillip earlier that day. But, instead, as I lay in bed, trying to sleep, I found myself full of sorrow. I finally understood why that past November night had been so painful. That was the night I'd lost the two men in my life that had meant the most to me.

Chapter Seventeen

RECALLING MY FATHER

My father was 93 years old when he passed away. Despite his age, it still felt inconceivable. His influence on my life was immeasurable. I idolized him as a child and my entire goal in life, back then, was to please him.

As a little girl, my dad favored me because I was the youngest. Whenever my older siblings wanted something, they asked me to go ask him, knowing he was more inclined to say 'yes' to me. As I grew older, I memorized Bible verses and tried to "save" all the neighborhood kids, seeking to convert them to his brand of Christianity. I knew it was what he wanted from me and I was happy to oblige. I adored my dad, and knew he loved me. I spent hours sitting in the background when his friends gathered at our house to sing and play their guitars. I listened with rapt attention to my dad's beautiful tenor voice and learned to sing harmony to all the hymns so I could be a part of his world.

He had that effect on others, as well. He captivated the neighborhood children by giving them rides on his motorcycles. He performed small magic tricks to entertain them. He worked with the youth groups at church, and they adored him because he was so charming and funny and an all-around lovable guy.

He was generous with his money and donated too much of his income to our local church. And yet, while he was overly generous with local charities, his children wore ill-fitting hand-me-downs, and my mother counted pennies and shopped thrift stores.

He never offered even one of his seven children rides on his motorcycle, and he cultivated relationships with teens from the church before taking time out of his busy schedule to spend with my older siblings. He was adored by so many people, but his own children and his wife saw a very different side of him.

To say we had a contentious relationship as I got older would be an understatement. When I hit puberty, he seemed to abandon me. My new interest in boys angered him, and nothing I did seemed to please him anymore. My good grades and obedient behavior were no longer enough to satisfy him. As I became a woman, he acted like it was a betrayal.

When I was around eleven, my dad convinced my mother that he should give up his job as a welder at a General Motors plant in Framingham so the two of them could attend Bible school in western New York. Although my mom had been diagnosed with rheumatoid arthritis and her health declined over those years, he sold our house in the small town where I grew up and moved us, first, into a trailer, then, into a duplex belonging to the school they were attending.

The entire family hated the change, but no one more than my mother. She, too, had to attend school and she resented her husband for it. She had been ripped away from her family and friends and the life we had back home in Massachusetts. Now, more restrictions were placed on her already restricted life. There were rules against just about everything. My father loved the spartan way the Bible school required us to live and the authority he gained as the man of the house. But my mom hated giving up her pleasures, like television, cigarettes, and red wine. I couldn't help but notice how quickly her health declined once we moved west.

On the other side of the duplex in which we lived was a

couple with five children. Mr. and Mrs. White were attending school as well, and my mom and Mrs. White became fast friends. Each night, however, our family could hear Mr. White beating his wife and throwing her against the wall. No one at the school stood up for her except my mom. My father said it was none of our business. My mother disagreed.

"It's not right!" she told him, all the time.

The hypocrisy stung, and soon I saw my parents differently. My father's image weakened dramatically in my eyes, and I had a newfound respect for my mom. Even at that age, what was happening next door, in the context of men going off daily to preach to others, turned my stomach. The purple welts I saw on Mrs. White's arms and face sickened me.

Maybe that was the catalyst that caused me to question the two different sides of both his beliefs and personal conduct. There was the public one, where he was a kind man, and then the personal one that didn't care about the behavior of a guy who was beating his wife because "it didn't concern him."

The screams coming through the wall each night taught me that not all men cherish their wives. By the time my parents graduated from Bible school, I had a new understanding of the relationship between husbands and wives. My perception had changed entirely, and I became closer to my mom because I understood the sacrifices she made for her children in a way I never did before. As my siblings left the house, I became her caregiver and talked with her more than I had growing up.

While she never said the words, I believed my mom thought it wasn't fair that her husband got to make all the decisions. She had frequent bouts of illness which stemmed from both her arthritic condition and a variety of gastric problems. I think the circumstances prohibited her from leaving my dad and, eventually, she grew to forgive him. Despite his faults, he showed his love and support in ways that made it more acceptable to her to tolerate the uneven power dynamic in their relationship. The longer they were married, I believe, the more they gained an understanding of one another, and I appreciated how attentive he became to her needs.

When Bible school was over, we lived in the town where it was located for another year before we moved to the Catskills. I was a junior in high school by then and my siblings were all out of the house. The move was the result of a job my dad took with a missionary organization located in Brooklyn, New York. Their goal was to convert Jews to Christianity. I was appalled at this, mainly because most of the boys I dated were Jewish. It was just one of the many reasons the undercurrent of friction grew between my father and myself.

As my dad became more and more devoted to his religious convictions, he tried to exert more influence over my decisions. He wanted me to attend Bible school so I could become a missionary like he was. I wanted to attend music school and received a full scholarship to do so. But he refused to allow me to go, and I gave in.

It was a constant battle to exert myself and what I desired for my own life. I didn't rebel by doing drugs or drinking. Instead, I started exhibiting physical signs of severe stress. At seventeen, I developed uncontrollable diarrhea.

Because of my mom's deteriorating health, my dad assumed most of the parental oversight during those years, including taking me to doctor's appointments. He was the one who accompanied me when the situation got so bad, I was having a hard time attending school. My mother finally convinced him to take me to the doctor to determine the cause.

At the appointment, the doctor began asking me questions.

"How frequently does this happen?"

"Well, I..."

My father cut me off. "Sometimes, I've noticed she has to get up from the dinner table. Maybe it's something she's eating?" he asked.

The doctor acknowledged him with a nod. "Do you notice that certain foods affect you?" the doctor asked.

"Well, I..."

My father cut me off. "Didn't you tell me mustard upsets your stomach?" he asked me, before turning to consult the doctor. "Could she have an ulcer?"

The doctor ignored him and nodded for me to respond.

"It seems like..."

My father cut me off again but, after answering for me a third time, the doctor had had it with him.

"Mr. Rogers, I am not asking you. I am asking your daughter, and I want you to let her answer for herself. Have I made myself clear?" he admonished.

My dad sheepishly nodded, but I could tell he was mad. He was used to being in control of even the words I uttered, and he didn't like the fact the doctor advocated on my behalf.

I spent my eighteenth birthday in the hospital, and after a week of tests, they diagnosed me with what they called spastic colitis. The doctor determined it was caused mostly by stress. While I battled with it on and off in my early twenties, the condition disappeared once I left home and didn't return until after I married Phillip.

My love for my father was as complicated as my love for Phillip. Until I had children, my relationship with him was filled with tension. I left home as soon as I graduated high school and only returned for a brief time after dropping out of college. The few times I saw him after that were usually because my parents were up from Florida, where they'd moved. I knew he loved me, but he would say things that were cruel and hurtful, so I avoided speaking to him.

For years, I called home once a week so I could check on my mom. She was mostly bedridden and hearing from her children brought her a great deal of joy. She understood how difficult her husband could be but tried to buffer our relationship by reminding me that, despite his harsh words, he loved me.

While I rarely spent much time talking over the phone with him, he kept trying to reach out by sending me heartfelt letters that I read with a hardened heart. But I found that I couldn't throw them away and often opened the shoebox where I kept them to remind me he was at least trying to make amends.

But he would sabotage all his attempts at reconciliation with his thoughtless comments as he did one time, when I called home. On that occasion, my father told me my mother was very ill and was in the hospital. She was so sick, he said, even if I called her, she wouldn't be able to talk on the phone.

"I hope she will be okay!" I said through tears. "Please tell her I love her, and I'll pray for her."

"God doesn't hear your prayers," he told me. After that, I refused to speak with him altogether.

My mom's health continued to decline, and nine months after the Beans were born, Phillip and I took the twins by train to see her for the last time. I was so grateful to him because he not only offered to make the arrangements, Phillip insisted we go.

I was only reluctant because it meant seeing my father and I was still keeping my distance. Even after years of barely seeing or talking to him, I couldn't imagine spending time in the home where he and my mother lived. But I was desperate to see my mom, so Phillip and I took the Auto Train, with the Beans, to Florida.

The trip healed the fractured relationship between my dad and me. Not because my father changed or did anything special, but because I realized, after seeing him gush over these two little beings that I loved dearly, that I wanted him in their lives, even if it meant I had to tackle the difficulties in our relationship.

I wasn't the only one he had alienated in the family, and I knew I was not the problem. This allowed me to tolerate some of his behavior, but it didn't mean I couldn't speak up. I just chose not to argue or fight with him over things we disagreed about. But I would state clearly that I disagreed.

Somehow, we navigated a relationship that grew more loving as the years passed. As the kids grew, he came and visited every year, making the trip with my older brother Ray, who was now caring for him.

I loved him in the ways I loved him when I was a child. I saw his good side, the humor he exhibited, his enjoyment of life, his intelligence and spunk. When he was eighty-four years old, he was still riding a motorcycle. I had to admire him, and work through the anger I had felt for years. When I received the news that he had died, I was heartbroken. My dad, the man who taught me how to sing harmony, the father who loved me with all his heart, if not his words, was gone.

Losing a parent is one of those times when we all become children again. It really doesn't matter how old we are, or how old they are, when they pass. We feel abandoned and lonely and long for the comfort of their loving arms. The fact that we will never see the person who brought us into the world again somehow leaves us numb. The anguish is different and changes our world forever.

When I lost my dad that cold night in November, the tension between Phillip and me robbed me of the time I needed to grieve, so I shut down and pretended not to feel the loss. Instead, I stuffed these feelings deep inside and carried on like I was expected to. But a year later, my two worlds collided, and I let all the grief I'd suppressed rise to the top, because my dad was gone and now—so was Phillip.

Chapter Eighteen

FALSE START

When Jenny and I were chatting earlier that evening, something she said helped me to realize that losing my father had been completely overshadowed by the pain inflicted by Phillip's reaction. As I tried to sleep that night almost exactly one year later, I began connecting the two events. The physical distance between my family and me allowed me to bury the feelings and ignore my sorrow. Instead of taking time off to feel my sadness the day after my father died, I simply carried on and suppressed my anguish.

Regardless of Phillip's response that night a year ago, I never lost concern for his well-being. It did, however, make me even more determined to leave him. I worried when I hadn't heard from him after sending him my carefully worded email the night before. I thought about calling him, but I couldn't face hearing his voice, so I decided against it. I lay in bed, trying to fall asleep, but was kept awake by fears of an uncertain future.

Starting over yet again was not something I looked forward to. Neither was the idea that I would hurt someone I had thought the world of at one time. But I couldn't continue to live with someone who thought so little of me, and this is what kept me moving forward.

I knew Phillip still wanted to push forward with the mediation idea. I was still convinced this was a power play. He knew my weaknesses, and this orchestrated event was more about exposing what he considered to be all my flaws than trying to solve the problems within our marriage. I believed he was rehearsing his side of a custody argument since he often said, "You'd never win in court." Was he practicing for that day?

Years earlier, we pursued counseling; however, it ended in a disaster because the counselor asked me to speak first. My candid response was met with Phillip's condemnation when we left the office.

"You're unbelievable, you know that?" he told me. "You sat there for fifteen straight minutes telling this guy what an asshole I am, and not once did you mention the shit you put me through daily."

"What did you want me to say, Phillip? Did you want me to go in there and say everything is just ducky? Isn't this the whole point of seeing someone? Aren't we supposed to tell them what bothers us about the marriage so we can address the problems? You didn't hold back. You painted a pretty clear picture of the issues as you saw them. The only difference is, I told him about my problem with the ways you treat me. You told him all the ways you wanted me to change into someone I'm not."

Until he came up with the idea of mediation, he'd never agreed to attend counseling again. Perhaps the scrutiny was too much. Since he had already asked his sister to be his mediator, I asked Jake to be mine. While Phillip wasn't aware of my plans to leave, I felt I had to move forward with his idea of solving our marital problems. Allowing him to voice his opinions would give me insight into how he was presenting his side of our marriage. Even though I was certain it would be brutal, at this point, I was hoping I could control my emotions and temper so I would be able to state my beliefs regarding what was at the core of our problems.

In the morning, I found his response to my email.

"Kasey-

I don't know if you have been trying to reach me thru the home phone, but I just discovered a little while ago that it had been unplugged.

Thought it was too late to call. So please call me tomorrow to let me know what is going on. ~ Phillip"

I still had to address a few more building repairs that cropped up that morning before the Beans and I left Canada to head towards Vermont. I called Jake to alert him of the delay. In our conversation, I confided in him I was fairly certain my marriage was over, and I had to leave Phillip.

Soon after my call, Jake reached out to Phillip's sister Rachel about coordinating our get-together on the weekend. In their conversation, Jake accidentally revealed my plans to leave Phillip. She then alerted Phillip. I was beside myself and panicked because now he knew I was planning to leave him. As soon as the repairs were completed, I returned to Jenny's, got Jack, Lucy, and Chubby into the car, and headed towards Vermont.

When I arrived at Jake's late that night, I checked my email, and sure enough, Phillip now knew my plans.

"Kasey,

I've been up all night thinking about all of this. I don't how we got to this point, but I don't want our marriage to end, nor do I want our family to break up.

So I would like to resolve things today. You don't have to come up with a list as we had discussed. We can either have Jake and Rachel discuss things, or we can talk directly.

Regardless of how and where this anger between us has come from, I want it over. I heard our new neighbor and her husband (boyfriend?) laughing with their children tonight and they seemed so happy to be together. Here they were, moving into a crummy little apartment and they were so full of joy to just be together. I broke down and cried for a long time.

I want my wife and I want my kids. Nothing else is more important to me. Let me know how you want this to proceed.

I do love you. I always have and always will. ~ Phillip"

I could imagine him sitting alone in the apartment in Cobleskill, wondering how things went awry. But I couldn't understand how he was so blind to the disintegration of our marriage. Was I the only one that was so unhappy? How could he think the issues between us would magically be resolved over the course of a day? While his remorseful tone touched me, I wasn't convinced that anything had changed just because it finally occurred to him it might be over. I composed an email response, trying not to further damage the relationship but firmly stating how I felt about his email.

"Phillip-

I honestly am very, very baffled at your statement, "I don't know how we got to this point."

I do not want to be cruel and level any more anger at you, as I feel you are beyond your capacity to deal with any more pain in your life. But you had to have known, on some level, that you could not simply say some of the horrid and hurtful things you have said to me without my taking them to heart. You have to have known you could not simply level all your anger and frustrations about things and have me just absorb them without them having an impact.

My decision to come here was not one made overnight. I tried for weeks and weeks to see some sign that things were going to change between us. Things did not get better, they got worse. I was never certain of what was on your mind, especially when you would say things like, "You just wait until you see what is going to happen to you," like you did the morning we fought over my laptop. The level of uncertainty I have been living with became unbearable. I could not remain there.

I came here because I needed to be with my family, specifically my brother who is kind and levelheaded and who I know loves me with all his heart. I needed the protection of his arms and the guidance he could offer because I am overwhelmed by the pain of this situation and could not be certain of anything other than the need to put an end to the suffering I have been feeling. Most importantly, however, I needed to remove the kids from the level of stress they were absorbing from both of us.

I knew this would hurt you and am truly sorry you are suffering. But you are always telling me that everything's my fault, we are where we are because of me, that I am responsible for your frustration and anger, and I have made every decision in our marriage, you simply have just gone along because I am so very persuasive.

My question to you is: if you feel this way, why in God's name do you want me to stay? Why do you want to remain married to me when you have expressed to me you have nothing left but disdain? You are now telling me you love me. Is this regardless of how flawed you think I am? I cannot process this emotionally or mentally with the vast majority of recent emotions and experiences in our marriage that have told me otherwise. I left because I had no other choice. I left because I could not survive the pain and destruction that I identify with our relationship.

Jake told me he feels I need to simply step back and not be reactionary. By letting some time pass, it will let me deal with things rationally. I feel this is sound advice because I always feel I am on the defense in our relationship. I think it would be good for both of us to reflect on things before moving forward.

You want things that have built up for years to be resolved in one day. That simply cannot happen. I would like you to consider coming here next weekend to talk. Jake is genuinely concerned about you and I know he will in all ways try to be as helpful as possible. I believe this would be the same for Rachel, who, if willing and able, should be here too.

I will await your response. ~ Kasey"

We arranged a meeting between the four of us on Saturday. To keep things neutral, we met in a conference room at a church about half way between Marblehead and my brother's home in Vermont. From my perspective, the entire thing was a complete fiasco. The genuinely concerned husband that wrote an impassioned email imploring me to set aside our differences did not show up at the meeting. The Phillip I had been battling for months, however, was there.

My journal of that day is blank because I had removed all those items from the apartment in Cobleskill, and everything was still at Maryanne's. My recollection of events is that it was an unmistakable disaster with mudslinging on both sides. All the recriminations from years of dysfunction were on display. The day left me in complete despair. Phillip returned to his sister's that night, and I went back to Jake's house. Now, I was more determined than ever to divorce him.

Phillip called me from Rachel's the next day and asked to visit the kids before returning to Cobleskill. I told him I was fine with that. I never wanted to prevent him from seeing his children. I knew he loved them. Jake and Meredith were also deeply concerned about Phillip's well-being, so no one had a problem with his visit.

The reunion was awkward because the kids knew what was taking place. They loved Phillip, but the years of constant separation had shaped their relationship as much as it had shaped his and mine. After a brief and loving visit, there was little to say, and the twins became antsy, trying to avoid any unpleasant conversation. They kept looking at me with questions in their eyes. I signaled my assurances that they were behaving appropriately, but it was uncomfortable when they both became silent.

Phillip turned to me and asked me if we could talk. I was reluctant, but I agreed. I figured nothing could be any worse than the day before, so we went out in the car to sit and talk. He couldn't stop crying; he sobbed for what seemed like hours. I tried not to be frustrated. Any time I cried, Phillip would admonish me for being manipulative. I tried not to let the past color the moment, so I comforted him. It was hard, however, not to feel played.

He apologized for his behavior during the meeting, and his regret seemed sincere. He spoke of how frightened he was at the thought of life without the Beans and me. He acknowledged his unfairness in placing all the blame on me for our problems. I told him I, too, was sorry for acting like a madwoman at times.

While he expressed his love and commitment to change, I held out little hope that things would ever be different. I desperately wanted to believe him, but my doubts were well-founded. We had resolved nothing. There was no new understanding of one another. We weren't beyond all the triggers that led to our unhappiness. He didn't take any responsibility for all the hurtful things he'd said for decades or for distorting the facts of my contributions to our finances. Not once did he even pretend to understand why I was so hurt when he told me in a thousand ways I was *unacceptable*. Why couldn't he see the enormous difference between calling someone out for bad behavior and attacking their personality or individual preferences? I couldn't see how we could pull through this horrible experience when we couldn't even be in the same room without spewing animosity towards one another.

"Why, Phillip? Why do you even want me to come back? I get that you miss the kids, but name one reason you want me back?"

"I just do. I miss you."

"That's not enough. You miss the relationship, but you don't miss me."

"That's not true. I love and miss you, too."

My mind was racing, waiting for his answer. It didn't come. He couldn't even name one reason he loved me. Why? I loved his crooked smile. I loved his sense of humor. I loved how smart he was and how he made me want to be a more accomplished person. I loved learning about the things that interested him, even if I didn't find them interesting myself. I loved his creative nature and how he excelled at just about anything he tried. I loved how he kissed me and the way he grabbed me from behind to hold me. I loved the way he walked with the oddest gait. I loved when he woke me up in the middle of the night to make love. I loved how dedicated he was to his parents and sister, and friends. I loved the fact he cherished his family's heritage. I tried, for years, to show him just how much I loved him. All I wanted from him was to love me back.

I understood he missed me. He was used to being in a relationship. But that was not the same as loving someone. When you love someone, you want as much, or more, for them as you want for yourself. I wanted the world for him, and yet, he didn't share those feelings. I wanted to ask him to explain how I could change everything about myself and still be the person I was. Why did it matter that I never finished college? Why did he complain about the way I drank my coffee? How could the music I liked be *stupid*? He seemed to understand a desire for friendships outside of marriage wasn't abnormal or harmful for him. Why was my desire to have friends such a problem? The list went on and on. How could he utter the words "I love you" when he didn't like anything about me anymore? Maybe he loved the attention and support our relationship once offered, but was that love? I wanted more for Phillip. I knew, without asking, that he wanted so much less for me.

At that moment, I wished I could see into his heart. I wanted to believe he truly loved me, but I didn't. I wanted him to accept me, warts and all. The love he gave me was conditional, and in his eyes, I constantly failed to meet those conditions.

"Kasey, I don't want things to end."

"What's ending, Phillip? We barely speak anymore without it ending in an argument. How am I supposed to react to your contempt? Do you even realize that, a year ago, you refused to even let me take off time to grieve for my father?"

He hung his head, and I could see tears spilling onto his jeans. He asked me if I would consider returning to New York. I told him I would think about it. He left to go back to Cobleskill so he could return to work the next day. I went in to talk with the twins about the hard decision we had to make.

Part Three

A REVISED APPROACH

Your strength doesn't come from winning.
It comes from struggles and hardship.
Everything that you go through prepares
you for the next level.

~ Germany Kent

Chapter Nineteen

RETURNING TO COBLESKILL

The Beans and I had a long talk that night. They both missed Phillip and their cats. We decided to give it one last try, and I promised to look into changing schools. The next day, I called Phillip to tell him.

"Hi."

"Hi."

"The kids and I talked about it, and we're willing to try again. But things have got to change, Phillip. I mean it. I'm not going to come back to the same bullshit that had me leaving in the first place."

"It will. It will change. I promise."

I hung up the phone and told the Beans we needed to pack.

Over the next few months, I noticed a significant change in Phillip's behavior. I was cautious, however, because this had happened before. I wanted to believe this time it was for good, but I couldn't. I'd been through these reprieves too often to trust it would last. I welcomed the calm but continued to expect the storm. During this time, I was the one who picked arguments, and I had to pull back because I found myself still in defensive mode. Part of this was because Phillip remained adamant about having me report every penny I spent. Even if he wasn't combative about it, I found it humiliating.

One thing that didn't change was his habit of closing himself off in Jack's room each night. He was still very private about conversations that I imagined were about something he wanted to keep from me. So even though he tried harder than ever to temper his frustrations when he spoke to the twins and me, I was apprehensive that anything had changed. I just couldn't do anything about it without money.

Knowing this, I began focusing my attention on getting a job. It wasn't easy putting a resumé together because my work experience was all over the place. Since I'd left the advertising industry, I had built websites, got my realtor's licenses, and had taught school. I also worked as a mobile notary, did some graphic design, and owned and operated the café. Finding a well-paying job after I'd been out of the regular workforce for years was going to be challenging. I was also middle-aged and looking for work in an economy that was still recovering. I briefly explored the idea of opening yet another café or catering business before realizing that it couldn't happen without money, and I had none.

My other focus was trying to get the kids the help they needed. Both kids were very smart, and seeing them struggle in school was heartbreaking. Redirecting my attention kept my frustrations about my marriage in check.

I made an appointment to meet with a man from the public school system who helped me navigate a transfer of the Beans to public school. I worked with the teachers at Sacred Heart to make the transition smoother than if we just yanked them out without considering all the aspects of their emotional and educational needs. There were things to consider, and we decided it would be best to wait until after the Christmas holidays.

In early December, I finally landed a small, part-time job, cold-calling potential clients for an insurance agent. It wasn't the best job in the world, but having even a tiny income of my own helped me relax a bit because I didn't always have to ask Phillip for money.

The holidays had a calming effect. We both tried to refrain from past feelings of anger and resentment. I told myself not to let Phillip off the hook for what had happened in the past, but I couldn't allow myself to punish him when he was genuinely making an effort to be pleasant.

I blasted off an email to my friends in Canada right before Christmas.

"Happy Holidays My Dear Friends,

I hope this email finds you well and knowing that I miss you all. Life has certainly taken some unexpected turns in recent months and I am in the States basically doing whatever I need to do to survive, play nice, and keep whatever sanity I left Canada with intact. Kate and Sharilyn are still running the Healthy School Lunch Program out of the café and the tearoom is being used by Glen for his business.

I am trying to remain philosophical about the changes in my life, do things time didn't permit when I was running the café! I have started to write again (which keeps me sane) and I am teaching a film course at the school Lucy and Jack are attending.

We all miss our adopted home more than I can express. It is very hard to say what our future holds, as the economy is holding us captive. But I am forever the optimist and hope my future brings me north once again. We spend as much time in Alexandria as possible, but time is always so short. Please know that while I may not always be in touch, I think of you all, and you remain in my heart and mind. Love ~ Kasey, and the 2Beans!"

In my mind, it was still the twins and me. While Phillip and I weren't fighting, we weren't behaving like a couple, either. We didn't sleep together, and we treated one another like two room-mates rather than two people who would be celebrating a mile-stone anniversary in less than a year. The upcoming event highlighted the dysfunction in our marriage because we couldn't celebrate it openly. Many people still thought we were married three and a half years after we actually had been. The secret still loomed over us, but I didn't know if a celebration was in order, anyway.

. . .

WE SPENT our holidays with Phillip's family. I felt awkward because I didn't know what had been said to Phillip's parents if anything. Thankfully, there was no indication of a rift between us, and his parents were as kind as always. I also felt that being around other people helped keep the acrimony at bay since the season brought back memories of wonderful times.

Shortly after the holidays, I had to return to Alexandria to deal with more tenant issues. Every month, I was chasing rent or dealing with a significant maintenance issue. Phillip appeared utterly uninterested in what was happening in Canada. As soon as the lunch program ended for the current school year, I decided it was time to cut ties with the business side of the building. I was tired of struggling to pay the mortgage and all the other expenses. I was falling behind.

I spoke with Kate and Sharilyn while I was up there, and Kate said she might be interested in renting the kitchen and continuing the program. I was thrilled because, by now, I knew that I wouldn't be able to go back there. Things had already changed. The hole I'd left in the community had already filled in, and life there was going on without me.

IN LATE JANUARY, Phillip got word that his Uncle Joe had died. He was very close to his father's identical twin brother.

"I'm sorry, honey. I know how much you loved him. I wasn't aware he was that sick," I said when he called from the office to tell me the news.

"My dad is really upset. He didn't get a chance to say goodbye."

I planned to prepare lasagna for dinner that night. It was one of Phillip's favorite meals. I hadn't made one for a while since the various cheeses cost a small fortune, and Phillip still insisted on shopping for groceries. When I saw that Ricotta cheese and fresh mozzarella were on sale, I asked him to get some on his way home. I already had some ground beef and ground pork, so I decided to make two lasagnas and freeze one for another meal. I had all the ingredients out when Phillip came in and asked what was for dinner.

"I'm making one of your favorites, lasagna! That's why I needed the groceries. Did you pick them up?"

"You know I can't eat that!"

"Since when?"

"The tomato sauce will kill my stomach."

Phillip put down the sack of groceries, then left the room in a huff. It was the first time in weeks he'd lashed out at me, leaving me confused. What was I missing? Why didn't I know he was struggling with eating foods like lasagna? I was cooking a lot of comfort foods because they were cheap, and Phillip and the kids enjoyed them. But I wondered when things had progressed to where he was struggling to eat. I knew I had to directly confront this news, but I knew it wouldn't be easy. He was on the couch, and I sat down next to him.

"Did you ever call that gastro doctor?" I said this with as little reproach as possible. But my question still made him angry.

"When am I supposed to schedule an appointment? Barry laid off Debbie a few weeks ago, and she had no notice at all. For all I know, I could be next. I can't afford to take time off, Kasey."

I knew better than to press the issue. It was a flashpoint, and we were avoiding those. I went to put the cheese and other ingredients away. I wasn't in the mood to cook anymore, so I made a quick frittata and, when it was done, I called everyone to dinner. I watched Phillip out of the corner of my eye, wondering, again, what I was missing.

Chapter Twenty

HAPPY BIRTHDAY TO ME

Phillip was gone for the weekend to his uncle's funeral. The kids and I stayed behind because the funeral was on a Friday, and attending would have meant missing more school.

I was in an excellent mood because I didn't have to try hard to be on my best behavior. Jack read a book while Lucy watched something on TV in the living room. I sat at the kitchen table, creating invoices to bill the schools in Canada for the school lunches. I stopped what I was doing and called to the Beans, "You guys want some hot chocolate?"

"Sure," they shouted in unison.

I put on some music, pulled a saucepan out of the cabinet to warm some milk, and then gathered the container of Hersey's cocoa powder, the canister of sugar, and the salt shaker. I'd begged Phillip to buy a can of whipped cream and knew we had some left. I grabbed that and placed it on the counter as well.

I hummed as I stirred the warming milk and found myself thinking about what had happened the night before, with the whole lasagna incident. It stunned me that Phillip was having so many problems with his stomach that eating one of his favorite foods was now off-limits.

I had urged him for so long to address the issue, and I recalled reading an email he sent to Rachel months ago about some tests he'd had done. Surely if anything was wrong, it would have been picked up at the time.

When the milk was warmed, I added the cocoa powder, sugar, and a pinch of salt. Before pouring it in mugs, I did a little digging in the cabinets above the sink to see if I could find them a snack. There I found some microwave popcorn, a few bottles of red wine, and a bottle of Glenlivet, Phillip's favorite scotch. Everything was unopened and had gathered dust. It made me realize it had been quite a while since I had seen Phillip partake in a glass of wine or a few fingers of scotch, neat when he came home. I wondered when that stopped. I put the booze away but left out the popcorn to give the Beans a snack with their hot chocolate.

Having a few moments to myself made me think about feelings I'd managed to shove aside for a while. Phillip's absence resurrected resentment in me. When my father died, Phillip had not permitted me to take a day off to grieve, yet he left for an entire weekend to attend his uncle's funeral. The matter underscored the continued hierarchy in our relationship. I didn't resent him for going to his uncle's funeral. I resented the fact that if I was in a similar situation, he would determine if I could go or not. I began to think again about our marriage. I realized the only difference between now and November was that we were acting more civil towards one another. I avoided wondering where it would all lead, so I could enjoy my time with the Beans.

The following weekend, things were "back to normal," whatever that was. I was washing the dishes after dinner while the Beans were doing homework so they could watch TV later. Phillip came into the kitchen and leaned against the counter, watching me for a minute before asking, "What do you want for your birthday this year?" The casualness of his question caught me off guard. I was not prepared to answer him, mainly because I had no funds of my own to buy him anything for his birthday, which was on Valentine's Day.

In recent years, birthdays had seemed more obligatory than celebratory. We usually traveled to Phillip's parents' home because his mother's birthday fell between Phillip's and mine. Since we weren't going back to see his folks this year, I assumed we'd be staying in. I wasn't thinking of doing anything more than maybe having an enormous glass of wine while I made something special for dinner. I spent time looking through grocery store circulars trying to find crabmeat on sale so I could make him Maryland-style crab cakes or seafood stuffed scallops. It was something I was sure he could eat, and I thought he'd enjoy.

When I heard Phillip's question about what I wanted for my birthday, even I was surprised at what flew out of my mouth.

"I want you to see a doctor." I spun around to face him. "I want you to take whatever is happening with this whole swallowing thing more seriously than you have. That's what I want for my birthday," I said sincerely.

"Don't go there," he warned me. "I'll go to the doctor when I damn well please, and in case you haven't noticed, I barely have time to take a shit these days because I'm working non-stop to keep this family afloat. I know how to treat this, so mind your business." He stormed out of the room.

"Well, I guess I'll just have to make do with a big ole glass of wine for my birthday," I said under my breath.

As I washed the dishes, my mind raced, wondering what he meant by, "I know how to treat this." As concerned as I was, I knew better than to bring it up again. Not only was he working a full-time job, but he was also taking in freelance writing projects for Marco. When he was working, he was focused on his freelance assignments to the exclusion of everything else. He always worked over and above the call of duty, hoping to stay employed. I emptied the sink and watched the water go down the drain, hoping my concerns were unfounded.

As weeks passed, I tried to believe that if something were wrong, my husband was smart enough to seek the advice of a trained professional. But I couldn't stop wondering if I'd overlooked something. The more I thought about it, the more I became troubled. A war waged inside me. We'd lived apart for years, and part of me insisted Phillip had ample opportunity to address his health issues on his own. However, the other part saw him struggling, and my instinct to love and protect him took over.

Finally, I decided if he wasn't going to do anything about his health, I was. I called and made an appointment to see our new family doctor. Since he was booked for weeks, I agreed to see his nurse practitioner. A few days later, I sat there doing a Sudoku puzzle in the waiting area until she was able to see me. I was nervous that she wouldn't agree to tell me anything relating to someone else's health, so I rehearsed what I would say in a way she couldn't refuse to answer me.

I was so thankful she was seeing me because I was sure I wouldn't have had the confidence to explain my mission if I'd seen our regular doctor. In her office, I told her why I was there.

"I know that you can't discuss my husband's health with me without his permission. I know that," I said bluntly. "What I'm asking you is what advice would you give me if I came to you with these symptoms," and I began reciting what I'd observed in Phillip without giving her a chance to cut me off. "I've had acid reflux for many years now and am taking omeprazole. But I'm having a very hard time swallowing, and sometimes I regurgitate into my mouth unexpectedly and sometimes spit up a kind of white foamy liquid. It doesn't seem to affect my energy level, but I still have persistent heartburn even with the medications. What could cause these things?" I asked her and started to tear up, finally acknowledging to myself how concerned I was.

She looked at me with great compassion and gently leaned towards me.

"He needs to seek treatment now," she warned me. "As soon as he can." She drew a breath and reached out, and took my hands.

Then she said, "Look, I don't want to scare you. Without seeing him and running tests, there is no way to know what's causing the dysphagia, but this could be very serious. When I was in school, one of my favorite professors had similar symptoms. It turned out he had cancer, and he died within six months." She again assured me that there was no way of knowing if this was the case with Phillip without further testing. I couldn't help but hear the concern in her voice.

My heart was heavy as I drove back to Cobleskill that day. I knew if I told him about going to the appointment, I risked alienating him further since it still pissed him off that I asked him to see a doctor. But I knew not telling him would be irresponsible. I was determined to have a tough conversation with him when he got home that night, regardless of his anger.

When I got home, I still had hours before I had to pick up the kids, so I did some research on the internet. I'd written the word "dysphagia" on a piece of paper since I was unfamiliar with the term. None of what I was reading about dysphagia was good.

"See your doctor if you regularly have difficulty swallowing or if weight loss, regurgitation, or vomiting accompanies your dysphagia," warned the Mayo Clinic.

Holy shit! The weight loss! These were all symptoms he was experiencing! I'd assumed he'd dropped a few pounds because he'd started jogging again, or worse, he was trying to be more attractive to a secret lover. He'd really trimmed down. Except for not being able to swallow sometimes, he looked healthier than he had for years.

I studied a picture I had of him in my wallet. He was holding our Beans as toddlers, cradling them, one in each arm, sitting in an oversized chair in their nursery in Blairstown. His radiant smile beamed from the past, capturing the emotion he felt as I snapped their picture. These little beings were his pride and joy, and he loved them.

Hot tears streamed down my face as I confronted my fears and the emotions I'd felt about him in recent months. There were times I resented him. No, I hated him. Our relationship had fallen apart, and it was still extremely fragile. Sometimes I still suspected he had planned to file for divorce and could have been having an affair. Perhaps my threat to leave him made him decide against divorcing after all. I still thought he stayed in our marriage out of habit and wanted to maintain the status quo. But he was trying. He was trying harder to get along with me than he ever had before, and that counted for something. I needed to tell him what I did and report what the nurse practitioner said.

When I told him, he was angrier than I'd seen him in months. He didn't speak to me for days. He never spoke of the incident, but he sent me an email from work a few weeks later.

Can you call and make an appointment with that doctor you saw?

After that appointment, they scheduled some tests. Phillip was very closed-mouthed about everything with me. I suspected he was sharing the news with Rachel. I considered checking his emails to see if he'd said anything to her but refused to do that again. I had to be satisfied that, even though he was angry with me, for once, I got what I wanted for my birthday.

Chapter Twenty-One

SIGH OF RELIEF

The Beans' birthday was at the end of March. I was catering a murder mystery dinner theatre event for Sacred Heart on the day of their birthday, so Phillip and I decided to celebrate the following weekend. We took them into Albany for the afternoon, visiting a bustling Museum of Science and Technology, or *CMOST*, which offered a range of activities we all enjoyed. It was a tremendous hit, and we allowed each of the twins to get a small gift at the gift shop. They even enjoyed seeing *Hop*, a movie they were initially reluctant to see, complaining it would be too childish for their thirteen-year-old sensibilities. We topped the celebration off by going out for dinner, something we rarely did on our tight budget and concluded the day with a homemade cake, ice cream, and the opening of their presents. That day was the first time in years that it felt like we were a real family. Phillip uncharacteristically had held my hand as we walked and seemed full of tenderness as we ushered the kids through the city.

Shortly after we got back to the apartment, Phillip went into Jack's room and closed the door. I tiptoed closer to the door and heard him leaving a voice mail for his sister.

"Just an update... I have a Gastro and GP consult tomorrow. I have a surgery consult on Thursday. Still don't know when they will actually do the biopsy. According to my doc, they were supposed to do it this week. I don't think I should tell Mom and Dad till next weekend when I know more. Call me later. Love you." I heard him hang up the phone.

I quickly went into the kitchen so he wouldn't know I was eavesdropping. On the one hand, I was glad to hear he had reached out to Rachel because he needed the support. Usually, I would have been upset that he wasn't telling me this news. That no longer mattered. I was just happy with the thought he had seen a doctor and would soon be feeling better.

Some of my relief also came from the knowledge that I'd made it through the worst of the winter months with the property in Canada. Soon, the chaos of trying to maintain the property long-distance would be behind me. Once the lunch program was over, I planned to list the property.

The next morning, I took Chubby for a walk. I noticed that a bright yellow and purple crocus was poking through the last mounds of dingy grey snow in the winter-fatigued backyard. This harbinger of spring raised my spirits. I started to think perhaps everything was finally changing for the better and wondered if maybe my marriage wasn't heading for a divorce after all.

When Chub and I returned, I went into the kitchen and called to the kids in the living room watching TV.

"Hey, do you guys want scones for breakfast?"

They responded with a resounding, "Yes!"

Because there were few foods Jack and Lucy both liked, I decided to make chocolate chip scones because chocolate chip anything was the exception to their divergent food preferences. I began assembling all the dry ingredients onto the counter, then grabbed the heavy cream from the fridge and took a stick of unsalted butter out of the freezer. I looked for and found an orange to grate the peel into the batter for extra flavor.

I grated the frozen butter into a bowl, working quickly, careful not to scrape my knuckles on the rough edges. Soon, I was floating in and out of thought about the world I'd left behind seven months earlier. I realized that cooking of any kind was such a trigger for reminiscing about all the hours I spent in the kitchen of my beloved café. Aromas wafting from the oven had me thinking about the days when I called Alexandria home. It wasn't just cooking, however, that brought back thoughts of the café. The dishes I used to serve my family were the same ones I'd once placed in front of my customers. It was so much easier to desire something that no longer existed than to appreciate the present moment, making it hard to let go of the past.

With the oven warmed and the scones ready to go in, I placed them on the middle shelf and closed the oven door, setting the timer for twenty minutes—plenty of time to shower and get dressed. I hollered to the Beans.

"Last call if you need the bathroom." I hurried in before anyone could respond.

As the water covered my body, I lathered my hair with shampoo. I tried to break away from my earlier thoughts of the past. Even though I'd done a few catering jobs for the kids' school, it was much different, carving out a niche for myself as a caterer in Cobleskill. Many well-established businesses had their own kitchens.

I'd looked into the possibility of opening a small shop, but there were too many obstacles. Then I considered joining forces with another woman I'd met who also had thoughts of operating a café. We even looked at a small shop that was for rent. But all that took more money than I could come up with, so I had to finally acknowledge that opening a new business wasn't a reality.

As I showered, I continued to wonder if that was what I really wanted anyway. While I loved owning the café, it was never my dream. I loved to cook simply because it was a way to express myself. I'd done that throughout my life by writing, painting, acting, and singing. Cooking was another outlet for my creative expression.

As I toweled off, I glanced in the mirror. I barely recognized the woman looking back. My obligations over the past few years had consumed me. No, I didn't want to start another business that had me working fourteen hours a day just to make ends meet. I wasn't sure what I was going to do, but I knew, someday, I'd get back to the things I was passionate about, like writing. I just wasn't sure when.

I HAD a job interview in Albany scheduled the next day but saw an ad in a local paper for a restaurant not far from our apartment. I emailed Phillip and let him know I was going to apply for the position. He replied, asking me to check on the details for the two tests he was having performed on Wednesday. I quickly obliged and reported back that, according to the doctor's office, the procedure would take less than two hours, and he would most likely feel well enough to return to work.

I went to the library to print out my resumé and was excited about the opportunity of landing a job as a sous chef at one of the area's many restaurants. It wasn't exactly what I wanted, but I thought about the need to take baby steps. It was a job that paid better than the other positions I'd looked at, and I loved the fact it was closer to home. It was a start.

MEANWHILE, in Alexandria, Kate and Jenny helped create a list of personal and business possessions that still remained there. Jenny helped price them for sale. I was reluctant to sell some items we had purchased for our former home in Blairstown but knew it was time to let them go. Since Hydro One in Canada was breathing down my neck for back utility payments, I needed the money.

I still had to deal with retrieving the things I'd left with my friend Maryanne up in St. Johnsville. I didn't see her often since her granddaughter no longer attended Sacred Heart. We exchanged calls and emails once in a while, but that became less frequent because she had sold her house and was busy organizing her move. Trying to make arrangements for me to retrieve the belongings allowed us to catch up, and I shared my news about what was happening with Phillip's health issues.

It all seemed like ages ago that I'd packed those things and stashed them at her house. I could barely recall what I brought there. I feared that if Phillip found out I'd removed items from our apartment, it could open old wounds. I was determined not to let that happen.

Chapter Twenty-Two

THE ANGUISH OF APRIL

April 8

P hillip's tests were scheduled for the morning. The facility was about an hour from home. We decided to take the kids with us because they would have no one to get them to and from school.

After we arrived at the testing facility and Phillip was checked in, I decided to take Jack and Lucy for breakfast at a diner close by. The nursing staff assured me that Phillip wouldn't be ready to go home for hours. I alerted one of the nurses that I was carrying Phillip's cellphone, asking them to call if, for any reason, I needed to come back.

I tried to appear nonchalant at the diner because I didn't want my deep concerns to register with Jack and Lucy. After we ordered our meals, they read books they brought along while I did a puzzle from a newspaper that someone left behind. Our meals were just delivered when I got a call from a nurse telling me I had to return immediately. As I paid for the food, my heart was in my throat, arguing with the waitress I didn't want the food to go.

All the way back to the facility, I feared the worst. I assumed they found something horrible during one of the procedures. By the time I arrived back, there was no hiding my anxiety as I rushed into the testing facility lobby. I waited for the kids to catch-up. At the desk, I was told, "We can release your husband once he wakes up from the sedation. When the results of his tests are in, they will be sent to his doctor." I pushed my anger aside, thinking they had alarmed me over nothing.

The Beans and I sat in the waiting area until Phillip was ready to be released. I sat there looking at the twins playing and talking quietly. Maybe it was the waiting that drove my thoughts to dark places. But now that the testing was done, the situation seemed far more serious. I kept trying to shove aside all the reasons I had to be concerned, convincing myself that the doctor would suggest some minor procedure and Phillip would mend in no time. After all, I reasoned, Phillip was an intelligent guy. I told myself he would never have let things get too far without addressing his health issues.

Before heading back home, Phillip wanted to get something to eat. The Beans were still hungry, too, so we headed for a Subway® in a nearby strip mall. We sat opposite one another, avoiding eye contact, as he methodically ate a turkey sub. I busied myself by fidgeting with the placemat that listed all the local businesses they recommended. By the time we left, I couldn't recall even one.

I CONVINCED Phillip to take the rest of the day off work as he didn't look well enough to focus on writing copy for one of his clients. For once, he agreed with me and called in sick once we got home.

He sat on the couch, dozing on and off. I called Jenny to occupy my time. She and Roberto had recently agreed to occupy the old tearoom since Glen had abandoned it shortly after renting the space. Their idea was to use the space for a joint venture selling antiques. Having them there to keep a watchful eye on the place gave me a sense of relief. They also agreed to sell some things that belonged to Phillip and me to help us out financially.

Jenny reminded me that even without test results, it was great that Phillip was following through on getting answers regarding his medical issues. Maybe after his health issues were addressed, he would be more like himself, she told me. Her positive spin acted as the antidote to the malaise that hovered over my heart that day. By the time we hung up, I was convinced I was just letting my imagination get the best of me.

Later that evening, I heard Phillip telling Rachel over the phone that all the way back in February, he had developed a small but persistent and progressive nodule in the area of the neck just above his collarbone. I began to wonder why he never said anything about this to me. I found myself wondering, *Were the tests he'd had that morning related to this issue?* Hearing him tell Rachel about his concerns raised my anxiety over the uncertainty of his condition. It didn't ease as the next few days passed without any news regarding the tests that were taken.

April 10

As I made breakfast that morning, I was beside myself that we still had no results from Phillip's tests on Friday. He was still asleep, and I decided not to wake him when breakfast was ready.

The phone rang a little while later, and I picked it up in the living room, hoping the noise wouldn't wake Phillip. As I brought the portable phone into the kitchen, I was glad it didn't seem to wake Phillip, and he remained asleep.

The call was from the human resources department of the resort I'd applied to, offering me a position as a sous chef in one of their many kitchens. We discussed some dates for training, and I offered to confirm my availability once I had a chance to discuss my proposed training schedule with Phillip.

It was hard to contain my excitement. As I returned to the living room to put the portable phone back on the charger, I almost knocked on the door to Jack's room to tell Phillip but chose to let him sleep instead because a part of me wanted to relish my good news alone.

As I cleared the dishes off the table, I decided to take a long shower. It was still my go-to thing to relax and have some time for myself. As the water washed over me, I smiled, thinking about the fact I would finally have some real money of my own. The frustration of always asking Phillip to buy or provide the funds for even the simplest of things, like groceries, gas, or other house-hold items, had fueled my anger. My new job would give me some of my independence back.

Knowing I'd have options allowed me to relax a bit. I knew that even if things remained the same in my marriage, they would stay that way because I chose that for myself. I wasn't just doing it because I was stuck in a quagmire. And if the marriage was over, I would have the resources to extricate myself and the Beans after the property in Alexandria was sold.

I had just finished rinsing my hair when I suddenly heard Lucy banging on the bathroom door.

"Daddy needs help," she shouted over the sound of the running water.

"I've been saying that for years," I thought sarcastically as she interrupted my moment of solitude.

"Tell Daddy I'll be right there, honey." I wanted to stay in my wet cocoon, but I shut off the water and toweled off.

When I went into the bedroom and saw Phillip's face, I felt guilty for making light of the situation. "Honey, what's wrong?" He looked pale and was clammy. "Do you want me to call an ambulance?"

"No. It's my neck. I'm in so much pain," he said through tears. "I might have pulled a muscle, but it feels worse than that. Can you take me to that walk-in clinic?" he pleaded.

"Of course!" I told him. I instructed the kids to get their Game Boys for the car, and we left a few minutes later.

As I drove Phillip to the urgent care clinic, I wish I could say that I was the model of compassion and grace. I was not. I wish I could say I focused solely on my husband's well-being. I did not.

No matter how many times I wished I'd risen above the negative impulses that sometimes consumed me, as we traveled to an urgent care facility nearby, I stewed. The words that came out of my mouth were in direct conflict with what I was thinking inside.

"It will be okay," I assured Phillip. "Once we get there, they'll give you something for the pain, and you'll be all right." What I kept thinking, however, was, "This is so typical. If it were me, he'd accuse me of faking it or tell me to just take a few Motrin®."

One of the major obstacles in our relationship was our invisible scorecard. I justified my thoughts with the recollections of the countless times I was hurt, ill, or emotionally bereft, and he would not offer me an ounce of compassion or sympathy. Even if I'd just spent days nursing him back to health, if I came down with the same cold or flu, anything Phillip did to help me was done begrudgingly.

However, this was not just in moments of illness. Whenever I needed a "favor" from him, Phillip would ask, "What are you going to give me for it?" While his words were always framed as a joke, he was serious. There was always a price tag attached before he was willing to do what I asked or needed unless it benefitted him somehow.

Almost more annoying was his need for one-upmanship whenever one of us was sick. If I had a headache, he had a migraine. If I had a cold, he had the flu. When I was diagnosed with carpal tunnel and needed surgery, he began wearing a wrist and hand brace, too. As I rushed him to urgent care, I relived the moments when he told me I was lazy. Even after the diagnosis and surgery were performed to remove the tumors on my parathyroid glands, he continued to insinuate my claims of exhaustion were just an excuse for tasks left undone. It was as if the surgery corrected the problem, and I was completely well again the following day. The concept of recovery seemed to be beyond his grasp. As I drove, the memory of this left me keeping score instead of sincerely being there for him. I convinced myself what was happening that day was purely Phillip. He probably just slept with his head in an awful position, I thought. Not once did I connect the dots to the tests he'd had that past Friday.

For an entire hour, we sat in the waiting area for his turn to be seen. Because I was convinced it was a minor problem, I was initially more concerned about how much time it took than about my husband's well-being. The Beans sat quietly in the corner, playing, while I sat close to Phillip, trying to contain my frustration.

However, after a while, it was difficult to watch him struggling to cope with the pain while they took others in to see a physician. Finally, I told him I'd be back in a minute, and I approached the nurse's station.

"Excuse me," I said to a petite young woman behind the desk. Her name tag read "Liz," but I called her "Miss," almost hissing the word. "I brought my husband in over an hour ago, and it seems like people that just came in recently are being seen ahead of him. He's in a lot of pain. Can you tell me what's going on?" She looked over her shoulder at another nurse who was standing a few feet away with a clipboard.

"His doctor is aware he is here, and they are consulting with him," she told me.

"What the bloody hell?" I said to myself as I returned to the waiting area. I wondered if that was the standard procedure. That didn't seem right, but I really didn't know how to express my concerns.

Ten minutes later, I was back at the nurse's station. "Is there anything you can give him, at least?" I inquired.

"That's why we called his doctor," she said politely and walked away.

A while later, they sent him home, loaded up on painkillers, and told us to return the following morning.

When we got home, Phillip went to sleep in the chair, so I checked my email. Jenny was having some issues identifying keys for the building, and I updated her on Phillip's condition. I told her I assumed the agony was caused by a pulled muscle or the awkward positions he slept to deal with the persistent stomach acid. I was horrified when I learned the actual reason Phillip was in so much pain.

April 11

Despite the heavy painkillers, Phillip called me into his room the following day and told me he felt worse. I decided that the kids would either miss part of or an entire day of school yet again. I was at a loss for what else to do. I had no idea how long we would be gone.

We piled into the car and went back to the clinic. The nurse I had spoken to the day before informed us Phillip's doctor, the one who had ordered the testing, wanted to see us. We were escorted through a series of corridors connected to the medical offices in another area of the complex.

Once we arrived at the doctor's office, Jack and Lucy made themselves comfortable in chairs in the almost empty waiting room. They huddled close together for support, looking at me nervously. I tried my best to assure them everything would be okay, even though the pit of my stomach was doing flip-flops.

Phillip held his neck stiffly as he sat down. He almost seemed relaxed. I wondered if that was because the medication had finally eased his pain. I stood, unable to remain calm enough to take a seat. I was bracing myself for what the doctor had to say.

He began, "I have some unpleasant news." Phillip and I exchanged a look.

"I'm sorry it took so long to get back to you, but we needed to make sure of the results. In reviewing the images, we found hundreds of small white masses. The needle biopsy is consistent with adenocarcinoma, which is a type of cancerous tumor. The endoscopy revealed lesions that extend all the way down to your gastric body. A large mass could be the cause of the pain you're experiencing. We found that it is dangerously close to your spinal cord. The only way to know, with absolute certainty, what we're dealing with is to do further testing. At this point, I would advise you to check into the hospital immediately so they can conduct more tests. I've reached out to an oncologist on your behalf, and he will order additional tests. I am so sorry to be telling you this," he said, handing me some paperwork.

Phillip remained composed, while I couldn't say anything that wouldn't lead to falling apart. "Is there any chance that it's something other than cancer?" Phillip asked him.

"I wouldn't count on it," the doctor replied, shaking his head. We left his office in a daze.

I drove to the hospital in silence. What was there to say? I couldn't trust myself to speak. I was bombarded with the widest array of emotions I'd ever experienced. The guilt of my private thoughts haunted me. The magnitude of this diagnosis was devastating. And yet, I was so angry at Phillip. Why had he waited to get treatment? Now he was gravely ill. I realized it was time to put away the scorecard. I put those thoughts to the back of my mind and had the good sense to know that whatever I was dealing with regarding our fractured relationship meant nothing at this point.

Chapter Twenty-Three

ST. JOE'S

As we headed west to the hospital, I couldn't imagine life moving forward. It was as if everything had come to a grinding halt, and we were caught in some sort of time warp to allow us entry into a hidden dimension. When we arrived, the sound of the receptionist's voice was muffled and distorted. The lights were too bright, and I wanted to squint. I moved my arms and legs, my eyes and mouth, but they did not feel like they were a part of me. Then Lucy reached out and grabbed my hand as we rode the elevator up to the floors above, and I was once again grounded in the moment. The Beans needed me, and I had to be strong for them.

When we arrived on the floor where we had been instructed to go, a nurse escorted Phillip to some unknown destination. I could feel the urgency now. I wanted to go with him, but I didn't want to leave the kids behind. I wasn't even sure where they had taken him or even if they would have let me accompany him. Instead, I allowed myself to be led to the hospital room they'd assigned to him.

The Beans and I walked into a sea of blue: light blue walls, blue vinyl floor, striped blue curtains, navy blue visitor's chair. There was a laminated oak bedside table and a TV mounted high on the wall. I looked for the remote, so I could turn on the TV, hoping to take our minds off of what was happening.

The curtain was drawn, dividing the room. There was snoring on the other side. I didn't know what to say or how to act. I kept thinking, *"What am I going to tell Phillip's parents and sister?"*

I flipped around the channels, looking for anything the kids might like to watch. I settled on the Animal Planet channel, airing reruns of *The Crocodile Hunter*. They shared the navy-blue visitor's chair and watched the episode with rapt attention.

When the nurses wheeled Phillip into the room, it hit me. This was real. He wasn't coming home with us tonight. I waited while the nurses helped him settle in, then retreated into the bathroom to wipe away tears I couldn't contain. We stayed all day, eating dinner in the cafeteria, playing cards, and watching too much TV. The news programs were never so interesting.

We were told they planned to conduct more tests later in the evening, followed by another battery of tests the following day. However, based on what they knew from the tests conducted earlier, Phillip had esophageal cancer. A CT scan of his neck showed a large calcified mass. An MRI revealed multiple enlarged lymph nodes, and there was a pathological compression fracture of his C7 vertebra with an approximate 30% compression. They started him on steroids and morphine immediately.

I could barely keep up with the medical jargon. Phillip wrote copy for pharmaceutical clients for years. He had to explain most of what was being said. It seemed cruel to make Phillip go into depth about how this disease had infiltrated his body and was consuming his life. But, I wanted to know as much as possible about his condition because, later on, I would have to tell others about the gravity of his illness. I took notes, hoping it would help me keep things straight as if somehow, getting the information right would improve his chances of survival.

In the morning, they would be doing more ultrasounds and X-rays, something called an esophagram, and an EGD, along with some other tests I didn't have time to write down. Until they were done, we didn't know the exact extent of his illness —we knew it was cancer but not the prognosis.

I had to get back to Cobleskill at some point. Chubby was at home and hadn't been walked all day. I also had to bring Phillip his belongings because he only had the clothes he had been wearing. The only thing he brought with him to the hospital was his work laptop since he'd taken that with him for some reason.

"I guess I should let Barry know and try to wrap up my work," he said as I was about to leave.

I leaned over and kissed his cheek, trying to avoid breaking down. This was purely Phillip, I thought. He's facing a major health crisis, and he's still worried about his job.

Phillip asked me to call his sister when the twins and I returned to Cobleskill. Knowing all the negative things he'd been telling her about me made it difficult to imagine how she would receive the news coming from me. From this point on, I knew I just had to suck it up because it wasn't the time to focus on our marital problems. We were all officially trying to save a life.

Chubby greeted us at the door when we arrived back in Cobleskill. I'm sure if he could have, he would have been crossing his legs. "Hey, guys. Can you walk Chub and then feed both Chubby and the cats? Just take him over to the bushes. I'm going to go upstairs so I can call Auntie Rachel."

I sat on the bed, staring at the small notepad where I had scribbled all the notes I had taken earlier. None of it made sense. I put it on the nightstand, grabbed the portable phone, and then got a long-distance phone card I kept in my wallet. The card's number was a bazillion digits long. However, I opted to use it because my laptop's power cord was worse and barely held a charge.

I kept entering the card numbers wrong. I couldn't see through my tears.

"Damn it!" By the time I finally entered all the numbers in the correct sequence, I was frazzled. When the call went through, Dennis and Rachel's answering machine picked up.

"Hi. It's Kasey. I just got back from the hospital. Phillip has cancer. It's bad. Call me when you get this message," I blurted out. I hung up the phone as if an electric shock had passed through the lines. *What did I just do?* I screamed in my head. *How could I have left such a message on her answering machine? What a dope!* I felt horrible. I sulked into the living room, where Jack and Lucy sat on the couch with Chubby, and collapsed in tears. They both snuggled close and hugged me. Chubby climbed onto my lap. I let the tears flow because there was no reason to stop them.

When I finally calmed down, I made everyone a snack. I tried to think of something we could do other than just watch more television, so I grabbed a book I'd given the twins for their birthday. The title of the book was *Kasey to the Rescue*. The picture on the cover was of a handsome young man with a blazing smile and a small Capuchin monkey on his shoulder. When I had looked closer at the book in the store, I realized that the author, Ellen Rogers, and I had the same last name. Ellen wrote the book, a memoir, about her quest to get help for her 22-year-old son Ned after a devastating car accident in June of 2005. Lucy, Jack, and I needed to hear about miracles, and Ellen's story was about all the obstacles she had to overcome to get Ned back East for treatment. Their story was the inspiration we needed. I had no idea then how much of a role this book would play in our lives in a few short months.

Regardless of the fact they were both excellent readers, we often snuggled on the couch, and Phillip or I would read out loud to them. When they were little, we went from the *Trumpet and the Swan* to *Watership Down* and, later, to *Harry Potter and the Sorcerer's Stone*. We journeyed from chapter book to chapter book, one evening after another. It was one of my fondest memories from their childhood. I loved reading *The Pokey Little Puppy* or *Good Night Moon;* however, when we still lived in New Jersey, it was the longer pieces that left us snuggled in the oversized chair in their room for hours, and we savored each moment.

I had just started to read when the phone rang. It was Rachel. Given my abrupt voicemail message, she was much more gracious than I would have been as I related what we'd learned at the hospital regarding Phillip's test results. Rachel would have me pause every so often to convey the information to her husband Dennis, who was listening in the background. They were both willing to do whatever they could to help. When I got off the phone, I felt a bit of hope.

Shortly after I hung up with Rachel, the phone rang again. This time, it was a doctor who Barry, Phillip's boss, had reached out to on Phillip's behalf. He guided me through the various questions I needed to ask tomorrow regarding Phillip's treatment plan. Since Phillip was in no shape to advocate for himself, I needed to be there to speak for him.

The kids were back on their Game Boys by the time I hung up with the doctor. I suggested they get into their PJs, and we could continue reading upstairs. I offered to prepare some hot chocolate while they got dressed. We continued our reading on my bed and, before I knew it, they'd both fallen asleep. I put the book down and closed my eyes, too.

I heard Chubby scratching at the door downstairs and got out of bed to take him out. I walked down the steps to the first floor as quietly as possible to avoid waking the twins. I slipped on my jacket and went outside with Chubby.

The night air was warm but refreshing. Chub peed and used his back legs to lift the dirt, scattering his scent behind him. With a wagging tail, he looked up at me, signaling he had completed his mission, and I brought him back into the apartment.

He made himself comfortable under the table while I fixed myself a cup of tea. I was too awake to go back to bed, and the night was calling me to immerse myself in something that would take my mind off the events of the day. As was my habit, I decided to bake.

I searched through the kitchen and saw I had everything needed to make some banana bread. It was a recipe I knew by heart, so I went to work assembling the ingredients and placing them on the counter.

COOKING AND BAKING were my go-to things whenever life got too complicated. It eased my mind to have a sense of purpose. Rolling out dough for a pie or watching the butter brown when I made a roux calmed me, allowing me to focus on a task that was within reach rather than trying to fix something that was beyond my control.

Phillip never seemed to understand my love for cooking and baking. This led to many petty arguments after we married. Our upbringings were so different. I grew up with seven siblings and learned to cook at my mother's knees. There were always big family meals, or gatherings of relatives or friends, around the table or the backyard fire-pit. My dad and his buddies would play their guitars and sing. The kids would play tag or hide-and-seek. It was something that happened at least once or twice a week during the summer.

While there were many family events in Phillip's family, he never connected my love of preparing food with my family's traditions. Phillip thought (and often expressed this verbally) that taking the time to make food from scratch was pointless when you could save time by purchasing it already made or partially prepared.

Phillip tried to eat well, but more often than not, he settled for convenience. His hectic work schedule left him eating at drive-through windows and pizza joints. For years, his thrifty nature had him opting for canned or frozen meals over freshly prepared foods. When the Beans were born, and Phillip began working full time, he set a food budget of a hundred dollars a week for four. It wasn't until I broke down the cost of items and showed him what our regular grocery bill was that he loosened the purse strings so I could buy most of what I was accustomed to feeding our small family. Since moving to Cobleskill, he was once again in control of buying groceries, and fresh foods and produce were often ignored in favor of cheaper processed foods.

Despite his complaints, he always seemed to enjoy the end results of my cooking or baking. It was the time and expense it took that he resented. He had a totally different perception of the value of food. After a while, it finally occurred to me that it was also a way he could control my time and energy.

I put the loaf pan in the oven. It would take an hour to bake. I couldn't just sit there, thinking, so I got out some yeast to check the expiration date and, since it was still good, I made some bread dough. I got out my large mixing bowl and measured the ingredients, thinking about all the times a loaf of fresh bread had come out of my oven. I didn't get back to sleep until about 5 a.m.

When my alarm went off at seven, I fired off an email to Tammy at Sacred Heart about the kids being absent from school again and explained what was happening with Phillip. Typing out the words made it more real, and I started to cry.

I needed more sleep but knew it would be impossible, so I got up instead. I woke the Beans and told them to shower and get ready to go. I packed some drinks and snacks and put some plastic wrap around the banana bread to bring to the hospital in case Phillip was able to eat some. I hoped the small loaf would express my love.

Chapter Twenty-Four

ERASING THE TALLY LINES

B y the time the Beans and I arrived at the hospital, it was mid-morning. Phillip wasn't in his room when we arrived; however, I was told he would be back shortly. While waiting for him, I tried reading Phillip's medical report. Even with my limited understanding of medical terminology, I knew the news was grim.

The report read, "The gastric tumor showed a glandular pattern, with a locally cribriforming pattern, and other areas of an irregular, invasive glandular pattern. The tumor cells show a moderate degree of atypia and some areas of abnormal mitosis. In the esophageal tumor biopsies, there appears to be a relatively greater volume of the tumor, with this adenocarcinoma under-mining intact benign squamous epithelium in some areas. One fragment shows the tumor cells to show mucin production, with individual "signet-ring" tumor cells invading through the stroma. This is indicative of a high-grade adenocarcinoma. The tumor may have started in the esophagus, given the greater volume of tumor noted in this location."

Phillip was wheeled back to the room as I was reading. After he was settled in, I asked him for a translation so I could relate the information as accurately as possible to his family. I tried to write everything down. As difficult as it was to keep up, it was more painful to know that these terms would explain why he was dying.

He then asked me to send out emails on his behalf to clients he was freelancing for on the side. I powered-up his work laptop and thought about the irony that he was now giving me his email passwords. I typed as he dictated a brief note, letting them know the situation.

"Hi guys,

My biopsy came back this morning as being cancerous, so my life just got more complicated. They found another mass in the esophagus and stomach. That said, until I know more, I will be unavailable for any more freelance work. The docs are presenting options tomorrow, etc. I am in the hospital so Kasey is going to be handling any loose ends. (EG, I have invoices that I still need to send your way, etc.). Please keep good thoughts and prayers coming my way. Many thanks again for all your previous good thoughts, prayers, and the card. I will try to keep you posted when I can."

Once I emailed everyone, I put down the laptop and made an excuse to leave the room so Phillip wouldn't see me cry.

THE RESULTS of some of the testing didn't come back until late afternoon. The expression on the doctor's face when he came into the room indicated he would be delivering more dreadful news.

"The cancer isn't your only problem, I'm afraid. The fragility of your neck is quite serious. Further tests have revealed the extent of the damage. An MRI of the cervical spine showed a destructive lesion involving the C7 vertebral body extending into the epidural faccia. While there is no evidence of spinal compression, the bone scan we performed demonstrates abnormal activity near the left thoracic inlet that probably involves the rib. What I'm trying to tell you, Phillip, is that you've been walking around with a broken neck."

As he continued to speak, I wanted to throw up. He explained that a sneeze, a fall, or a sudden movement could sever Phillip's spinal cord, leaving him unable to breathe. While I sat, listening to the doctor tell us this, all I could think about were the times recently that Phillip had been out jogging.

We also learned that his team of doctors felt Phillip's neck was so fragile that they couldn't release him. The conundrum was, St. Joe's specialized in cardiac care. There was only one part-time oncologist on staff, and he told us Phillip should be moved to a hospital that specialized in the treatment of cancer. However, the question was, how would we get him there? Consulting with his colleagues, they felt it would be best for Phillip to be seen by a doctor at Massachusetts General Hospital in Boston. But, for the moment, they wouldn't release him until something could be done to stabilize his neck.

After I contacted Rachel with the latest news, she graciously offered to let us move into her finished basement in her home in Marblehead, Massachusetts, about an hour north of Boston. I reached out to one of the doctors that came highly recommended and waited to hear if she would consider taking Phillip's case.

Phillip's parents and sister still lived in the same town where he grew up. It was the place we visited for holidays and other family events. I was reluctant to move yet again, but our options were limited. Phillip's doctor made a couple of phone calls on our behalf. Once we were given the green light for him to be released from the hospital, we planned on traveling to Marblehead, hoping the proximity to Boston would offer more treatment opinions.

While there were benefits to moving back to Massachusetts, there were problems, as well. On the plus side, the Beans weren't adjusting to Cobleskill and Sacred Heart. As lovely as the people were there, the twins felt alienated. The plan to get them transferred to the Cobleskill public school system was on hold. At least Marblehead would be familiar to them. They had a cousin their age, so Phillip and I thought it might make for an easier transition. In the past, Lucy, in particular, seemed to have difficulties transitioning to new situations. However, it was now apparent it was also challenging for Jack. This was one reason we'd always kept the kids in smaller schools like Sacred Heart. I hoped that if they attended a public school for eighth grade, they would get more of the help they needed.

My sister-in-law was the principal at an elementary school in Marblehead too, and that could help us navigate the system and help them catch up on all the work they'd missed. She was also fantastic with the kids. They loved their fun, Auntie Rachel. Without a doubt, it would be so much easier for them to be surrounded by family.

Something else I had to consider was the reality that moving into my sister-in-law's home would be an enormous adjustment. It would be the first time I would be living under the same roof with other adults since I left my parent's home decades ago. In our twenty-five years together, Phillip and I had always lived far from his parents and sister. He liked the independence that distance brought him.

But at the heart of my concern was the fact that when we visited his family in Marblehead, Phillip had a way of making me feel like an outsider. There was a noticeable shift in his attitude. After our visits, he often became highly critical of either the twins or me. He not only implied that the twins and I didn't measure up to whatever ideal he had of a family unit, he told me without reservation that his parents and sister should be the model for the family he and I had created.

Recalling these instances, I struggled to figure out how I would preserve my renewed sense of self while doing what I felt was right for the sake of the man I had married. I knew the challenge would be to balance what was in our mutual best interests without allowing Phillip to exploit my insecurities. I was determined to remain vigilant and guard myself and the twins regardless of whatever I might face. Despite my fears, I agreed to move to Marblehead because, in the end, it was the right thing to do.

Chapter Twenty-Five

MORE BAD NEWS

The next day, they gave us even more dire news when his doctor told us Phillip's cancer had progressed to the state where he might only have a few weeks to live.

"The cancer has spread too far for treatment options, and given the complication of Phillip's neck injury, there is little we can do," Phillip's doctor explained. "Since I know you've contacted a physician at Mass General, I've consulted with a neurosurgeon specialist about how to deal with transporting Phillip, considering the severity of his neck injury. The only way to prevent further injury is to provide him with a specially constructed device called an Aspen® Collar before they can release him from the hospital."

I nodded my head when he finished, holding my emotions in check. I asked all the questions I'd written down the night before about the treatment options.

"The bottom line is, none of those options are viable considering the extent of Phillip's cancer and the fragility of his neck," his doctor responded. "Your best option is to wait for the Aspen Collar and see about having him transported to Boston by ambulance." He walked over to Phillip, who was listening intently and rubbed his arm. As he started to leave the room, he turned to us briefly.

"I wish you both the best of luck." I wondered if he wanted to add, "you're going to need it."

WHILE WE WAITED for the specially constructed device to arrive, the kids and I traveled to the hospital to visit Phillip over the next few days. It made no sense to have them in school, anxiously wondering if he would be alive when they got out. For the first time in years, the Beans were spending almost entire days with Phillip. Watching them huddled together by his bedside helped me set aside all the troubling issues we had in our marriage. It didn't erase them. It didn't change what had happened. It just allowed me to put everything into perspective. The three things that mattered most were right in front of me.

I scoured the Internet for information about his disease when Phillip was out of the room for additional tests. When he returned, Phillip wanted to reach out to his best friend, Kevin. Phillip knew Kevin from their high school days. Kevin was a very gentle man with a kind of quiet grace, a quick wit, and an easy-going demeanor. His intelligence was apparent to anyone who spoke with him, and yet, he never seemed snobbish or overbearing. Over the years, the two friends stayed in touch and swapped stories of all their teenage years' mischief. I'd always liked Kevin and especially enjoyed his wife, Stephanie.

Unable to move his neck, he asked me to send an email that he dictated.

> "Hello, my friend,
>
> As has been the course of my life for the past few years, I have some more bad news.
>
> I have been diagnosed with esophageal cancer and, unfortunately, it has spread to the point where I'm told it's incurable. I don't know how much time I have left. I haven't asked, and don't want to know just yet. I've

always been a very deadline-oriented individual (now there's a pun) but this is one date that I'd rather not rush toward.

I'm currently at St Joseph's Hospital in Albany, but I am being transferred to Mass General. The staff here at St. Joe's are great, but their specialty isn't oncology. Kasey and my family think there's hope for a miracle at Mass Gen. Also, there is little to no support system here in Albany. The many perils of constantly moving for work is not making many solid emotional connections. Most of our family and friends are back in Massachusetts so, like a salmon, I'm coming back home.

As I am quickly realizing, dying is not an experience shared by those around you. I had a nice chat with a Franciscan nun here about the topic of hope, which is shared by all those involved in stories like this. You know I'm a born pessimist so you know how long a stretch this is for me. While my docs here agree that Boston is better for treatment, they believe there's no missing the final "deadline." My brother-in-law Dennis has connections that lead to the Head of Oncology so they are hoping to grease the skids, getting me in there ASAP. I might be transported by ambulance later today. (Contingent upon my insurance company's decision.) One of my cancer complications is that there is a tumor near my upper spine that is touching the spinal cord. The fear is that a bad road bump or fender bender could also leave me paralyzed from the neck down, so immobilizing me till I can get the tumor shrunk, or cut out, should save me from that threat.

I'd like to see you when I'm back. I will have a lot of check-in protocols and other procedures when I first arrive so I don't know what my "schedule" will be like over the next few days. The spinal issue and nutrition issue (some sort of feeding tube) have to be addressed immediately so I may not be available much. But, hopefully, beyond that, I have some quality time. Either I or Kasey will be in touch.

Love you, man. ~ Phillip"

As I typed the words he dictated, I erased all the uneven tallies on my invisible scorecard. Later, while Phillip dozed in the bed beside me, I vowed to reconcile the past and present. I knew one day, I would have to look back at thes moments, I needed to know that I had risen above all the dysfunction of our fractured relationship. I knew I wasn't always easy to live with and that I'd contributed to some of the problems I reeled against. But there were two separate issues here, and I had to be mindful of that to get through our ordeal.

All marriages have to work through a set of dynamics to create a successful partnership. I'd read book after book early on, trying to master the essential elements of a good marriage. Things like communicating, having trust, respecting boundaries, etc., were all fundamental. For a short period, after I'd left him, he appeared willing to confront his part of our problems. I wanted to believe he would continue to be respectful. But knowing our past, I had to be vigilant about making sure that I didn't allow his illness to become an excuse for his mistreatment.

Guilt is for the guilty. I was not responsible for Phillip's cancer, and I couldn't allow my sympathy for him to pardon his poor conduct. I acknowledged that I had to work to get past the grief I still carried over losing myself and not allow self-doubt to creep into my soul. I needed to care for myself the same way I cared for others. I promised myself not to want less for myself than I wanted for him. What I wanted was for him to know I loved him. But I needed to love myself, too.

I started by mentally listing all the positive things about Phillip and highlighted those things instead of focusing on the past. I recalled some of our favorite times together. Our trip to Tombstone, Arizona; our passion for scary movies; the way we both laughed at *Calvin and Hobbes*; silly things that defined us. Phillip and Kasey. Kasey and Phillip. What made us a couple? I looked over at the Beans, who were now reading. It wasn't hard to find.

I SPENT every moment of those horrible days trying to find ways to help him through this horrendous experience. The only reason I left at all was to walk Chubby and feed him and the cats. Each time I left the hospital, I could barely breathe. I tried to learn as much as I could about his disease because knowing what we were facing helped. I bought used books about ways to boost the immune system, grasping for any hope offered.

As we stared into the abyss that first week after the diagnosis, I was full of bitterness over a system that seemed to work against us when every moment mattered. Every answer the doctors gave us about transporting Phillip to Boston seemed to be in the context of the cost to either the hospital or the insurance company. Even after the Aspen Collar arrived and Phillip was using it, the hospital hesitated to release him.

I was beside myself with rage. It was now directed at the people that prevented us from getting the help Phillip so desperately needed. I told the nurse at the desk I'd arranged for an oncologist to see Phillip at Mass General, one that specialized in the very type of cancer Phillip had. I was told that Phillip could only be released after the hospital got the insurance company's approval. I wanted to shout, "This is his life, you ass-wads!" Instead, I threatened to call the press if they didn't let him go.

"You realize no one can come up here on this ward without passing security?" she scoffed. She'd called my bluff. I felt hopeless.

The next day, I was determined to somehow resolve this situation. Shortly after I arrived, I told Phillip and the kids I would be at the nurse's station until I received news regarding his discharge.

"I understand you're both eager to leave, but our insurance company has instructed us that we have to get approval from his provider to pay for the ambulance to transport him," the first nurse I spoke to told me impatiently.

"I get it," I told her. "His insurance company doesn't want to pay for it. They're happy to take his premium payments each month, but, hey, let's not go wild and cover the cost of an ambulance for a guy with a broken neck," I vented.

She looked at me with a withering smile.

"I'll let you know as soon as we hear back."

"I'm not leaving this desk until I get an answer. I know you're just doing your job, but my husband has so little time, and I'm not wasting the only chance he has while some penny-pinching bureaucrat keeps us waiting. I'll sit right here and wait, thank you."

She turned her back and continued speaking with whoever was on the other end of the phone. I wanted to scream, but I was afraid I'd never stop.

While I sat there, I tried to remain calm because getting worked up wasn't helping. Finally, the nurse gently told me she'd have an answer by noon, and she would come and tell me when she heard back. I had to use the bathroom, so I agreed and practically ran down the hall.

When I got back to his room, I offered everyone some goodies I'd baked, and even Phillip could enjoy some. The Beans and I sat side-by-side next to his bed, and we took turns telling them stories about our funny adventures before they were born. They often asked Phillip to tell them about our cat, Squirt. It was one of their favorite stories.

"Mommy and I rented an apartment in Blairstown before we bought our old house. It was in the same neighborhood, just a few blocks over. One day, when Mommy was taking a walk, she found a little gray kitten. He was about twelve weeks old. We already had Boo Boo Kitty, our Maine coon cat, so we didn't want another," he explained. "Your mom and I put up flyers, trying to find his owner, but no one called us so, finally, we placed an ad for a "free kitten" in the paper. Someone came and got him, but they brought him back later that day because their son thought he was too old. So we kept him," Phillip told them. As often as they had heard the story, they leaned forward to hear more.

"Mommy was gone early in the morning and didn't come home until late at night, so Squirt became my pal. He used to sit on my keyboard when I was trying to work, and every time the phone rang, he jumped at it. At night, he'd bite my toes, and, sometimes, I'd find pencils from my desk on the floor next to my bed. And whenever I had to go out, Mommy said Squirt would somehow find one of my socks and drag it from one end of the hallway to the other, meowing," Their favorite part was still to come. "Sometimes, I'd tease Squirt by blowing into a bottle. He hated the noise," Phillip continued. "After I did this, Squirt would wait for me at the far end of the upstairs hallway banister and, when I'd walk up the stairs, Squirt would hit me in the head and run away!"

No matter how often he told the Beans about Squirt, they always laughed, imagining our silly cat's antics. But as I sat, hearing him regale the twins with Squirt stories, I had to leave the room. Memories of our sweet, funny cat were filled with both joy and sadness. While I was pregnant with the twins, we discovered a lump on his back. The vet diagnosed him with cancer. For months, we took him into Manhattan for treatment at the finest veterinary clinic in New York City, but he ultimately succumbed. I had to wonder if Phillip was thinking about that, too.

Finally, a little after noon, the case manager came to his room to deliver the news. The hospital agreed he could leave. However, the insurance company refused to spring for an ambulance.

"You're free to leave," she told us, "as long as you agree to sign the papers releasing the insurance company of any liability should anything happen because of his neck injury." The stack of papers must have been a half-an-inch thick. There would be no ambulance. Instead, after we returned to Cobleskill, I would have to drive him to his sister's home in Marblehead.

By three that afternoon, I had my family in the car, and we headed back home for the evening. I could feel my heart in my throat each mile I drove. Our apartment was a long forty-five minutes away. I wasn't sure how the hell I would make it, driving him, the kids, our dog, and three cats all the way to Marblehead, let alone get him into Boston. But I was going to try.

Chapter Twenty-Six

BACK TO MASSACHUSETTS

Phillip's appointment with the oncologist at Mass General was the morning of April 18th. Upon arrival, I pulled into the Fruit Street garage, one of the hospital's many parking structures. Phillip and I exited the building at street level.

We could see the Massachusetts General Hospital building directly in front of us, clearly identified with large metal lettering. It was framed by two other buildings—the steel and glass Lunder Building on the left and the red brick Wang Building on the right. There was an expanse of concrete between the three structures that could easily be navigated by foot if one walked straight ahead. The horseshoe-shaped area was large enough for several cars or ambulances. Visible from where we stood was a sign pointing to the emergency room entrance and patient Drop-off area.

Even with Phillip's slowed gait, we could have walked the approximate two hundred yards to the revolving entrance door within a few minutes. However, after reviewing the medical records forwarded by the hospital in Albany, Phillip's new oncologist, Dr. Allison, was deeply concerned for her new patient's safety and instructed us to call her office when we arrived. After calling, we were told to wait where we stood by the garage and that Phillip would be escorted to the emergency room.

Soon, an ambulance pulled up. A three-person EMT crew unloaded a stretcher and approached Phillip and me. He explained to them he could not lay down on a gurney. Apparently, no one told them before they arrived what they were dealing with regarding the fragility of Phillip's neck. They were at a loss for what to do. They moved out of earshot to discuss options while Phillip and I stood there waiting.

They decided to use a type of gurney that would allow Phillip to sit up and planned to carry him to the hospital. After further discussion, however, they determined it would jostle him too much. We stood there waiting.

One of the three attendants called a manager expressing concern about their liability if something tragic happened while they transported Phillip. A return call from someone higher in management was expected any time now, they assured us, while we stood there waiting. Almost an hour passed. After numerous phone calls were exchanged and after much deliberation, they ended up surrounding Phillip on all sides and walked him into the emergency room. Our introduction to Mass General left me with a sinking feeling.

DR. ALLISON WAS right to be concerned. The fracture of Phillip's neck made his care more complicated. She wanted the Emergency Department to further evaluate the fracture. We weren't there long before they whisked him away to review the situation while I stayed there waiting.

After Phillip was seen, they admitted him. We already knew that the severity of his condition warranted being hospitalized. We were also aware that the extent of his cancer meant they would not offer him surgery or a procedure called kyphoplasty, which would stabilize the bone. They offered him a feeding tube, but Phillip opted not to have it implanted since he still had some ability to swallow and wanted to enjoy the simple pleasure of eating. This was how Phillip began his journey as a 52-year-old male with metastatic gastroesophageal carcinoma.

I TRAVELED from Marblehead to Boston daily. When I arrived, Phillip eagerly reported everything that had happened during my absence. These interactions made me believe we were moving past some of our marital conflicts, and I listened patiently to everything he recounted about what he experienced.

As I sat on a chair next to Phillip's bed, he began describing an incident that had occurred after I had left the day before, relating the details of being seen by a herd of physicians with various specialties.

"So, you missed all the drama after you left yesterday," he said.

"Why? What happened?" I asked.

"There was some confusion when they conducted the procedure," he told me.

"Honey, which procedure are you talking about? You've had so many of them," I asked, growing more concerned.

"They were supposed to put in a port, but they put in a PICC line instead," he told me.

"What's the difference again?" I asked, keeping my voice in check.

"PICC's an acronym for a "peripherally inserted central catheter." It's different from a port, which is a small medical device placed beneath the skin. They wanted me to have a port before I get chemo, but, somehow, they initially put in a PICC."

"So, how did this get messed up?" I said, trying not to sound alarmed.

"I'm not really sure, but you should have seen all the doctors here consulting with my primary team of physicians. They decided to go ahead and put in the port anyway, but then they put it in the wrong place," Phillip explained. "I heard them talking to Dr. Allison, and they said that a chest X-ray showed that the line terminated in the right atrium. One of the doctors they consulted with recommended that they 'pull it back' to make it end at the Cavo atrial junction, but someone else advised her that was too risky."

I was silently seething as Phillip concluded by telling me that there was now a potential risk of arrhythmia or infection if they tried to adjust the port or replace it. Deep inside, I was equally irate that every term rolled off his tongue in a way that informed me he was cognizant of so much about his medical condition, yet he had waited so long to seek treatment. I shoved these thoughts aside and continued to listen.

"I had them leave it in place," Phillip told me with a bit of recrimination in his voice. "The vascular interventional radiologist assured my primary care team that the PICC was okay to use, so they'll just use that for the chemo instead," he finished.

I didn't know how to respond. I nodded to show I shared his concern about all that was happening to him, even though much of it was over my head. As Phillip continued to relate the situation to me, I felt like I was underwater and knew someone was talking but couldn't make out what was being said.

"Well, I'm glad they could resolve things," I told him, hoping I'd struck the right tone. When he remained silent, I checked to make sure he hadn't fallen asleep and saw he was awake. After a few moments of silence, I began telling him about what was happening back in Marblehead. As I related how the rest of the family was doing, I held his hand and tried to quell the dueling emotions raging inside me.

Within days of being admitted to Mass General, Phillip developed a deep cough. This was alarming because it could further injure his neck. They gave him a drug called Levaquin to relieve the irritation that caused his modulated voice to become thick and hoarse. A side effect of taking the medication gave him nausea and diarrhea, which left him unable to eat. Being unable to eat left him weak. His health was falling apart.

LIFE BEYOND MASS GENERAL had to go on. The world does not grind to a halt over these types of diagnoses, and a great deal is expected of both the patient and their families. Beyond Phillip, my most immediate concerns were getting the kids into school and traveling back to Cobleskill, mainly because we'd ended up leaving the cats behind with multiple bowls of food and water and extra litter boxes.

My Aunt Lil had agreed to take our two older cats while the kitten would be coming to Marblehead with us. The anxiety of leaving Phillip during this time was almost too much to bear. I didn't want to be that far away but had no choice as I had to tie up all the loose ends, both in Cobleskill and Alexandria.

Phillip's palliative care social worker called me while I was in New York. I was overjoyed to have someone to speak to about what was taking place, who understood how to traverse the insurance and healthcare systems. I was learning first-hand that navigating any type of catastrophic illness or injury was like picking through the wreckage of a house after a tornado. There are bits and pieces of a life previously lived that you're trying to salvage, but you can't find all the fragments.

I told him I was trying to figure out how we would survive financially, as Phillip would get his last paycheck at the end of April. Our financial realities were bleak since we had canceled our life insurance policies back when Phillip lost his job in 2005. When things got more financially stable, he balked at taking out new policies.

"I don't want you profiting from my death," he joked.

I didn't find it funny back then, and I certainly resented that decision now. But there was no way I could go back and change things, so I had to live with the knowledge that I was facing some real financial difficulties even if I sold the building in Canada. The social worker told me he could connect me with someone knowledgeable about the questions I had. He also informed me that Phillip would also be eligible for social security disability, something I wasn't aware of previously.

While I was only gone for two days, I was so relieved when I could once again travel to Boston to visit Phillip. I saw that he was doing better and was in an excellent mood. I attributed this to visits from Rachel and his best friend Kevin while I was away. Having access to his family and friends seemed to make a tremendous difference in his outlook.

Even when he discussed his health issues, it seemed more about his irritation than his overall condition.

"My biggest concern is I'm having trouble sleeping," he told me. "My mind is always racing. It makes it hard to get enough sleep. I wish they would let me take off this damn thing," he said, trying to scratch under his Aspen collar. "My doctor is only letting them take it off when I'm being bathed, but that only gives me a few minutes of relief each day," he moaned.

I got out of the chair and stood behind him. Using my nails, I scratched his neck under the collar as gently as I could.

"I feel imprisoned by this fucking device," he groused as I scratched.

While the brace kept his neck isolated, I knew it must be terribly uncomfortable. I kissed the top of his head and reached further down his back to scratch, hoping to ease his discomfort the only way I knew how.

Chapter Twenty-Seven

HOPE FOR THE HOPELESS

During my next visit, Phillip discussed his condition and treatment options with his oncologist. I heard him tell her what he had told Kevin in an email: "I don't want to deal with specific time frames regarding the prognosis of my condition. I'm used to working with deadlines," he joked with her. "This is one deadline I don't mind missing."

Someone coming in to check his vital signs interrupted their conversation, so I asked his doctor if I could speak with her in the solarium, which was a short distance from his room.

"I know Phillip doesn't want to be told if the chemo and radiation will improve his chances, but I do," I blurted out. She looked at me through thick glasses, and in a calm and slightly condescending manner, told me, "There is less than a 5% chance it will be effective. He is a Stage 4B cancer patient. There is only the slightest hope it will help. He has months, not years, to live. But we have to do as he requests. If he chooses to have the chemo and radiation, we'll honor his wishes."

I didn't know what to say. I believed Phillip needed to spend time with his family and his friends. I wanted to tell her that every moment he had remaining should be filled with joy and doing things that reminded him of how much we love him. I felt like asking how much money the hospital would make treating a man who was a "Stage 4B cancer patient," using air quotes and getting right up in her face. I didn't say any of this because I had to support him, even if I disagreed with his decision. I nodded, unable to say what I was thinking.

THAT SAME DAY, I met with Phillip's social worker in person. He came to visit Phillip when someone from the brace department arrived to see about making some adjustments to Phillip's Aspen collar. While Phillip was speaking with this technician, I asked the social worker if we could go into the solarium to talk privately.

He was as warm in person as he had been on the phone. He made me feel heard and didn't talk down to me, like some of the other health care workers I had to deal with, regarding Phillip's treatment. While we spoke, he looked at me unflinchingly. I felt I could trust him to level with me about what to expect. I told him what the oncologist had said earlier, that Phillip most likely had months, not years, to live. I questioned the wisdom of not telling him. He agreed with Phillip's doctor that it was best not to tell Phillip if he really didn't want to know. The social worker's compassionate attitude helped me understand this honestly had to be about Phillip's wishes. I was very grateful for his insight and the way he addressed me with kindness. His approach to alleviating the anxiety I faced was beyond helpful.

By the time I returned from speaking with the social worker, they had taken Phillip out of the room for his first radiation treatment. The hope was to stabilize Phillip's C7 vertebra by calcifying the tumor, strengthening his neck. I wasn't sure how any of this would help, but this was my understanding of why the radiation treatment was suggested. An ongoing course of chemo would follow this, along with a chemotherapy regimen referred to as FOLFOX.

He saw nutritionists and dietitians for his continued weight loss and psychiatric doctors to assess his mental health and emotional well-being, on top of seeing his oncologist. He was getting the care he needed despite the screw-up with the PICC line. I was very grateful.

THE FOLLOWING WEEK, the Beans came with me to visit Phillip at Mass General. It amazed me how fortuitous it was that we had read the book *Kasey to the Rescue*. Ned, the young man who was the central figure in the book, had become a quadriplegic after a car accident. He, too, had received treatment at Mass General. Most importantly to the kids, however, was that while reading the book, we learned that Ned's family could bring their dog on visits to the hospital. It would never have occurred to me, otherwise, that we could bring Chubby with us into Boston.

His presence certainly made the outing more pleasant. The twins beamed with pride, walking their charming pup down the hall to visit their dad that day. They held his leash tight and lead him through the hallway from the elevator to Phillip's room with a bit of swagger. The nurses and other patients commented on our sweet pooch, and Jack and Lucy were over the moon.

Having Chubby with us made it easier for everyone during this visit. At their age, it was hard to know what to say to their father. When the small talk evaporated, uncomfortable silences remained. With Chubby as the focus of their collective attention, Phillip and the twins were able to pass the time enjoyably instead of enduring an awkward visit.

While I knew Phillip wanted to see the twins, he was very weak because of his rapid weight loss. Concerned he was overexerting himself, I suggested we leave. Phillip smiled and blew them kisses as we left his room, not knowing how long it would be before he'd see them again.

On the ride home, I promised the Beans I would send Ellen Rogers, the author of *Kasey to the Rescue*, an email about this experience and thank her for writing a book that helped ease my children's challenging encounter with a large hospital. (She replied with an invitation to visit her, Ned, and of course, Kasey, their trained Capuchin monkey that was Ned's service animal, when things calmed down. The twins were stoked!)

At the end of April, they finally discharged Phillip from Mass General. By that time, I wasn't sure how anyone coped when a loved one was diagnosed with cancer, especially if they didn't have the kind of support our families gave us. I was more determined than ever to stay hopeful that his life could somehow be extended, and whatever time he had remaining would be absent of our marital dysfunction. I promised myself that, regardless of what lay ahead, I would try to have more patience. I knew that would be challenging, but his oncologist's words regarding Phillip's prognosis loomed large in my mind.

As harsh as it was to hear, what she said moved me to change my relationship with Phillip. More than anything, I just wanted to give him my better self, one that was more honest, compassionate, and loving—without being a doormat. I wanted to be there when he needed me most. I kept thinking about a quote I'd read once from Erich Fromm in his book, *The Art of Loving*: "To be loved because of one's merit, because one deserves it, always leaves doubt. Maybe I did not please the person whom I wanted to love me, maybe this, or that—there is always a fear that love could disappear.'

For much of my marriage, I strove to feel that Phillip truly loved me. I tried to prove I was worthy of his love from the day we married. I was finally learning that it was an illusion to believe my entire self-worth was based on whether he loved me. This shift in perspective gave me more control over my own happiness. I knew if my self-esteem was no longer in the hands of another human being, I could let go of so much of the insecurity that kept me chained to the repeated negative messages I received from him. I was determined to learn that I didn't need to prove myself worthy of his love. In the end, that is truly what saved me.

Chapter Twenty-Eight

LOOKING FOR MIRACLES

After Phillip was released from the hospital, I refused to face reality and was very skeptical of anyone who suggested otherwise. Despite the midnight trips to the emergency room because Phillip was vomiting blood or experiencing unexplained pains, I remained convinced that a miracle was just around the corner. I had to stay positive. I wanted to believe we could beat this.

I resented anyone who painted a grim picture of his prognosis because he seemed so much healthier and looked terrific. I convinced myself, they would never have released him if he wasn't getting better. Even when one of my closest friends tried to reason with me, advising that I should prepare myself for the worst, I scoffed. I told myself there were cures; I just had to find them. I started looking for signs that a miracle could occur. I truly believed that Phillip would end up in medical books as having been the most severe cancer case to have survived.

It didn't take long to figure out my thoughts and beliefs weren't grounded in reality. Looking back, I know I was in denial. Those who are suddenly faced with the type of diagnosis Phillip received frequently experience similar notions. There was a part of me that truly believed he would somehow get better.

There was another part of me that knew it was hopeless. I vacillated between these two conflicting thoughts hourly.

In the back of my mind, I kept looking for a place to hang my hope. I reminded myself of how disheartened I felt when we first moved to Canada, and Phillip left the Beans and me behind. In those early days in Alexandria, I started feeling better because I was sure someone was looking out for me from above and protecting me in those weary first months.

It started with minor things. For instance, I would notice, each morning, that when I went to the grocery store, the odd item I needed for the café's lunch special was always on sale. Like the time I wanted to use up some roast beef and had decided to make sandwiches as a lunch special. I looked for horseradish sauce to use on the side. Usually, the price would have prohibited me from buying it, but it was on sale that day. Initially, I wasn't convinced it was anything more than a coincidence, but this happened so frequently, it was uncanny.

Then there was a series of events that should have or could have ended in a tragedy but didn't end badly at all. For example, shortly after we had opened for business, I got a call from Solange, who managed a thrift store, a few doors down from the café. She was always alerting me when something became available that I might need for the café. That day, it was a refrigerator. I had no idea how, or if, she knew that our fridge was on the fritz, but her call was welcome. She said that the men who moved furniture and appliances for her could deliver a practically new fridge that afternoon. They would even remove the old fridge and pick up a check after the café closed. We sealed the deal.

After the men left, I realized the fridge's door swung from the left, not the right. It frustrated me because the counter we used to assemble food was to the fridge's right in our galley-style kitchen. Having it swing open from the left meant I would have to open and close the door more frequently to remove items I needed. One of my employees assured me that it could be switched to swing the other way, so I relaxed, knowing Phillip could do that the next time he came to Canada.

I made the kids nachos for dinner that night and prepared them in a Pyrex dish I'd used a hundred times. The Beans were seated at a small table outside of the entrance to the kitchen. I took the nachos out of the oven and placed them on the top of the stove. Then I crossed to the fridge for the various condiments. I had just opened the door and ducked down to grab some things off the bottom shelf when the Pyrex dish exploded. There were shards of glass all over the kitchen. Some even reached the ceiling. We dug enormous pieces out of crevices for days after this happened. I was completely unharmed because the fridge door shielded me entirely.

There were other things, as well. In the spring of 2008, I rented the farmhouse, the one we eventually used for the music festival. Shortly before I was ready to move into the place, I had a conversation with Yves, the man that owned the coffee roasting company where I purchased my beans. I asked him why he called his business Justin Café. I thought it was an odd name for a coffee roasting company. He explained that the name came from a café he and his wife had owned years ago north of Alexandria. When I asked why they closed, he told me that he and his wife were off to their baby shower one day before their son's birth. On the way out, he heard an odd crackling sound. They were in a rush, so he didn't check to see what was causing the noise. When they returned later, their place had burned to the ground. The crackling noise had been an electrical fire in the walls of their old building. His story gave me the chills.

A week later, I moved into the farmhouse and planned to hand over the keys to our apartment above my business to the new tenant. I had a catering job the night before, so, early the following day, I went to finish cleaning before the tenant was scheduled to arrive.

I left about 7 am and brought Chubby with me because he hadn't been walked earlier. I opened the outside door to the foyer area that led to the apartment and climbed up the stairs. I was about to put the key in the apartment's lock when I noticed Chubby in the corner of the landing. His head was cocked to the side. I tried coaxing him into the apartment, but he just stood there and refused to come in. Then I heard it. There was a crackling noise—the conversation I'd had with Yves only a week before came to mind. I called the fire department, two doors away from the café. They were there in minutes and put out an electrical fire that had started in the wall. Somehow, it felt like I had angels watching over me.

There were other instances as well. When we moved to Rachel's home in Marblehead, that happened so rapidly, we still hadn't moved out of the apartment in Cobleskill. We couldn't afford to continue paying for an apartment we weren't using, so I had to develop a plan to move out before the end of May.

With the help of my brother Jake on one trip and my niece Ronnie on another, I was able to return the keys to the landlord by Memorial Day weekend, with Rachel tending to Phillip's needs while I traveled back and forth.

As the rental truck got full, I realized there were many things I couldn't take with me, so I offered them to Greg and Patrice, the lovely young couple who had purchased the house next door. It thrilled me they could use things, and they even helped Ronnie and me load the rental truck and empty the rest of the apartment.

While we loaded the truck, Greg told me he worked on antique cars. I said I'd keep that in mind since Phillip still had a 1966 Mustang in a garage back in New Jersey. Weeks later, when Phillip and I were trying to figure out what to do with the Mustang, I thought about Greg. I couldn't recall his last name, so I put our old address into the Google search engine, trying to locate a phone number. I was appalled to learn that Greg had recently been released from prison, where he had spent time for raping his six-year-old niece. I shook, thinking about my young daughter playing in the backyard at our apartment, the one that connected to theirs. I had to wonder if we had miraculously escaped some horrible event by moving away when we did.

I knew deep inside none of these things proved miracles happen. But I had to have hope. It was the only way I could

240

avoid being overwhelmed. At that moment, I had to hang on to something. I'm glad I didn't have a crystal ball because sometimes an illusion of hope is better than no hope at all.

ANOTHER THING that kept me going during that time was the communications I regularly received from my friends up north. While I still had to address selling the property in Canada, our accountant (who was also our attorney) advised me not to sell the building yet. He was concerned that the influx of income might disqualify us for some financial help we were getting for Phillip's medical expenses. He suggested letting go of the building's contents instead, which would also help drive down the cost of moving things once the building sold.

I sent my friends and those on the café's email list a notice, telling them of my plans. They met my email with warm responses that once again illustrated why I desperately missed my life up north. I truly appreciated all the support and outreach that came via calls and emails.

"Hi Everyone-

I have decided to sell many of the belongings I used to furnish the 2Beans Café and Tea Room and some of the other things that I can't hang on to any longer. Yes, even the granite tables are available! Jenny has lots of larger pieces. Roberto has items for sale in the Café's tearoom. As silly as it sounds, knowing that these things that brought me much pleasure while owning my little business are in the hands of people I know and love is more comforting! Thanks, bunches, ~ Kasey"

Days after I sent out the email, I heard from Sondra, one of my favorite customers. She had a thick Scotch-Canadian accent and a wry smile. She often wandered into the Café to join me for a cup of coffee late in the afternoon as she shuttled from one project to another.

She wrote,

"You are learning one of the most difficult lessons life teaches...' letting go'...No one in this world goes through life without ever having learned, in some way, this lesson's meaning..We fill our lives with so much unimportant nothings, just to avoid learning this most difficult lesson of all. Your life will take on new meaning and in the process, so will the lives of your children...This is how the world functions...You are doing the best a person can do, Kasey, by responding to what life requires from you at this time. Go with the present and always remember, 'all is exactly as it should be at this time'...Thanks for your kind offerings...I have already mentioned it to a few of your 2 Beans Café patrons...Bye for now...Sondra."

Her kind words and sage advice boosted my spirits and gave me encouragement when I needed it desperately. It occurred to me that there really were angels protecting me—just not in the way I first imagined. As painful as it was to let go, it was what needed to be done. I read and reread this email repeatedly to remind me that life was exactly as it should be.

Part Four

LETTING GO

Life is a series of natural and spontaneous changes. Don't resist them; that only creates sorrow. Let reality be reality. Let things flow naturally forward in whatever way they like.

~ Lao Tzu

Chapter Twenty-Nine

SAME OLE, SAME OLE

As much as I wanted to believe Phillip and I had managed to put aside our problems, they reemerged after he was released from the hospital. It didn't happen all at once, but cracks appeared, especially when I returned from being away for a few days.

At first, the things he said and did weren't bad enough for me to call him out on his behavior. But his actions were hurtful and reminded me of our past conflicts. By the middle of June, however, something happened that made me realize nothing had changed. It was only glossed over because of our circumstances.

That night, I heard him call out to me well after midnight.

"Honey, what's wrong?" I said, rushing into his room.

"I don't know. I have a sharp pain in my lower back that's coming in waves. I can't stand it. I need you to take me to the ER."

By now, I was used to the sudden trips to the hospital, and we traveled into Boston so frequently, it was almost routine. But that night, the intensity of his pain forced us to opt for a hospital in Beverly, a small city that was much closer.

The doctor came into the cubicle where Phillip was waiting to be seen. He reviewed his charts from a previous visit.

"Hello, I'm Doctor Misri. Can you tell me what you're experiencing? Where is the pain?"

While Phillip described what he was experiencing, I ducked out quickly to use the restroom. When I came back, the doctor was still reviewing Phillip's chart. Noting the situation, he asked Phillip if he were to go into cardiac arrest, did he want to be resuscitated.

"Yes."

"Have you designated a healthcare proxy? We need to make sure everything is in order," the doctor told him. Phillip nodded.

Moments later, a nurse came into the room with papers for Phillip to sign. He read them, filled out the appropriate information, and signed them as routinely as he signed dozens of other documents.

While we were waiting for the doctor to return, he said, "Just so you know, I've made Rachel my healthcare proxy. The last thing I want is to have you be in charge of pulling the plug," he told me matter-of-factly.

I turned and looked at him, my mouth agape. I couldn't respond. I felt a chill, even though it was the middle of June. I clutched my purse closer to me, then glanced at the floor, determined not to cry. When I finally composed myself, I told him, "Whatever you want is fine." And it was.

He was whisked off for some tests. It was determined he had a kidney stone, and it had passed. I didn't see him again until they were ready to discharge him.

On the ride back to his sister's, there was a palpable silence. After arriving home in Marblehead, we both went to bed without saying goodnight. I climbed into the bed I shared with Lucy, trying not to wake her. Sleep eluded me for much of the night. I couldn't understand how Phillip could be so callous. Then I realized that, in many ways, he had done me a huge favor. By choosing Rachel as his healthcare proxy, Phillip let me know how he truly felt about me and where I stood in our relationship.

What I learned that night was that Phillip's love was conditional. When I was needed, I was of value to him. When he didn't require my help, I didn't matter. When Phillip signed that paper earlier, it revealed something I had long suspected but couldn't admit to myself about my role in his life. It wasn't flattering.

The words, "The last thing I want is to have you be in charge of pulling the plug," echoed in my brain. At first, I blamed it on the impact of leaving Phillip eight months earlier. However, looking back, I realized he had made statements equally damning before that when he said things like, "I don't want you profiting from my death." Whatever his reasons were, his concern about my receiving money as a beneficiary of his life insurance obscured his concern to provide for his wife and children. Those were things he said long before I left him.

That night, I tried to reconcile that, for whatever reason, Phillip believed I was unworthy of his trust, protection, loyalty, or commitment to our marriage. Perhaps this was something I should have realized long ago when he refused to tell his parents we got married. However, that night, I finally understood that his words and actions more of a statement about his character than they were about mine. I may have loved him imperfectly, but I loved him.

I lay there, wondering if maybe he floated in and out of being in love with me all those years. Loving someone and being in love with them were separate matters. I thought about the years I'd given him enormous chunks of me. I'd sacrificed for the concept of us. I convinced myself we were a team, but for whatever reason, Phillip treated me as though I was a bit player.

Phillip's attempts to control me and change me weren't acts of love. When you love someone, you want as much, or more, for them as you want for yourself. Whatever he felt for me, it wasn't love. What I started to feel for him was pity. He could have experienced a deep and committed relationship, but he opted to marginalize me whenever possible. It made me sad instead of angry.

It wasn't possible to go back and change the course of our marriage. There wasn't enough time to alter what was now etched in the past. What I could do was to feel compassion for him. It was unfortunate that he only appreciated me or was grateful for what he had when it suited him.

Still, I decided I would not allow myself to become a score-keeper again. I had erased all the tally lines, but it wasn't the only thing that needed to change. I had to stop replaying his voice in my head. I knew the narrative had to change if I wanted to honor not only the vows I made to him but, more so, those I made to myself. I could be that better self if I could find forgive-ness for the self-doubt that started when I allowed him to define me. I was willing to take responsibility for my flaws but knew they didn't make me unworthy of his love. They made me human.

I kept thinking about all the things my friend Sondra from Alexandria had said. I'd read her email a bazillion times. "Go with the present and always remember, 'all is exactly as it should be at this time."

When morning broke, I was still awake. As I finally drifted off, I realized I had to stop myself from wallowing in self-pity and acknowledged that I could grow and learn from this horrible experience. It would not be easy to push aside the anguish of this recent revelation. But in the end, if I could acknowledge the pain and move past it, I would come out of it a better human being.

TOWARDS THE END OF JUNE, I was planning to go to Canada to clean out the apartment of a former tenant once again. I needed to get another renter into the apartment immediately because I needed the income desperately.

I would be leaving the day before our wedding anniversary—the one, his parents, knew about. I wasn't sure what to do about acknowledging the occasion. The special day seemed to blend into the background. I took it in stride because, with so many other things going on, it was hard to celebrate, anyway. But I kept thinking this was most likely the last anniversary Phillip and I would ever have and how ironic it was that I was mourning the marriage that, nine months earlier, I had desperately wanted to be over.

I went to the store and bought Phillip a card. I felt pangs of guilt because I knew he wouldn't be able to do the same unless he asked someone to take him. It was a no-win situation all the way around.

I wondered if he even thought about this milestone, considering how fragile our relationship was sometimes. A sense of grief crept over me. I grieved for what I thought we once had together. I grieved because I knew his days were numbered, and there wasn't anything I could do that would ultimately prolong his life. I grieved because he couldn't understand that I had a right to grieve.

"You're not the one who has cancer," he told me again and again.

The last time he spoke those words, we were downstairs in Rachel and Dennis's basement. I had entered the room where Jack and Lucy were sitting with him, reading. I asked if they would walk Chubby, and they readily agreed. When they left, I turned to Phillip.

"I'm leaving for Alexandria early in the morning. Amelia emailed and said she has no hot water again, so, on top of cleaning out the rear apartment, I'll have to get ahold of the plumber." When he didn't say anything, I tried to fill in the awkwardness. "I wish I didn't have to go north."

"Well, I can't go," he said with a tone of sheer contempt.

"Phillip, I'm not suggesting you can. Don't be like that, please."

"Be like what, Kasey? You don't understand what this is like because you don't have cancer. You're going to be seeing your friends while you're up there. Don't lie."

I was tired of holding my tongue. I realized Phillip was suffering, but I felt compelled to say something.

"Does your mother and father or Rachel have cancer?"

"What are you talking about?"

"You constantly tell me I can't possibly be suffering because I don't have cancer. And yet, you understand they're suffering because of your illness. How is it that you think I've escaped the pain of this?"

He looked at me with disdain. I wasn't arguing or emotional. I presented him with a valid statement. He pursed his lips and seemed to be about to object, but then he refused to comment.

"Just because I don't have cancer, Phillip, doesn't mean it doesn't affect me. It affects me in ways you refuse to recognize. You recognize their pain and suffering but, somehow, you think I'm immune. That's sad." With that, I left him alone and went upstairs.

The kids came back from walking Chubby. "Hey, you guys want to get some ice cream? Memere gave me some money for a treat."

The three of us piled into the van, and I took them to their favorite ice cream place. When we got back to the house, I asked the Beans to take Phillip a Chocolate Frappe we had ordered for him, but I stayed upstairs until I thought he was in bed. When I believed it was safe to go down, I made my way to the basement and was relieved to see the door to his room closed. I casually asked the Beans where he was, and they confirmed he'd gone to bed. Before I left in the morning, I put the anniversary card on his nightstand. He never acknowledged receiving it.

Chapter Thirty

A GIRL NAMED ELLIE

Phillip and I were making weekly runs into Boston for one reason or another: chemo treatments, check-ups, and sudden trips to the emergency room became routine. In each department we had to visit, the various personnel became almost like friends. There was Emma, one of Dr. Allison's nurse practitioners, who told us funny stories. Denise, an RN in the infusion unit, made us comfortable and showed extraordinary kindness each time Phillip went in for the chemotherapy. They made the day brighter because of their overwhelming compassion towards those they cared for each day.

Not only were his various caregivers considerate, but there were other patients on similar schedules that we chatted with regularly. While it wasn't exactly a social event, smiles were exchanged, and familiar faces were acknowledged.

One such patient was a young girl named Ellie. She had a wisp of bright red hair that peeked out of the colorful bandanas she wrapped around her balding head. Her beautiful smile was so engaging; it was impossible not to smile back at this young woman who, we learned, was battling brain cancer. She beamed at Phillip in a way that made me think the fight they shared was one I could never truly understand. To my knowledge, they never spoke, but Phillip always liked it when we were escorted to an infusion chair where he could see her and exchange a thumbs-up.

One day in mid-July, when he went in to have his infusion, we noticed Ellie wasn't there. He asked the nurse if she'd come in earlier because their schedules didn't always mesh. We learned she'd had a stroke, or something of that nature, and didn't make it. My heart was in my throat for the entire time we were there, realizing Ellie had died. Phillip left the hospital that day in a somber mood and went to lie down as soon as we got back to Marblehead.

While incidents like that had me finally accepting the inevitable, it also made me search harder to find ways to fight the cancer that was killing him. I realized I couldn't save him, but I could help preserve his strength.

Days later, I noticed a local Borders Bookstore was closing, so I ventured in. I found and purchased a book called *Anticancer, a New Way of Life* by Doctor David Servan-Schreiber. The book was about a doctor who, as a med student, discovered, quite accidentally, that he had a brain tumor. He beat cancer once but, eventually, it came back. The second time, on top of treatment, he changed his diet and lifestyle radically. He was able to live with his condition for another fifteen years. Sadly, I learned he died a week after I finished reading the book.

I also learned from my best friend, Leigh, that her sister-in-law had battled a very advanced case of breast cancer and had survived. We swapped book titles to further our understanding of how to help our loved ones. When I got off the phone, I was determined once again to support Phillip in any way I could to fight this horrible disease.

One of the most notable things about the book *Anticancer, a New Way of Life*, was that Doctor David Servan-Schreiber suggested avoiding sugar. When I reached page 61, I read, "The German biologist Otto Heinrich Warburg won the Nobel Prize in medicine for his discovery that the metabolism of malignant tumors is largely dependent on glucose consumption. (Glucose is the form of digested sugar in the body.) In fact, the PET scan commonly used to detect cancer simply measures the areas in the body that consume the most glucose. If a particular area stands out because it consumes too much sugar, cancer is very likely the cause."

I learned from other things I'd read that there was a growing body of information about the connection between cancer and sugar. All the statistical information regarding the increased risk of cancer because of lifestyle diseases, like obesity, was alarming. I was dealing with a man with cancer, and I was also increasing my risks by not addressing my growing weight issues that stemmed from diabetes.

WHEN I WAS five months pregnant, a routine test at my obstetrician's office had led to the discovery I had gestational diabetes. I was on insulin during the rest of my pregnancy and was a borderline diabetic for years before my bad habits caught up to me, and I developed Type-2 diabetes. I hadn't been to a doctor to check on my own health in many months, and I began chastising myself for being so careless. I wanted to present a better example of self-care to my kids, and that meant eating healthier. But without a source of income, we had slipped into poverty that summer and were struggling just to stay afloat. Trips to the grocery store were a constant source of anxiety because our budget and eating healthy were frequently at odds.

We were receiving SNAP benefits, but much of that money went to purchasing specialty food items that were easy for Phillip to consume. I will never forget the look of disdain the cashier gave me when I bought ice cream for him using this food program. I felt like smacking the self-righteous look off her face with the back of my hand. He could not swallow much, and if he needed, or wanted, ice cream, he would get it.

When we consulted with a nutritionist at Mass General about what Phillip should be eating, she gave us coupons for Ensure and a print-out of a diet, but that was about the extent of her input on nutritional advice. Unfortunately, the things she recommended, like the Ensure and Benecalorie, were not just expensive; they made him vomit because they were too thick. With her help, I learned how to change the consistency so he could tolerate them. I was now concerned that the amount of sugar in these drinks might help advance his cancer growth. One day, I decided to approach Phillip about the subject.

"I've been reading a lot about the connection between sugar and cancer, and they load those frozen drinks with it. Maybe we should see if something else is available?"

"What do you want me to do, starve to death?" he complained.

"Of course not. Don't be angry, Phillip. I'm trying to help you. Can't you see that?"

"You can help by letting me decide what I can and can't eat. You don't understand what it's like to even think about giving up the few remaining things I enjoy."

"Okay, fine," I told him.

Phillip agreed to ask his doctor about the link between his diet and his cancer. Dr. Allison came into the room for a moment before the nurse saw him, but he remained silent. After exchanging pleasantries, I piped up and took the opportunity to ask my lingering question.

"Dr. Allison, I have a question. I've been reading about the link between cancer and sugar. Do you think changing Phillip's diet will help at all?" I asked her.

"If he wants to eat cake, let him eat it," she told me.

"It's just that —,"

"Let's get your vitals, shall we? I'll have the nurse come in," she said, beaming at Phillip as she left the room.

When I turned to face him, he had a victorious grin on his face. I knew there would be no support for changing his diet to eliminate sugar. I wondered if Dr. Allison was telling me this because Phillip's cancer was at such an advanced stage she believed he should be able to enjoy whatever foods pleased him, or had it bothered her, I was even raising the question? I knew if

I pressed the issue, I would be opening old wounds. I let the subject drop.

Instead, I began trying to re-evaluate what I was cooking. I made soft starchy foods for most meals because they were easy for Phillip to eat, and they were also cheap. I never thought too much that these foods contributed to my difficulties in maintaining healthy blood sugar levels. When I learned about the glycemic index and how it measures whether a particular carbohydrate-containing food increases blood glucose levels, I was stunned. All the foods I thought were so healthy because they were low in fat or weren't sweet weren't doing much for either of us.

I sat on the couch in Rachel and Dennis's living room, reading the Anti-Cancer book's last chapters. I knew I had to address my own needs, but I struggled since Phillip's needs were the priority. It wasn't something that just happened because he had cancer, either. It reminded me that, as a child, I watched my mother always put her family's needs, especially my father's, before her own. That expectation was cemented long ago. As a woman, I, too, sacrificed my own needs for my family.

I looked over at the Beans, who were watching a movie as I read. It seemed like an impossible situation. Here I'd just finished reading a book that was mainly about self-empowerment. Servan-Schreiber's advice to his patients was that lifestyle changes can fight cancer. Yet, the needs of others drove my lifestyle. Servan-Schreiber's book outlined some fundamental reasons that nutrition, exercise, psychology, and meditation were essential to a person's well-being. However, I was constantly stressed, ate poorly, didn't exercise, or did anything else he recommended in the book. Regardless of what was going on in my life, I realized that, no matter what, I had to do better. I finally understood that taking care of myself was taking care of my family.

Chapter Thirty-One

MORE THAN THE LACK OF A CELLPHONE

Each day that summer seemed to bring either a fresh challenge or a revision of an old one. The medical moments had us coordinating and working together to provide Phillip with everything he needed to fight the cancer inside him. But the everyday moments, the ones between the frequent medical crises and routine treatments, left us confronting the problems in our relationship. Those days that we should have been cherishing were instead filled with conflict.

I struggled to keep my impulse to argue or even defend myself or the Beans in check, especially when Phillip made hurtful comments. I sometimes thought my tongue would bleed; I was biting it so frequently. I sometimes suspected Phillip's hurtful remarks were a bit of payback. After all, I had almost left him less than a year ago. I reminded myself not to allow him to define me anymore and refocused his attention or ignored the matter altogether when a quarrel brewed.

There were so many times. However, I wanted to stay right there and level the same anger at him that he leveled at me. I wanted to confront him with the frustration that was building inside. He tapped into my emotions and knew exactly what to say when he tried to drive me over the edge. But I knew when I was less salty with him, he lost steam and left me alone.

At the doctor's office one day, another pattern emerged. I realized, when we were in the company of others, Phillip always presented me as a saint.

"You wouldn't believe what an excellent cook she is!" he told Emma, his nurse, at one visit. "The other night, she made me a soup that was so delicious; I had three bowls," he continued. "When we owned our restaurant, customers came all the way from Montreal for her cooking," he bragged.

"I didn't know you guys had a restaurant," Emma responded.

"Oh, yes," Phillip told her. "For years. It was a small café, but we did a lot of catering and other things on the side. We even rented an old barn and hosted a music festival." As Phillip chatted with Emma and described the café and our time in Canada in such glowing terms, I simmered because it occurred to me how often he did this. To others, he offered a totally different view of circumstances than he had presented to me. I wasn't sure which portrayal was the more accurate one. Was he proud of the café and the music festival, or were they the massive failures he told me they were?

On the ride back to Marblehead, I thought about this and understood the significance of his conflicting presentation of situations. He didn't want to portray me negatively in front of others because I was, in ways, a reflection of him. By praising me, he was praising himself.

Realizing that Phillip kept his admonishments out of the earshot of others offered me a way to circumvent his callous words. I began avoiding being alone with him whenever possible. I would leave the room or take the dog for a walk or just pretend I had to use the bathroom. I wondered why he didn't ask if I had a bladder infection because I left to use the restroom so often.

My plan didn't work out all the time. At the end of July, Phillip ambushed me when I went downstairs to grab Chubby's leash.

"We need to talk right now," he told me from his room.

"What's up?" I asked him, trying to sound casual.

"When you go to Canada this week, you have to leave the phone in Marblehead, Kasey. I spoke to Dennis, and I promised him I'd have you give it back to me. He said he couldn't believe how irresponsible you are sometimes."

"Did he?"

"Yeah, he did."

"I've already apologized to Dennis. I didn't realize that I'd get roaming charges when I was in Canada. So, yes, I racked up a hefty bill. But I gave him money to cover the additional expense."

"Whatever your excuse, I want it back," Phillip insisted.

"So, you're telling me I shouldn't bring it while I'm traveling?" I asked him incredulously.

"It's not yours. Dennis gave it to me. Why you ended up with it is a mystery to me."

"Mystery? I took it initially because you handed it to me and asked me to hold on to it. I kept it on me because we don't have a cellphone of our own."

"This is so typical of you. You ran up an enormous bill, and now you're offering excuses."

"Oh, it's an excuse to want to have a cellphone on me while I'm the one who travels all over the place in a van that shouldn't even be on the road?"

"Don't tell me all those calls were made because of your traveling. That's a load of shit. You use it to call your friends, too."

"Yes, I call my friends. I call my family, too. But you're making it sound like I intentionally ran up Dennis's bill. You're the one that's blowing this up."

"I'm always the bad guy for pointing out how irresponsible you are. This is what you do to me. You make me out to be the villain. Even with everything I'm going through, you have to go there."

I left the room and grabbed Dennis's cellphone from my purse.

"Here. I won't use it anymore. I'm sorry I used it in the first place. I'm even sorrier that you have so little concern for my safety." I grabbed Chubby's leash, stormed upstairs, and took him out for a walk.

There was a pathway to the woods close to Rachel and Dennis's that I could access from behind their house. Over the summer, it had become a refuge I sought frequently. While Chubby sniffed at whatever scent he discovered, I looked out for flowers or birds as we meandered along the paths covered in pine needles. I headed there with Chubby, furious at what had just happened with Phillip.

I tried to focus on the moment instead of going over what Phillip said about the cellphone situation, but I couldn't let go of our argument. Instead, I berated myself because the whole situation made me feel inept again. But, as I walked Chubby, I had an epiphany. I had every right to use that cellphone! I had paid Dennis for the overage and had apologized. I took responsibility for my mistake. Phillip was wrong. I wasn't asking to use it just for pleasure. While I used it to stay in touch with friends and family, why did Phillip believe that was a problem? I also needed it to make calls to his doctors and have one if I broke down while traveling. Once again, I was allowing Phillip to get into my head. He turned the matter into an assault on my character.

I always tried to get Phillip to see the situation as I saw it. But by doing that, I was seeking validation from him. That was akin to asking him to love me. I had utterly sabotaged myself again. Of course, I wanted to have the ability to call for help if needed. But even if I'd only had a cellphone to talk to friends and family, there was nothing wrong with that. I needed their support, even though, in Phillip's mind, that didn't matter. No amount of arguing would change how he saw me. I'd been down that road too many times, and I knew where it ended.

As I walked along, I reminded myself to stop buying into his version of me. None of that was true. It was a reflection of how he thought of himself. His lack of self-esteem manifested in his need to boost his ego by deflating my accomplishments and assaulting my character.

Knowing this allowed me to be kinder to him—even when he was a dick. I wasn't tolerating his behavior as appropriate or acceptable. I just finally saw his outbursts weren't really a statement about me. They were about his own internal conflict. Showing others he was better than they were made him feel superior.

When I stopped letting him define who I was, I reacted less defensively. I also realized I shouldn't be hurt by it anymore. I refused to let what he said about me have the same influence on how I viewed myself. Much of it was a way for him to manipulate my behavior. When I gave in to it, I realized I was just hurting myself.

We never spoke about the cellphone issue again, even when I was about to leave for Canada again a few days later. He had either forgotten about it or just didn't care that I would have no way to get help if anything happened. But before I left the next day, I went to the store and purchased a cheap cellphone, so I would have one before heading north to return to Alexandria.

Chapter Thirty-Two

TRYING TO SURVIVE

By mid-July, Dr. Allison advised Phillip that continuing the chemotherapy was inadvisable. Tests showed that it was ineffective, and Phillip's cancer had grown. He declined to stop treatment, however. I understood that, for Phillip, stopping chemo meant giving up and acknowledging that time was growing short, that the treatment was what kept him going.

What kept me going, though, were all the little things. I realized the twins were better off in Marblehead than they had been in Cobleskill. They were thriving again. Having their cousin to hang out with and Rachel's positive influence helped tremendously. They both enjoyed spending time with their grandparents, Memere and Pepere, too. Whatever happened, I had to stay in the area because I couldn't move them yet again.

For me, knowing that it was what was best for them made the decision easy. I had let go of my thoughts of returning to live in Alexandria. I knew that all that mattered was to focus on getting through this ordeal without allowing myself to become despondent about the future.

At the end of July, I got an email from one of my former customers.

"Hi Kasey-

I was talking to our mutual friend Jenny about our Museum Fall Festival and asked about you. She tells me you are back in the States, in Boston, and this is and has been a very difficult time for you. Both Sarah and I are very sorry for the stress, worry, and the painfulness that you must be dealing with, considering the health of your husband and that you had to leave Canada. I know that you had high hopes for resettling here and launching a number of possibilities, including the restaurant and a more active arts program. I am sorry that some of that did not happen. Alexandria is a very tough town to crack into and it is hard on newcomers. I speak from experience.

I understand from Jen that your spirit is good, considering everything. I do remember you as someone full of positive energy and, I suspect, able to rely on those strengths in difficult times. I look forward to your return here or success in some new adventure. All the best, Andy (from Sarah as well.)"

I READ Andy's email a dozen times. I was so touched by the fact he had reached out to me. I was grateful that people were reminding me that I meant something to them. It wasn't all part of my imagination because there were times that my past life in Alexandria seemed like a lifetime ago.

The next day, I wrote back.

"Hi, Andy- Thanks so much for the kind and much-needed email. It always gives me a great sense of happiness to connect with friends in Canada.

While I must admit there is something that just doesn't translate down here about the pace and sense of well-being I had there, I have made a decision to embrace whatever life has in store for me, whether I am living here or there. I am trying to look on this as an opportunity to make some changes. I'm trying not to think of leaving Alexandria with the sense of loss or failure I initially felt. If nothing else, life certainly has a way of keeping me on my toes.

I am trying to find my "writer's voice" again, and although the moments I have to dedicate to this are few and far between, I have been managing to write a bit again. I had forgotten how much I love this, and it is something that has eluded me for some time. Writing for me is like scratching an itch, both are deeply satisfying.

Please let Sarah know I was thinking of her and send my warmest regards as well.

Onward and upward, ~ Kasey"

In composing my response to Andy, it occurred to me that for a long time, other than the quick notes I wrote in my journals, I had stopped doing something that had once been a significant part of my life: writing. So many of the things that were once so important to me had been shoved aside years ago. Every once in a while, I thought about trying to start a new project or begin reworking an old one. However, I never found the time to act upon my goals. I knew that had to change.

Regardless of my resolve to begin writing again, the events of the summer prevented me from doing much more than recording some thoughts sporadically. But in documenting even these tiny fragments of insight into the experience helped me feel heard, even if I was talking to myself.

DESPITE WHAT DR. ALLISON SAID, there were times the treatment seemed to work because Phillip's blood tests were so good. These minor indications of stability kept his spirits up because he maintained a positive attitude outwardly. In this way, his ability to cope was a constant reminder that arguing with him would accomplish nothing because it hindered his frame of mind. So when he strayed into areas that raised my defenses, I fought to remain calm despite the desire to tell him to go screw himself. I wasn't always able to resist temptation.

Phillip and I decided to get the kids to participate in more activities, so I looked into something I thought they would enjoy.

"Hey, I was able to locate a few places for fencing lessons. I don't want to promise something in case we can't afford it. But I reached out to the owners, and they can cut us some slack. What do you think?" I asked Phillip.

"Yeah, that could be good. I don't think Jack is enjoying soccer as much as I hoped he would. It could be his allergies. This is a terrible time of year for him," Phillip said.

"Maybe, because this is an indoor activity, he'll like it better? I'm going to see what type of discount they're offering and, if we can swing it, I think we should consider it." Phillip and I agreed.

"It's too bad you never enrolled them in more things like that when they were younger. Arianna is more advanced than they are with all her sports and dance," Phillip commented. I stopped myself from telling him that when the Beans were young, he told me those extra-curricular activities were too expensive.

Later that August day, things came to a head. It began with an innocent conversation with Rachel when I came out of the laundry room into the upstairs foyer.

"Oh, there you are. I was just going to go downstairs and tell you something," Rachel told me.

"What's up?" I asked her.

"My friend Laura is having a hard time selling her house. I think she might want to rent it. I don't know if I told you, but she got remarried, and her new husband is quite wealthy," she said. "It might be worth asking because it's just sitting there."

"That's interesting. I'll let Phillip know! Thanks!" I told her.

The brief conversation made me wonder if we were over-staying our welcome. Was this Rachel's way of seeing whether we could make other living arrangements?

Later that day, Phillip and I took the kids to the fencing lessons I worked out for them. I'd completely forgotten to tell him earlier about my conversation with Rachel until we were sitting in the car chatting with the Beans. I turned to him and said, "Honey, I forgot to tell you, your sister said her friend Laura might be willing to rent us her house."

"What? We can't afford to rent a house."

"We don't know that we can't afford it because we don't

know if she's willing to rent it. We can't stay with Rachel and Dennis forever," I joked.

"This is so typical of you. I'm always the last to find out."

"What are you finding out? Nothing has been done. I am relating a conversation Rachel and I had before leaving the house."

"You can't even understand simple math. We can't afford to rent a house," he screamed at me.

"Phillip, calm down. I never said we were renting a house. Rachel brought this up earlier. Now, I'm telling you about our conversation, that's all."

"You lie about everything," he screamed.

The entire argument came out of nowhere. By this time, he was screaming at me so loud Lucy and Jack were crying in the back seat. I believed the suddenly explosive conversation was over when Phillip said, "Don't blame this on Rachel. You never take responsibility for anything. You know you're going to hell for all the horrible things you've done to me."

I lost it. "Oh, yeah? Just wait until we get back. Ask your sister who initiated the conversation. You're way out of line, and I'll prove it, not that it matters to you." I screamed at him.

He got out of the car and called Jack and Lucy to go with him. They reluctantly followed. My outburst mortified me. I was getting so much better at controlling my temper and avoiding these types of conflicts. I didn't want to show my tear-streaked face to all the parents who were watching their kids pretend to duel, so I sat in the van, wondering why this touched off such a nerve. I suspected it went back to his need for control.

I kept wondering about what Phillip had said. What horrible things had I done? Was he referring to leaving him? Despite all the care and attention I lavished on him, it was never enough. I waited in the car until the Beans' class was almost over and then went in to watch the last few minutes. On the drive back, the twins filled in the silence by chatting about their first fencing experience. While I drove, I fumed.

When we arrived back in Marblehead, we entered the garage

to get to the laundry room. Rachel was taking a load of clothing out of the dryer. She had no idea of the horrible fight we'd just had. I was convinced that if Rachel set him straight about our conversation, he'd see how wrong he was about our argument.

"Hey, Rachel! I was just telling Phillip about our earlier conversation. You know, about your friend Laura's house," I said, looking forward to her reply.

"Oh, yeah! Did Kasey tell you?" she said, turning to Phillip. "Laura might be interested in renting her place. It's close to school, and maybe you guys can ask her about it?"

"Rachel, Phillip thinks I started this conversation," I said, feeling a bit self-righteous.

She made it clear to him that she brought up the subject. She looked at me as if to question why this was so important, but I didn't offer any additional explanation.

"Well, we'll have to think about it," Phillip told her as he disappeared into the kitchen for some reason.

I didn't wait for an apology because I never should have assumed there was one coming. When I was cold to Phillip later, he told me to "grow up and get over it." He lacked an understanding that the words he said cut through me. Sometimes, they were almost too much to bear. There was nothing I could say or do that would ever make things right. If I argued or fought with him, I risked doing more harm to him physically and emotionally. If I kept it bottled inside, I was harming myself.

The only thing I could think to do was to remind myself daily that I was not the person he portrayed me to be. I continued to reread emails like Sondra's and Andy's to remind myself of that. I retreated into hot showers and went on more long walks with the kids and the dog. I got out of his way whenever I could. He kept telling his friends he was doing his best to survive. I wanted to say to him, so was I.

Chapter Thirty-Three

GRASPING AT STRAWS

I t was clear by mid-August that Phillip was declining. The only thing left to pursue regarding treatment was either a clinical trial at Dana Farber Cancer Institute or some sort of alternative therapy. His old boss, Barry, was trying to help Phillip by slogging through insurance issues regarding their willingness to pay for the expense of a clinical trial, while his best friend Kevin was providing information on an alternative treatment called vitamin C infusion. We were all doing our best to hold out hope that something could be done to save him.

Phillip was at his best when he dealt with friends like Kevin. He presented the side of himself that everyone adored. It was easy to see why he was loved and respected by his family, friends, and colleagues. That side of him is what kept me loving him all those years.

As angry as I was with him at times, I didn't want him to die. He was my children's father. He was the guy I'd fallen in love with and married. I still didn't understand all the reasons why our relationship had unraveled. Still, I'd reconciled the problems we had with a greater desire for him to escape the fate that was unavoidable.

While Kevin was visiting one day late in August, he told

Phillip about a guy (in Canada, no less) who researched vitamin C infusion therapy and the impact on cancer with a strict alkaline diet. The information was coming from his own desire to help a loved one battling cancer.

After his visit, Kevin sent the information to Phillip, who wondered if this offered hope. He told us of his friend John Bridgeton who was involved in researching and developing treatment protocols using large doses of vitamin C given intravenously or orally. At this point, Phillip seemed eager to try anything. After talking with Kevin's friend, John, the possibility of a new treatment offered us a sliver of hope. In pursuing this alternative, Phillip once again acted as if we were a united front. It was as if someone had waved a magic wand and pronounced we were once again "Phillip and Kasey." I was astounded that, suddenly, he began treating me as an ally.

I wondered if part of his shift in attitude was because he wanted his friends to see him as they always saw him as a great guy with a loving wife. Or, maybe when he saw me in the context of those cherished friendships, instead of the distorted image that lived somewhere in his head and deep in his heart, he realized I had some kind of merit after all.

I didn't believe his lack of criticism was a renewed love or concern for me for one minute. I thought of it as a reprieve from his disdain and criticism. While I didn't want to get lured into believing he loved me for myself, the change in his behavior was a welcome reprieve.

KEVIN FORWARDED the email his friend John sent, along with an article from the Canadian Medical Association Journal that discusses the use of vitamin C in the treatment of cancer. We read it and found it to be interesting.

After reading Kevin's email, he told me. "I'm apprehensive about going down any path without Dr. Allison's approval. I'm not even sure I'm eligible for the clinical trial since the protocols are rigid, and the timing must be right. Maybe this thing Kevin's friend John is suggesting might be worth a shot. What do you think?" he asked me.

I was amazed that suddenly, Phillip was anxious to hear my opinion. "Well, the doctor at Farber is about to go on vacation, so everything is very tentative with the clinical trial, anyway. I think the vitamin C thing worth considering," I told him. "In the meantime, why don't you reach out to Kevin's friend with questions regarding this alternative therapy? That way, when you do have a conversation with Dr. Allison, you can give her all the information." Later, he had me type out an email that related some additional questions about John's credentials. I knew that the fact he was so highly regarded by Kevin that Phillip was reasonably open to trying this therapy.

I still wondered about the link between his diet and the cancer that had invaded his body. What I'd read made sense to me, but my understanding was so limited, all I had to go on was what I found in books and online. I knew that what was out there on the Web wasn't always accurate. But we were desperate by this time, and Phillip looked at every possibility as time grew shorter. I didn't believe that changing his diet would save him. My previous questions about cancer and sugar came to mind. I was willing to do anything that could help him live longer and provide him with more strength.

There were other things to consider in his overall health; his neck's fragility and the discomfort it caused sometimes overshadowed his cancer. He was still waiting for a follow-up with his neurologist at Mass General. The hope was that the targeted radiation had fused the mass on his C7 vertebra, stabilizing his neck. This appointment wasn't until mid-September, so Kevin's information provided a much-needed boost to his declining morale.

On the other front, his old boss, Barry, was instrumental in helping him navigate the complications of clinical trials. He even visited Phillip with one of his former colleagues in mid-August. I was in Canada dealing with the issues up there, so I never had a chance to thank them. While the visit was welcome, the news regarding the hopes of participating in a clinical trial was not. It disappointed Phillip to hear what Barry said about the financial coverage just one day after his visit.

"Hi, Phillip- It was good to see you yesterday. Regretfully, it looks doubtful that a clinical trial will be covered. Glad you are surrounded by family and friends. Your courage and spirit and grace is truly admirable. Know you are missed at PII.

Please keep me posted."

Barry might have been shocked to hear Blue Cross wouldn't cover expenses related to clinical trials. However, Phillip seemed to take it in stride. While Phillip was in the hospital in Albany, our experiences informed us early on regarding the healthcare industry's priorities: profit over patients.

Rachel helped Phillip returned Barry's email.

"Many thanks to both of you for the food! It was thoroughly enjoyed by all of us here. (We even decided to save some of the ice cream cake for my kids when they return.)

Also, thanks for your kind words. As mentioned, I truly appreciated the opportunity to have worked with both of you and hope things continue to forge ahead for everyone at work.

In the meanwhile, keep good thoughts for me. I plan on fighting as best as I can against the odds. Please stay in touch, and I will try and do the same. Sincerely, ~ Phillip"

While Phillip seemed outwardly optimistic, the realities were crushing him. He and I spoke by phone while I was in Canada with the Beans the last weekend in August. He broke the news that there was little hope the costs of participating in the Dana Farber trial would be covered if they accepted him.

I was at a loss for how to help him. I felt the pressure to sell anything and everything I could while I was in Alexandria, but my time was consumed with cleaning out rental units. Without the funds necessary to pay for the costs of a clinical trial, our hopes were fading.

"What about the vitamin C therapy?" I asked him when we spoke.

"I'm just reluctant to begin following the regimented diet John's recommending," he told me. "The clinical trial options are still up in the air. I know it doesn't look good because of the latest rounds of issues with insurance. But Barry is doing his best to fight their decision, and he wrote to one of his former colleagues about the matter."

"Well, I hope they respond soon," I told him, then changed the subject. "Hey, Honey. Before I forget, I got an email from your friend Mike. I'm going to forward it to you."

When the Beans and I got home the next day, he asked me to type out an email to him.

"Hi Mike! Kasey forwarded your email to me. Many thanks for your concern. Currently, I am hanging in there with no pain…only fatigue, and a bit of nausea when undergoing chemo.

While my prognosis is still not good, I am doing my best to battle this disease as best I can. My last round of chemo at Mass General was not effective so I will hopefully be switching to an alternate therapy at the Dana Farber Institute. With all the chemo and radiation I've undergone, I'm learning cancer is like having a part-time job.

One positive note in this whole mess is to learn how truly fortunate I am to have the support of so many friends and colleagues. Your email is very much appreciated.

Please give my best to all, and continue to send all your good thoughts and prayers my way. Sincerely, ~ Phillip"

As I typed the email for him, I had to think that, for a person who is dying, waiting to learn if you qualify and can afford to pay for treatment options has to be the worst kind of hell of all.

Chapter Thirty-Four

ANOTHER AUGUST

Alexandria, Late August

For a brief time, being in Canada was the reprieve the Beans and I needed. Being there kept reality at bay. However, while I was away, I became eager to return home. So we left Alexandria earlier than I had planned, knowing with certainty that Marblehead was where we should be.

Driving back, I couldn't help but wonder about all that had happened in just one year since the farewell dinner at Jenny's house. None of the things I thought back then came true. Instead, I faced a loss far more devastating than I ever imagined.

I emailed Jenny to let her know we'd arrived in Marblehead safely.

> *"Hi, Jen- I'm back.…. Got in at 11:30, what a trip. All the Beans talked about towards the end of the trip was going back to live in Canada. They are miserable with the thought that school starts in a few weeks. They are in pain over this and are simply too young to understand the complexities of the situation. I will be trying to move forward and figuring out how to proceed. It makes me crazy, but I will figure it out.*
>
> *Thank you so much for all your love and support. You are so important*

to my overall sanity. Even when I haven't spoken to you for weeks, I can think about sitting on your porch, having a glass of wine, and sharing some girl time with you and Carole, and it makes me smile. It is the oasis in my mind when I am depleted of my own resources and need to replenish my sense of hope and faith that life will offer me more than it does at the moment.

I will be in touch and keep you posted on this end. Love you bunches, ~ Kasey."

I'll never know what happened while I was away but, suddenly, Phillip was far more connected to me than when I had left. I accepted this with cautious optimism. Based on past experiences, I knew this wave of affection would not last. But because his remaining time was limited, the reprieve was welcome, if not ironic. Perhaps he realized that all the stupid fighting was diminishing the moments he had remaining. Maybe someone said something that registered, and he recognized I was distraught, as well. I don't know what it was. I didn't care. I couldn't bear the thought of our last days together being filled with acrimony. I was ecstatic when he began treating me more as a partner once again.

Phillip's friend Kevin and his wife Stephanie came for a visit over the Labor Day weekend. Everyone enjoyed their company. They brought food and drinks, and we sat around the dining room table, swapping stories and chatting late into the evening.

I marveled at the smile on Phillip's face and the ease of his conversation with Kevin. Their shared history gave them easy access to stories told in brevity because they knew the middle and end. It was so good to see him in the company of his friends, people he loved so dearly and who loved him equally.

While I was in the kitchen refreshing our drinks, I heard Kevin bring up the idea of speaking with his friend about the vitamin C therapy with Phillip. I stopped what I was doing and listened as they discussed the matter. Weeks earlier, Phillip had shut me down whenever I brought up the subject, but now, he appeared open. This would have pissed me off before, but it didn't matter anymore. It thrilled me he was willing to try the diet.

We spent the rest of the evening chatting, and I got to know Kevin's wife Stephanie a bit more. She was also a joy to be around. Even with all the insanity of the current situation, her outlook made me laugh. While I didn't know her well, her candor was refreshing, as she stated things so matter-of-factly without an iota of judgment. She'd been through a messy divorce and had two girls from a previous marriage. Some of her personal history's horror stories allowed me to put my relationship with Phillip into perspective. She also told me, "this too shall pass." At first, her frank remarks took me aback. I didn't want Phillip's life to end. Even after all the adverse reports on Phillip's health, the trips to the emergency rooms, and the visible wasting away of his body, I still held out that sliver of hope that something could turn things around. The mere thought that there would come a day when my marriage complications and Phillip's illness would end stunned me at first. But I realized, after they left, I had to be prepared for what was inevitable. Even if the vitamin C therapy worked to slow the progression of Phillip's cancer, Stephanie was honest instead of sugarcoating the reality of our situation.

The next day, Phillip got an email from Kevin.

Hi Phillip and Kasey- It was wonderful to see you and the kids last night. Steph and I had a great time. I hope we didn't keep either of you up too late.

John is currently up in the Laurentians but will be back in Ottawa tomorrow. I plan to call him and let him know that you'll be phoning. And, as always, please let me/us know if we can be of any assistance.

We love you guys, and we'll see you soon. Kevin

The fact that Kevin still thought of us as a couple acting in concert touched me. While I was not going to rewrite our history or take full responsibility for our marital problems, I was making more of an effort to put the past behind me to tend to his needs.

It wasn't a denial of self. It was an acknowledgment that there was no longer any time to address past behaviors, his or mine. I had to focus entirely on the present, as I had vowed to do.

While there was little hope that this regimen would cure him, there was a hope it would allow him to live longer and stop wasting away. He was down from 195 pounds to 130 pounds. His face looked skeletal. He officially weighed less than our thirteen-year-old son.

John sent us a list of all the vitamins required and a list of dos and don'ts. The basic concept was aligned in many ways with the Anti-Cancer diet I had looked into months earlier. The idea was to starve the cancer and stop it from spreading. There wasn't much scientific data to support results, but we reasoned that eating healthier wouldn't cause Phillip any harm. That made us both feel like it was worth a shot.

It was hard for Phillip to eat anything that wasn't pureed, and he had had to have surgery to stretch his esophagus multiple times to swallow. I tried using my culinary skills to make what he was eating palatable. I knew that products like the Ensure that had been recommended had loads of sugar in them, so we abandoned those types of products. I found ways to incorporate berries and vegetables high in antioxidants into smoothies and soups that he could still drink.

The added benefit of this project was it helped distract us from personal issues. It brought me back to the days we worked on film scripts or produced videos together. We discussed and planned our meals together because this diet was very regimented. I wondered if Phillip realized we behaved better towards one another when we worked as a team.

In September, I'd accepted a part-time job at a catering company. I wasn't happy to be away from Phillip because I never knew what would happen while I was gone. But expenses were piling up, both in Marblehead and in Alexandria, and we needed to purchase the various items for this new diet. The money I earned helped in this way.

By actively taking part in his health care, Phillip seemed

happier, too. Having radiation and chemo treatment was a passive method of treating his disease. With this therapy, he could take part in the process. He was a brilliant man and enjoyed learning about things by searching the internet. This was made possible by a special pair of glasses we purchased that didn't require him to strain his neck. Still, it was difficult for him to hold his head in a comfortable position to work on the computer, so he started taking off his Aspen collar. This troubled me at first, but I could see how difficult it was to be in this contraption 24/7. I also had to wonder how much wearing it contributed to his foul moods.

Sometimes, he still had me type out emails. A few days after he began the treatment, he caught me off guard as he dictated one such email. It began…

"Hi, John…

Phillip had me type out several questions he had about each vitamin John's individual dosages instructed us to purchase. We needed more clarification about the amounts he was to take and sought recommendations about alternatives to some of the items John had listed. I just typed away at the keyboard and wasn't really paying much attention to this communication's mundane nature. What got my attention was how he asked me to end the email.

He had me type,

"Many thanks again, Phillip & Kasey."

I can't explain why asking me to sign both our names made such a difference. I can only tell you, it did.

THE BEANS WERE ADJUSTING to their new school in Marble-head, but the issues in Alexandria remained hard to deal with effectively from such a substantial distance. By late September, I just wanted to pull my hair out. My coffee guy Yves asked about leasing the entire building, and I agreed since I'd no longer be responsible for the many issues involved in owning the property. We discussed a triple net lease. Once I worked out the details, I forwarded him the information he asked for and kept my fingers crossed that I wouldn't be spending another winter dealing with the many issues presented with owning the building.

Between Phillip's needs, the building up north, the Bean's new school regiment, on top of my part-time job, there was little time for anything other than tending to the various things on my plate. Days passed with little progress on any front.

Phillip was trying to hang onto the thread of hope this new diet gave him, and I was more than willing to support him. However, even the healthier, pureed foods were difficult for him to swallow. Each night that he reported his progress to John, it became clearer that our efforts were fruitless. Even though both of us were doing our best, in my heart, I knew that Phillip's cancer had progressed beyond the point where even a promising new diet would help to stave off the disease that was ravaging his body.

As September sped by, I realized that six months had passed since we learned of Phillip's illness. When we first learned about his cancer, we were told Phillip had less than two weeks to live. Then, at Mass General, Dr. Allison told us it was perhaps just a matter of months. When you're dealing with a fatal disease, these milestones have a tremendous significance. On the one hand, it seemed like we were victorious. He'd survived well beyond what we were initially told in April. On the other hand, it was a reminder that there was little time remaining.

Chapter Thirty-Five

A BITTER HOLIDAY WEEKEND

In late September, Phillip had a follow-up appointment with his neurologist. It was a significant setback for him emotionally. He learned there was no improvement in the stabilization in his neck. I think he was also very insulted that his doctor didn't even attend this appointment. Instead, we waited for an hour to meet with his assistant. Phillip had hoped that the radiation treatments had somehow fused the bones in his neck, allowing him to remove the uncomfortable Aspen Collar. I could tell, from his silence on the ride back to Marblehead, he was not in the mood to discuss having to wear the brace indefinitely. I found some music on the radio, and we rode home without talking.

The next day, I gave notice at the catering company. It's not a good thing to be required to use sharp knives and hot surfaces when your mind is a million miles from where you are.

I finally caught a break with the issues up north when Jenny announced she wanted to buy the building under the same triple-lease arrangement I was willing to make with Yves. I was thrilled that she would be there to handle the maintenance and repair issues.

It took days for me to get all the information to Jenny. By that

Thursday, October 13th, I was so glad she was acting on my behalf to handle things up north because life in Marblehead was getting more and more difficult by the hour.

"Jenny- Here's the document I sent to Yves. It's absolutely not set in stone.

Since we spoke this morning, things have taken a turn for the worse. After countless telephone calls, I scheduled Phillip's appointment for the intravenous vitamin C therapy that John and Connor recommended. Even though he was part of that decision, when the moment arrived, he refused to go because we had not consulted with his oncologist, Dr. Allison.

Dr. Allison called me back after I spoke with you and said a feeding tube is no longer an option. She wants me to take him to the hospital on Saturday or Monday for hydration, and we're supposed to meet with her on Wednesday to determine how he can get nutrients, etc. She told me that the only way to do this may be this thing called TPN, which is an intravenous feeding that should be carefully monitored, and that may mean hospitalization.

He told me earlier that if that's the case, he wants to go into hospice care. He is talking about death in the next few weeks, and I do think he may be right, that he won't be able to hold on beyond that. He is weak and is depressed. I don't even have enough money to plan for a funeral.

If buying the building is something you want to go forward with, I would want to do things soon. I will make sure it is something that benefits us both. I just have so little left to deal with this.

Call me if you want to discuss details, etc. Call me on the home phone because I don't know if I'll have the computer on, aka magicJack.

Love you. ~ Kasey

I felt utterly lost. In subsequent calls to Dr. Allison's office, I was told to take Phillip into Boston to administer him fluids. It was Friday of the Columbus Day weekend. I was relieved he would get help. But I was furious that I would be driving our van in holiday traffic into the city and back again with my extremely fragile husband. I was miserable Phillip was being subjected to the possibility of the van breaking down, on top of the knowledge of what we would face once we got there.

On the 14th of October, we arrived at the treatment center late in the afternoon. With a heavy heart, the nurse told us, there would be no more hydration treatments after today, even though it was the only thing keeping Phillip alive. After giving him a saline solution intravenously, Dr. Allison stopped in, gave me a prescription for liquid morphine, then pulled me aside to give me some advice.

"Take him to hospice care. Find someplace comfortable. There's nothing we can do from here," she said and quickly left the room.

Ignoring jaundice in his eyes, I wanted to ask her, "Why was there hope last week but no hope today?" It wasn't the cost of tolls, parking, and gas that taxed me. It was her dismissive tone as she sent us out at five in the afternoon into holiday traffic. Why had they offered him months of treatment that robbed him of time with his family? My anger informed me that there would be another patient tomorrow, filling the void in her schedule.

Once I filled his prescription at the hospital pharmacy, I got Phillip to the van. I promised God I would do anything if it didn't break down on the way north. The drive home in rush hour holiday traffic took us three hours. Just before arriving back in Marblehead, I pulled over because I couldn't drive another mile. I needed to release the overwhelming sorrow of knowing that my husband's life would soon be over. There was no more hope. It was the end of the line.

We sat, parked in a rest stop, and I sobbed uncontrollably. When I finally gained my composure, Phillip took my hand. I looked across at him, trying to stop the flow of tears.

"When we get back home, I want you to take the kids to the park or something," Phillip told me.

"Why?" I asked.

"I need to tell my folks what Dr. Allison said, and I have no idea how they'll react. You know how my mother is. It could be a real shit show," he said with a slight smile. "I need to ask them if it would be OK to be buried in their plot at Notre Dame. I want to be cremated, so it will only be an urn. I think that's best," he explained.

I didn't know what to say.

"Don't you want us to be together?" I asked him haltingly.

"Look, you don't know what will happen from here out. You're still young. Chances are you'll remarry. I don't want my ashes sitting in a closet somewhere. This isn't about us. It's about my last wishes, OK?" Phillip said matter-of-factly.

I hated him a little at that moment. He was forcing me to accept reality when I wasn't ready. I nodded, unable to argue with anything he said. I started the van, and we continued the trip back to Marblehead.

When we arrived back from Boston, Rachel took the kids out so he could tell his folks. I disappeared downstairs to make the necessary phone calls. I called dozens of places that provided hospice care without luck.

"We're full," Life Care told us. I got the same answer wherever I called.

After Phillip told his folks, it seemed like he lost any strength to carry on. He came downstairs, went into his room, leaving the door ajar. I debated whether to go back upstairs so I wouldn't wake him as I continued to make calls. I tiptoed to the bedroom, where I assumed he was trying to sleep, to check on him. I noticed the Aspen collar on the table beside his bed. He'd removed it so he could rest better. It was a startling reminder that his fight was nearing an end.

I sat in the next room, calling any place that might have an opening. Phillip's moans between doses of morphine kept me dialing. By a sheer miracle, there was a bed at a hospice center in Beverly that would be available the next day. My good luck was only because of someone else's loss. I wondered who would be jumping for joy when my husband's bed finally became available.

Phillip wanted me to let his friends know the situation. He

didn't want them to find out after he was gone. I wrote, with great emotion, all the things I felt and believed about him, with complete honesty, because all anger had passed, and only compassion and love remained in my heart.

"Hi Everyone- I just wanted you to know that my husband Phillip is currently in hospice care at a facility. He is gravely ill and not expected to survive beyond the end of the week. He asked me to let his friends know he loved you all, and to thank you for your love and support in his life.

At his passing, there will be a funeral Mass, but also a memorial service in a few weeks so people can gather and celebrate the life he lived.

He is a wonderful man, a loving father, and an exceptional husband. He will be missed beyond belief.

I don't know how practical it is for any of you to visit him. He is able to have visitors but it might be best to call ahead, if anyone wishes to see him while he is still able.

I, too, want to thank everyone who has meant so much to him. It is unbelievable to me that he will no longer be here, but I have made peace with things, as he is in too much pain to want him to remain here on earth. His love and spirit will remain with me until we can be together again.

If you need to contact me, please send me an email or call my cell. Love to all ~ Kasey"

I meant every word I said.

It was harder reaching out to those who called to express their love and sorrow. His favorite cousin Rob called when we'd arrived home from Boston, and I was beside myself, trying to speak when words got caught in my throat. The tenderness in Rob's voice was too much for me, and I hurried off the phone. I followed up later in an email so he would understand I simply couldn't speak through the emotional turmoil.

"Hi, Rob and Sandi-

I wanted to say something when you called the other day, but at that point, Phillip's folks were in the room and were not up-to-date, and I didn't want to say anything until he'd spoken with them.

Today we are bringing Phillip to a hospice facility so he will be more comfortable. He is experiencing more pain and is now not able to take in even fluids. I am so sorry to have to relate the news, but Phillip's end is very, very near.

He was doing so well up until about three weeks ago and we thought he had much more time ahead of him, but a CT-scan revealed that the cancer has impacted his liver and other major organs. I can't even begin to tell you how sad this makes us all feel, and I know you share in our sorrow.

I am hoping you could relate this to the other members of your family because I simply cannot say the words. I am not able to speak of these things without emotion overcoming me and, right now, I need to bear up for the kids. I've wanted to visit your mom so often but knew it would be impossible to stay composed.

Please know that you mean so much to both of us. He loves you dearly, and you're not only his cousin, but a dear friend.

I don't know the time frame in which things will happen in days to come, but the doctor doesn't think he has much time at all because he is not taking in fluids at this point. Call me or email me if you want to be in touch. We are most likely bringing him to the hospice facility sometime later this afternoon.

Love to you both - Kasey. "

In the morning, I gathered Phillip's bags, Bible, and some pictures of Jack and Lucy—our Beans. I packed whatever I thought would bring him comfort. It was the longest seven miles I'd ever driven. We checked Phillip into the hospice center, knowing he would never return to Marblehead.

Chapter Thirty-Six

A FINAL FAREWELL

October 25th

Phillip signed the papers granting the hospice caregivers permission to administer the drugs that would put him into an irreversible coma. For days, he had said his good-byes to dozens of people who had traveled countless miles to see him. His best friend, Kevin, and his wife, Stephanie, had offered to take the kids overnight. I was glad, as it would distract them for a while. It was the first time in days Phillip and I were alone.

We sat together, holding hands, waiting for the nursing staff to come and give the drugs that would accomplish the end-of-life sedation. I sat with him, trying hard to hold in the waves of emotion. He still hated it when I cried. He looked down at his hand.

"I guess I won't be needing this anymore," he said and handed me his wedding ring. I slipped it on my thumb, afraid I would lose it. "I wrote the kids some letters. They're on a flash drive in the top drawer in the desk downstairs in the basement. Could you print them out on nice paper and give it to them on their twenty-first birthdays?" he asked.

"You bet," I promised.

"I also wrote down what I want to be put on my grave marker. Don't get anything fancy. I know you can't afford it. Just something simple, all right?" Phillip instructed.

I couldn't say anything, so I nodded.

"I'm so tired," he said, looking away. "I'm so sorry I hurt you," he said, squeezing my hand.

"Please don't. Let's just hold on to all the best things," I told him. An hour passed as we sat, recalling, with broad strokes, the most significant moments of our lives together.

"Remember that day we learned I was pregnant?" I reminded him, choking back tears.

"How about the night the Beans were born?" he responded.

We talked of joys we shared and the life we'd created together, for better or worse. There were so many. We reminisced over some of our twenty-seven years together, trying to forget the anger that had built up and led to our happiness going astray. I forgave him for being unable to recognize my deepest desires, to bring him joy and happiness by giving of myself. I forgave myself for all the times I couldn't rise above my anger and deal with situations more calmly. I stopped myself from thinking about ever wanting to walk out on him months earlier. Not because I didn't have the absolute right. I did. At that moment, I needed to push aside all the wasted time spent on things that no longer mattered as we reached the end of our journey. We held hands, and the love we once shared rebounded.

When the nurse came into the room, I turned away, unable to look as she put the drugs in his IV. I knew soon he would fall into a coma and never wake up. I nodded through tears, holding his fragile hand while he drifted off to an unending sleep. Before the Propofol took hold, I leaned over gently and kissed his mouth.

"I love you," he told me, blinking through tears.

I looked deep into his weary eyes and told him what was in my heart. "I love you too." He turned his head and closed his eyes. I sat down beside him and waited until he drifted off.

I sat in one of the lounge chairs in his room until he fell

asleep. I looked over at him, lying a few feet away. He moaned. I wondered if he was dreaming. Was he haunted by his final goodbye to our twins, his sister, and his elderly parents?

I stayed in a soft lounge chair in the corner of the darkened room, knowing the end was near. I was thankful Phillip's suffering would soon be over, but I was angry, too. I kept wondering if he'd received treatment earlier if it would have made a difference.

"There's no way to know," I consoled myself.

I reflected willingly on all our days together. I didn't back down in facing the truth, as ugly as it sometimes was. Our relationship was highly flawed, but it didn't make either of us bad people. I was the fortunate one because I got to learn from the mistakes made along the way. Phillip had to go to his grave without the benefit of self-reflection.

Throughout my life, I struggled to love the two men that meant the world to me. I thought of my dad and how it never occurred to me how much Phillip and my father were alike. They were both loved and admired by so many people throughout their lives. But those people saw only the wonderful qualities. It made those of us who witnessed their weaknesses up close question ourselves.

I suppose it was because, to the world, we all show our better selves. We trust that the face on display at work and church, or out in the community, is identical to the one at home. But there, in our most intimate setting, we cast aside the masks we put on for the world, only revealing our underbellies to those who we believe love us the most. We hope those who are closest to us will love us regardless of how poorly we behave. We expect it. Sometimes we demand from our loved ones what we would never tolerate ourselves.

Phillip and I started out with some heavy baggage early on. Because we were often happy in those earlier years, it was difficult to see how much those issues infiltrated and shaped our relationship. Until I began to look back, it was hard to see how detrimental the lie about our first wedding had set the stage for future events. It became the catalyst for the imbalance of power that drove a wedge between us.

For so long, I avoided confronting our problems head-on because we were apart so much of the time. By the time Phillip's patterns of behavior emerged, I was so used to weathering the storms in our relationship, it was easier to wait until they were over so we could get on with life. His capacity to be so loving endeared him to me, and the cost of confrontation was often more than I could afford emotionally.

Throughout our marriage, I'd done my share of complaining and arguing. Sometimes it was justified. But other times, not so much. While I couldn't define the exact reasons why there was an enormous difference between my approach to addressing our problems and his, I just knew there was. But in that moment, while my husband was about to take his last breaths, I did what I had to do to get through those moments. It wasn't the time to thoroughly examine that reality.

Instead, I reasoned that we had both changed as we aged, and it was hard to keep up, year in and year out. Our goals changed. Our interests changed. We had children, and that changed everything. We were two people who merely wanted to find happiness. Sometimes that was together. As time passed, it was not.

No one teaches you how to be married. We'd both come from families where patriarchal standards were the norm. We played into these notions without ever realizing just how deeply they were ingrained. While we both believed we escaped the imbalance, it was there all along, hiding right beneath the surface.

I also accepted that I would never know the depths of Phillip's personal struggles. For whatever reason, something skewed his perception of how others treated him. I admit there must have been things I didn't know about his life. His perception of events was often quite different than what I witnessed. His accounts of his past, too, made me wonder about what was real and what was imagined. The questions that remained would never be answered. I recognized that it was probably for the best.

Sitting in the darkness, I realized I had much to be grateful for, as well. I acknowledged all Phillip had given me as my husband. He'd taught me many things in our time together. The lessons I learned weren't always easy or even pleasant. And he didn't always teach me these things through acts of kindness. But what I'd learned made me a more compassionate person. It made me more resilient and more self-aware. I had a better understanding of the suffering of those with major illnesses and appreciated my health more. I knew what love was and what it wasn't. I didn't want my painful experiences to be lost in bitterness. I only hoped that in the end, Phillip realized that I had enriched his life the way he had enriched mine.

I woke with a start as the nurse draped a blanket over me. I forgot for a moment where I was. Then I heard the familiar sounds of the machines that monitored my husband's vital signs.

"He's still with us," she told me. "You should go home and get some rest. You can't be very comfortable in this chair. He might stay like this for quite some time."

I thanked her for the blanket, and she left the room. I was afraid to go. I wanted Phillip to know I loved him, even when I didn't like him sometimes. But, mostly, I felt the need to be there with him so he wouldn't die alone.

I sat there for a few more hours, thinking about all the times we laughed together because those were safe moments, moments I could think about him and not be overwhelmed with grief. His keen sense of humor was one thing that drew me to him. It was the place I retreated to as his life slipped away. I remembered something I'd almost forgotten about. It made me smile, and cry a little, too. I remembered one of Phillip's most endearing moments.

≈

OUR LAST SIGNIFICANT renovation before listing the property in Blairstown was finishing some upgrades to the kitchen and laying some slate in the backyard to create a more finished patio. We had purchased some slate, and it was sitting in the yard under a blue tarp.

One Saturday morning in late April of 2006, Phillip went out to work on the patio to install the slate when I heard him shout, "Oh, my God!"

I wondered if he had a heart attack! I ran out to see what was happening. I saw him standing over the tarp with the edge lifted up, staring at something on the ground.

"Are you okay? What's wrong?"

"Come here. Look at this."

I crossed the yard in seconds and was staring at four tiny kittens under the tarp. They were about 2-3 weeks old and mewing for their momma.

"Holy shit! What are we going to do?" I asked him.

"Well, we can't just leave them here."

By this time, Jack and Lucy were in the yard, and Phillip told them to go get a box sitting on the back porch and a towel from the bathroom. I wasn't sure if the mother cat had abandoned her babies, but the Beans had seen them, and I was reluctant to take a chance they would still be alive if we waited to find out.

We gathered the four kittens into the box and brought them into the kitchen. Soon, I was calling every place listed in the phone book and online that rescued animals, only to find no one was available to take them. Each shelter I called was full. I called the woman who rescued our older cats, Duncan and Felicia. She offered a ton of information and suggested we prepare to feed them as soon as we could. Off I went to the pet store to buy kitten formula and the bottles and gear to save these little creatures.

Phillip's involvement really surprised me. He was more of a dog lover, and the only cat we ever had that he was attached to was Squirt. For weeks, we took turns getting up in the middle of the night to feed them. However, what made me smile was thinking back to a picture I took of Phillip holding the kitten Lucy had named Milky. Phillip was holding the tiny thing in the palm of his hand while it sucked on the tiny bottle. He was so zoned-out that he didn't even realize I had grabbed the camera and taken his picture. It showed a side of him that was gentle and kind. It warmed my heart, watching him half asleep, trying hard to help save them.

THOSE WERE the memories I cherished as I sat in the chair. I recalled how tender Phillip could be and wondered how that side of his personality somehow got buried sometimes. It hurt to think about these things, but I needed to feel the pain of losing him so I could truly appreciate what was being lost.

I finally dozed off, unable to stay awake any longer. The nurse came in again, and I could feel her pull the blanket up around me. I opened my eyes and smiled in appreciation.

"Maybe he's holding on until you leave," she said. I was famished and needed to eat, and I wanted a shower desperately, too. I finally let her convince me my vigil was unnecessary.

I left about 2 am to grab a quick shower and change my clothes. As I rushed back to Marblehead, a cop pulled me over to give me a speeding ticket. He let me off with a warning when I told the officer why I was going 30 in a 20-mile an hour zone.

"Really?" I thought as he ran my plates. I slowed down for the remaining trip and made it to Marblehead with no further incident. I was just grabbing some clean clothing when my new cellphone rang. The night nurse at the hospice center told me that Phillip had passed moments ago.

"He died alone after all," I thought as I sobbed.

I showered and dressed, then returned to the hospice center to say my final goodbyes. I stood over Phillip's cooling body and thanked him for all the love we shared. I told him I wished him peace on his journey. When I could finally compose myself, I went to the nurse's station to hand over the vial of morphine that had remained in his room in the basement at his sister's. I didn't need that hanging around. They took the vial and placed it in a baggie with a seal.

As I left the place, I could see my weary reflection in the door's glass and smiled through my tears. I noticed the writing on the tee-shirt I was wearing and tried to make out what it said. I must have grabbed one of my brother-in-law's by mistake. The tee-shirt read *Free Agent*. The irony wasn't lost on me. I left the hospice center, knowing that Phillip's story was over, but my journey would begin with an ever-changing epilogue.

Epilogue

The most beautiful people we have known are those who have known defeat, known suffering, know struggle, know loss, and have found their way out of the depths. These persons have an appreciation, a sensitivity, and an understanding of life that fills them with compassion, gentleness, and a deep loving concern. Beautiful people do not just happen.

~ Elizabeth Kubler Ross

Final Reflections

I n the aftermath of Phillip's death, I barely had time to breathe. Beyond the weight of the sorrow I was experiencing, I had to cope with many practical issues. This included finding an apartment, a job, and dealing with the property in Canada.

I buried my emotional turmoil, just like I buried the sadness of my father's death years ago. This time I was more aware that I wasn't dealing with the pain, but it was the only way I could make it through each day. Eventually, the experiences I've detailed caught up with me, and I had to reconcile what happened to finally leave the past behind.

The twins and I stayed in Marblehead until they graduated from high school because I wanted them to live someplace familiar. They needed to be around family, and that mainly meant Phillip's family. I was able to rent an apartment with a small payout from a long-term disability policy Phillip had taken out through work. That was the first step to escaping all the painful memories.

Staying in Marblehead, however, often fed the despondency that consumed me. I passed the venue where our wedding reception was held—the second wedding, to get to the grocery store. The cemetery where Phillip was buried, his parent's home, the park where we took the Beans were all places that brought him back to life in my heart. I retreated into the new apartment and stayed there as much as possible, unable to confront our relationship's ghosts.

I began avoiding all the ways in which I was emotionally connected to the past. I barely had any contact with the outside world. I stopped writing in my journal, scarcely spoke to friends, or communicated with anyone who might bring the despair I felt to the surface. It wasn't the best way to cope, but I didn't know what else to do.

One obstacle after another presented itself, which forestalled the need to confront what had happened between Phillip and me. The situation in Canada went from bad to worse when Jenny suddenly changed course and decided not to buy the building. Communicating with her became more difficult. I found out she wasn't collecting rent from a couple that was occupying the café. Essentially, they were using the space for free while I was paying for the oil and electricity they consumed. The answering machine picked up every time I called her. Bills that I thought were being paid weren't. Since she had taken over the accounts for many of the utilities, I had to wrestle back control of the situation. Without a reliable vehicle, I couldn't get up to see what was happening in person, so I hired a company, long-distance, to collect rents and handle the maintenance on my behalf. This cost me all I had remaining from Phillips's small disability payout.

I still had hopes of selling the building and focused on getting my tax returns in order. Since Phillip and I didn't file the previous year, the records were a mess. I sent our long-term accountant, Lenny, all the original documents and receipts from Canada to organize everything relevant to my complicated tax returns for both the U.S and Canada. Then things really fell apart.

First, Lenny mailed back all my original receipts to my new street address in Marblehead but put "Marblehead, New York" instead of "Marblehead, Massachusetts." I never could locate the package. He assured me it wouldn't present a problem unless the IRS audited me, so I tried not to worry, especially when he told me I most likely had a substantial refund coming. I was hoping to buy a used car, so I could travel safely. The lost documents didn't seem insurmountable. But like all things in my life at that point, fate decided otherwise.

By mid-February, Lenny completed the tax returns and submitted them on my behalf electronically. He called me when he received a notice from the IRS that my tax return was flagged as fraudulent because someone had already filed a return and received a refund using Phillip's stolen social security number.

Lenny said he would try to straighten things out and would call me back on Monday. It was President's Day weekend, so I assumed he would call Tuesday when I heard nothing. I impatiently waited until Wednesday because I knew how busy he was. When I finally called him, a woman answered the phone. She identified herself as Mary, Lenny's wife. She told me Lenny had died of a massive heart attack over the weekend. I'd known Lenny for years at this point and felt the loss both personally and professionally. I expressed my condolences and hung up.

As the days passed, I was torn between being insensitive about Mary's loss and the need to proceed with obtaining my records. I waited a week and then called again to inquire about my tax return, only to learn Mary had no access to any of Lenny's computers or files.

Dealing with this issue dragged on for months as I reconstructed records to prove I was entitled to the refund. Although I eventually sold the building, got the tax refund, and moved on from the mayhem, the quagmire of circumstances that needed my immediate attention added to my stress and postponed dealing with my emotions.

I found myself sliding into depression. I'd tried so hard to rise above the many problems I encountered, and yet, it seemed like the entire universe was against me. It allowed me to avoid thinking about Phillip because confronting the layers of emotion over his passing on top of everything else was too much to bear.

At that time, I just wanted to forget the past. But there was so much that I cherished and missed about my husband even though it was all overshadowed by his acidic outbursts. Before I could move on, I first had to sort through the pain of losing him while experiencing the relief of never having to hear him utter remarks that left the deep emotional scars I still wore.

TO REFOCUS MY ATTENTION, I decided to go back to school to complete my bachelor's degree online. By pushing all my problems aside to address coursework, I avoided confronting the emotions I tried to bury. I eventually got a part-time job as a life coach for a severely autistic man. Between work, college, the Beans, and my day-to-day tasks, I had little time for reflection.

Believing I was over the anguish of the past, I slowly started to communicate with friends and family again. When the few conversations I had with those who knew Phillip veered toward the truth of our marriage, my words were met coolly and some-times with outright disdain. The reactions ranged from an eye-roll to suggestions that implied I needed to "move on" or "shouldn't you be over it by now?" It was as if the moment Phillip's life ended, the way he had treated me became completely irrelevant. I found myself unable to express my thoughts about what had happened because I feared being alienating.

Phillip showed a deep love for his family and close friends, and it was reciprocated. He could be exceptionally kind and generous. That made it hard for others to imagine that he had treated me quite differently from what they experienced. Even if they only saw him once or twice a year, our mutual friends didn't want to accept that my relationship with him was unlike theirs. Initially, I wanted to tell them that they weren't married to him for twenty-five years. But I realized that they, too, were grieving, and they had every right to respect their memory of him. But knowing this left me avoiding having these difficult conversations.

When I did again try to find the words to talk about the problems within my marriage, friends asked, "If it was so bad, why did you stay?" I kept asking myself that, too. Even before the kids were born, there were multiple occasions when I considered leaving the marriage. There were many reasons I stayed back then. I loved Phillip even though I also hated how he treated me. I pushed aside thoughts of splitting up whenever it seemed like the bad patch was behind us. Even though the longer we were married, the more intense and frequent those moments occurred, none of this was apparent to me at the time.

FIVE YEARS AFTER PHILLIP DIED, the kids graduated from high school. Lucy opted to attend a college on the other end of the state while Jack decided to take some time off school. I decided to explore real estate closer to where Lucy would be living on campus, and I ended up purchasing a home not far from the college she would be attending.

Not finished with my own studies, I applied for grad school. For one of my courses, I revived a story I wrote, *A Layman's Journey* for an undergraduate non-fiction writing course. The early version dealt only with my condemnation of the *for-profit* medical system that sometimes prevents people from getting care due to their fear of high medical costs. In the revised version, I expanded it to include more of our marital issues and why Phillip's illness made our already difficult relationship so challenging. I avoided writing about much of the emotional turmoil I still felt.

It wasn't until a classmate, and I exchanged our stories to critique that I realized a connection between her story and mine. She wrote about the abuse she experienced and what she did to overcome her troubled marriage. I got uncomfortable reading her work. It was as if she peeked inside my marriage and saw things I had never revealed. The language she used, her former spouse's behaviors, and his need for control were so familiar.

Initially, it was easier for me to talk to her about what she experienced rather than relating it back to my own marriage. But eventually, through long conversations over the phone, I opened up about what I experienced with Phillip.

She suggested I turn my work into a full-length memoir and gave me a list of books about how to write one. She also suggested several books on abusive relationships, one of which is called, *Why Does He Do That*, by Lundy Bancroft. I bought them but put the ones about abuse aside while completing the first draft of this memoir.

Writing my book enabled me to examine what had happened in my marriage. Yet, in the beginning, I resisted using the word "abuse." Initially, I referred to the problems Phillip and I had as "miscommunications." Our relationship was "dysfunctional"—and it was. Describing Phillip's behaviors as abusive made me uncomfortable even though they were identical to some of the behaviors experienced by my classmate. Yet, I had no problem recognizing her husband's behaviors as abusive.

One day, I got out Bancroft's book and began reading. There is no way to express how I felt as I turned the pages. His book documents stories of women who lived through events that were similar to what I'd experienced. It was both validating and devastating. Then, I got out my journals and reread entries. I had to confront what I'd always denied.

As I read through page after page of journal entries, I was shocked at the raw emotions I had while trying to understand why I was so unhappy. It crystalized all the times I circumvented the truth. Yes, Phillip was a kind and loving husband and father much of the time. What became evident, though, was how many times I tried to convince myself that Phillip got angry and reacted poorly because I got too emotional. He told me often enough that my behavior had fueled his outbursts. It didn't matter that I was responding to his verbal assaults and demeaning comments. He had convinced me that his eruptions of anger were essentially my fault.

After reading Bancroft's book, however, there was no going back. I finally had to accept what I had repeatedly skirted around. My old journals and email exchanges showed a consistent pattern of Phillip's control, manipulation, gaslighting, lying, and financial restraints. It was all part of his desire to have power over me. His need for absolute control fueled his increasingly abusive behaviors.

Because Phillip never hit me, I didn't connect how he treated me to what I knew about abuse. While I was aware that people could be verbally abused, that never seemed as damaging as the physical abuse my neighbor Mrs. White had endured when my parents attended Bible school. Her bruised face and nightly screams connected the word *abuse* to the word *victim*.

The lengthy periods between each blow-up left me believing, time after time, that it wouldn't happen again. The expressions of love and tenderness Phillip exhibited in the aftermath of these emotional upheavals lulled me into a false sense of security all over again.

When Phillip left the kids and me in Canada, it allowed me to connect my overall sense of well-being to Phillip's absence. Without his barrage of disparaging remarks, I wasn't "walking on eggshells." The contrast of my journal entries before and after we moved North helped me connect his behavior and my emotional scars. The humiliation and psychological impact of his words were assaults. Until I began reading about verbal abuse, I couldn't comprehend that Phillip's words and actions were as equally damaging as the physical harm Mr. White inflicted on his wife.

WHILE I AM FAR from an expert on the subject, in reading and talking with others about the issue, I've learned things that gave me a better understanding of how and why these unhealthy relationships develop. Perhaps the most influential factor that allows abuse to occur is all the societal myths about victims and their abusers. As I continued to learn about this subject, I realized that what made the obvious so unrecognizable was that I, too, had believed them.

As a society, we're taught to believe that abusers are monsters. A creepy-looking guy in the raincoat comes to mind instead of the well-dressed man in the suit. We're shocked when a member of our communities or a well-known public figure is accused of these behaviors. We often hear the perpetrator is *not capable* of what they're accused of. The outrage and certainty of those who know the individual in the context of an entirely different type of relationship often weigh more heavily than their intimate partners' experiences. Shock and dismay usually follow, and the accuser's character and behavior are questioned more significantly than the individual who has committed the abusive acts.

Of course, abuse happens outside of domestic relationships as well. The revelations of sexual predators exposed by the *MeToo Movement* come on the heels of those uncovered in the Boy Scouts, the military, and various religious and athletic organizations. Those unmasked are often revered community members, public figures, media or entertainment personalities, and political leaders. A victim's claim of abuse is often rejected even when multiple people come forward, delaying the perpetrators' prosecution. Simultaneously, the abuser is vehemently defended as innocent by people who have never even met the abuser personally. Opinions often outweigh personal experiences and influence the public even though those involved have a more intimate knowledge of the individual accused. Knowing how the public will most likely react after someone comes forward to disclose their abuse is a factor that keeps many victims silent.

It is essential to understand that an abuser's private behaviors often exist concurrent with exemplary public actions. If we continue to think of the perpetrators of abuse as the outliers of society, we make it harder to accept that one in three women are victims of abuse. When we think of abusers as monsters, they take on the characteristic of a rare creature lurking in unknown places ready to pounce. And because we think of them this way, we believe that their behavior is uncommon. However, those who perpetrate abuse can be found throughout our daily lives. We refuse to see that ordinary men and women can inflict abuse and then go about their lives undetected. Such cultural indoctrination makes it hard to break through the cycle reinforced by an unwillingness to accept that people can act differently in private than they do publicly.

We also want to believe the myth, "it could never happen to me." I secretly thought I would never fall into the trap of an unhealthy marriage, "allowing myself" to get stuck in a relationship where I depended on a husband until—I was dependent on Phillip and couldn't understand what happened and why. Once I understood how destructive these myths were, I gained a better understanding by reading and writing about what happened.

WHAT I WANT my readers to know is that abuse can happen to anyone. There are well-documented abuse cases among people of all income levels, those who are famous or ordinary people, and education and one's accomplishments don't exclude someone from finding themselves in an abusive relationship.

My relationship didn't start out as abusive. As Phillip lost control over his own life, he began trying to control mine. Initially, his behavior didn't seem threatening. Eventually, however, his need for control turned his actions into abuse.

His portrayal of being the *black sheep* of his family was repeated to establish a faulty perception of his upbringing. He used that narrative because he felt justified when he could not confront any difficulties in his life. Long after he reached adulthood, he blamed others for his problems instead of accepting responsibility for his own failings.

Phillip often joked about a place he called "Phillip's perfect world." In this island retreat, he would describe how he would change things to accommodate a better life for himself. For example, after doing yard work, he would say something like, "In Phillip's perfect world, there would be no weeds or even trees," or "In Phillip's perfect world, there would be free cable TV." He was always half-joking when he mentioned this, so I never really thought about it as a sign of his mindset. But one of the more frequent comments about Phillip's perfect world was, "In Phillip's perfect world, you would always do exactly what I say." In Phillip's perfect world, he had unbridled power over me.

ONE OF THE most important things I learned in writing this memoir is the impact of financial abuse. While financial abuse isn't discussed as often as other types of destructive behaviors, it has a devastating effect on a victim. When a person is financially abused, they are often powerless to escape. Their dependence on their abuser for many of the most essential elements for survival prevents them from fleeing, especially if there are children involved.

When Phillip forced the kids and me to move to Cobleskill, his erratic behavior escalated. As I examined our history together, Phillip's attempts to keep me isolated and restrict my access to money were part of a pattern that emerged. All his actions and reactions, especially regarding financial transactions before and after the kids and I moved back to the States, made his intent clear. In his mind, he had every right to dictate how I spent both time and money. That was the only way Phillip could achieve what he wanted: to maintain control over the relationship. It wasn't until I realized that my experiences aligned with everything I'd read; however, I understood the impact of financial abuse. When someone uses access to money to control their partner, that is abuse.

Now that I understand this, I want to be an agent of change. I believe speaking up about matters such as financial abuse will make the world better for my Beans. While what I reveal in this memoir might be unpleasant to those who knew and loved Phillip, I believe staying silent helps perpetuate abusive behaviors. By speaking out and revealing the problems I encountered, I hope to change people's perception of abuse by challenging the myths and telling the truth. I do not want my children to live in fear of honesty. Despite the adversity I experienced, there are lessons to be learned that I can only share with them only if they know what happened.

It is often easier to identify something in others than it is in ourselves. I do not want to hide or feel shame because of my experiences. Coming out of the shadows and speaking up has allowed me to move forward. I believe that if my memoir gives someone else the ability to confront their abuse, it's worth revealing what happened to me.

ABUSE IS A TRAUMATIC EXPERIENCE, and those who are victims frequently suffer from a form of PTSD. People who have been abused have higher levels of depression, anxiety, suicidal tendencies, and mental illness. While the impact of this type of trauma on the brain is now more fully understood than it was in the past, it is rarely taken into account regarding a victim's behavior. Instead, the victims' confusion and inability to articulate their experience are viewed with skepticism and, even worse, claims that the victim is deceitful or untrustworthy.

We need to consider that along with the experiences they've endured, victims of abuse are grieving the loss of a relationship. Someone they loved and trusted has hurt them repeatedly. They've lived in doubt because of promises made by their abuser to change. Even if they've managed to leave, their self-esteem has been erased, and society often provides little recourse to cope with what they experienced. The lack of understanding about the impact of abuse ends up adding to their suffering.

IF YOU SUSPECT someone you know is being abused, help them get the support they need. If they're not ready or unable to leave their relationship, help in other ways. Sometimes just knowing someone has your best interest at heart is enough to keep a person going until they can break free.

Sharing my story helped me to extend forgiveness. I forgave myself for all the things I could have done better. I realized that my marriage, dysfunction and all, is a part of who I am. I can't escape that. Nor do I want to. My experiences have helped me to have a greater insight into other's struggles. I dare say that the adversity in my life has made me a more compassionate person. I continue to strive to be that *better self* because my experiences opened my eyes and changed my perception of the world.

We all can strive to become our better selves and grow despite the adversity we face. Without the challenges we experience, we remain stagnant in our thinking and perceptions. In embracing the truth, we can move through life's challenges by coming out of the shadows and standing tall.

Onward and upward!

Kasey

Please visit my website <u>kaseyrogers.com</u> for more information. Thanks for reading!